Just One Pot

Just One Pot

Over **320** Simple and Delicious Recipes,
from Hearty Stews to Tasty Tagines

Reader's
Digest

The Reader's Digest Association, Inc.
Pleasantville, NY/Montreal/Sydney

First printing in paperback 2010

A READER'S DIGEST BOOK

This edition published by The Reader's Digest Association, Inc.,
by arrangement with McRae Books Srl

Copyright © 2007 McRae Books Srl

This book was conceived and designed by McRae Books Srl
Via del Salviatino, 1 – 50016 Fiesole (Florence), Italy

FOR MCRAE BOOKS
Project Director: Anne McRae
Design Director: Marco Nardi
Texts: Carla Bardi, Hajra Makda, Ting Morris
Photography: Brent Parker Jones
Food Styling: Neil Hargreaves
Layouts: Laura Ottina
Editing: Helen Farrell, Anne McRae

FOR READER'S DIGEST
U.S. Project Editor: Andrea Chesman
Canadian Project Editor: Pamela Chichinskas
Australian Project Editor: Annette Carter
Associate Art Director: George McKeon
Executive Editor, Trade Publishing: Dolores York
Vice President and Publisher: Harold Clarke

LIBRARY OF CONGRESS CATALOGING IN PUBLICATION DATA:

Just one pot : over 320 simple and delicious recipes, from hearty stews to tasty tagines / from the editors of Reader's Digest.

    p. cm.

  ISBN-13: 978-0-7621-0683-7 (hardcover)

  ISBN-13: 978-1-60652-160-1 (paperback)

   1. One-dish-meals. I. Reader's Digest Association.

TX840.O53J96 2006

641.8'2–dc22   2006049310

Address any comments about *Just One Pot* to:

  The Reader's Digest Association, Inc.

  Adult Trade Publishing

  Reader's Digest Road

  Pleasantville, NY 10570-7000

For more Reader's Digest products and information, visit our website:

  www.rd.com (in the United States)

  www.readersdigest.ca (in Canada)

  www.readersdigest.com.au (in Australia)

  www.readersdigest.co.nz (in New Zealand)

Printed in China

5 7 9 10 8 6 4 (hardcover)
3 5 7 9 10 8 6 4 2 (paperback)

On the front cover: Tuscan Minestrone with Italian Sausage (page 22)
On the front flap: Spicy Lamb and Vegetable Stir-Fry (page 90)
On the back cover: Top: Beef and Potato Tagine with Moroccan Preserved Lemons (page 138); Center: Butternut Squash Soup (page 56); Below: Baked Pasta and Vegetables (page 216)

CONTENTS

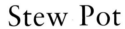

INTRODUCTION

Cooking with just one pot is convenient and fun. It also opens, quite literally, a "world" of possibilities, since all the major cuisines have traditional dishes that are prepared in a single pot. This book includes recipes for soups, chowders, minestrones, risottos, paellas, stir-fries, stews, curries, tagines, casseroles, fondues, hot pots, and much more. With classic recipes from American and international cuisines, this is a cookbook with recipes just right for every occasion, from family lunches to elegant dinner parties.

SOUP POT

SOUPS AND CHOWDERS

What is more satisfying than a steaming bowl of hearty soup—a meal in itself that nourishes the soul as much as it does the body? The wonderful thing about soup is that it doesn't take hours to prepare or require lots of exotic ingredients, yet it always provides a bowl full of wonderful aromas, textures, and colors. The 65 recipes in this chapter have been gathered from around the world—with an array of selections from the Hearty Beef Soup to the delicately fragrant Leek and Potato Soup. These simple but delicious soups offer something for all tastes and every occasion.

GOULASH SOUP

Goulash is the best-known Hungarian dish outside Hungary. It comes from gulyás, *the Hungarian word for "herdsman," but the dish Hungarians call* gulyás *is a soup, descended from one traditionally made by herdsmen. What we call goulash is called* pirkilt *or (if sour cream is added)* paprikás *in Hungary, and originally consisted of paprika-spiced beef or lamb cooked with onions. Versions that include a variety of vegetables, such as carrots, bell peppers, and tomatoes, are considered by Hungarians to be goulash soup (gulyásleves). Paprika, the ground spice made from a variety of sweet red peppers, gives this dish its typical fragrance and red color. Be sure not to roast the paprika because it turns dark and bitter! Add 1 pound (500 g) cubed potatoes 30 minutes before the end of the cooking time for an even heartier dish.*

1/4 cup (60 g) butter or lard

1 3/4 pounds (750 g) lean beef (stew beef), cut into small chunks

3 medium onions, finely chopped

3 cloves garlic, finely chopped

1 teaspoon dried thyme, or 1 tablespoon finely chopped fresh thyme

1/2 teaspoon caraway seeds, crushed

2 tablespoons hot paprika

Salt

1 1/2 tablespoons all-purpose (plain) flour

8 cups (2 liters) beef broth or stock + more as needed (see page 28)

1 tablespoon tomato paste (concentrate)

1 green bell pepper (capsicum), seeded and thinly sliced

3 ripe tomatoes, peeled and quartered

1/4 cup (60 ml) light (single) cream

1/4 cup (60 ml) dry red wine

Freshly ground black pepper

1/2 cup (125 ml) sour cream, to serve

Melt the butter in a large soup pot over high heat. Add the beef in small batches and cook until the meat is seared, 1–2 minutes. Set the seared meat aside.

Add the onions and sauté until softened, about 5 minutes. Add the garlic, thyme, and caraway seeds and sauté for 2 minutes more.

Add the paprika and 1/2 teaspoon of the salt. Sauté over medium heat until all the paprika has been incorporated, about 5 minutes.

Sprinkle in the flour and mix well. Pour in 1 cup (250 ml) of the broth. Cook over low heat for 1 minute, stirring constantly.

Stir in the tomato paste, bell pepper, and tomatoes and pour in the remaining 7 cups (1.75 liters) of broth. Return the meat to the pan. Bring to a boil. Cover and simmer over low heat for 1 1/2 hours, or until the meat is tender. Add more broth if the soup begins to thicken in the early stages of the cooking time.

Stir in the cream and wine and cook for 1 minute. Season with salt and pepper to taste.

Serve the soup hot, with the sour cream passed on the side.

Serves: 6–8 • Prep: 20 min • Cooking: 1 3/4 hr

CORNISH FARMHOUSE BROTH

2 pounds (1 kg) beef brisket

2 1/2 cups (250 g) yellow split peas

8 cups (2 liters) water

Salt and freshly ground white pepper

2 sprigs parsley

2 sprigs thyme

1 bay leaf

4 carrots, finely chopped

2 medium onions, finely chopped

2 stalks celery, finely chopped

1 small rutabaga (300 g) (swede), peeled and finely chopped

4 cups (1 liter) beef broth or stock (see page 28)

2 medium leeks, white parts only, trimmed and thinly sliced

2 cups Herb croutons (see page 246)

1 tablespoon finely chopped fresh flat-leaf parsley or mint, to garnish

Place the brisket and split peas in a large saucepan. Pour in the water and bring to a boil over medium heat. Skim off the froth and simmer for 10 minutes.

Add 1 teaspoon of salt, parsley, thyme, and bay leaf. Partially cover and simmer for 2 hours.

Add the carrots, onions, celery, and rutabaga. Pour in the broth and bring to a boil. Cover and simmer for 20–30 minutes more, stirring occasionally.

Remove the pan from the heat and season with salt and white pepper. The beef and vegetables should be tender. Remove the meat from the pan and cut into bite-sized pieces. Return to the pan.

Add the leeks to the soup and return the pan to low heat. Simmer until the leeks are tender, 10–15 minutes.

Remove the bay leaf. Serve the soup hot with the croutons and meat garnished with parsley or mint.

Serves: 6–8 • Prep: 20 min • Cooking: 3 hr

Beef Soup with Chiles and Tamarind

This wholesome soup gets its delicious tangy flavor from the tamarind.

- 6 cups (1.5 liters) beef or chicken broth or stock (see pages 28 or 56)
- 6 new potatoes, halved
- 6 carrots, cut into thin lengths
- 1 cup (100 g) chopped water chestnuts
- 4 ounces (125 g) broccoli, chopped
- 3 tablespoons dark soy sauce
- 2 tablespoons tamarind paste
- 12 ounces (350 g) beef filet, cut into strips
- 6 ounces (180 g) shiitake mushrooms, thinly sliced
- 4 ounces (125 g) mung bean sprouts
- 4 green scallions (spring onions), white and tender green parts only, chopped
- 2 fresh green chiles, seeded and finely chopped
- 2 fresh red chiles, seeded and finely chopped
- Salt and freshly ground black pepper

Bring the broth to a boil in a large soup pot over medium heat. Add the potatoes, carrots, water chestnuts, broccoli, soy sauce, tamarind, and beef. Cover and simmer over low heat for 15 minutes, stirring occasionally.

Add the mushrooms and cook for 5 minutes. Add the bean sprouts, scallions, and chiles. Cook for 5 minutes more.

Season with salt and pepper. Serve hot.

Serves: 4 • Prep: 15 min • Cooking: 25 min

Chicken Noodle Soup, Asian-Style

This delicious soup contains tamarind, from the reddish brown, curved pods of the beautiful tropical tamarind tree. Each pod holds several large seeds encased by moist, sticky, dark brown flesh, which is used as one of the primary souring agents in cooking, imparting a deliciously fruity tartness to soups, salads, stir-fries, and sauces. Curry leaves are shaped like small bay leaves and impart a wonderful aroma. They are available in Asian food stores, but if you cannot find them, omit or replace with bay leaves.

- 2 tablespoons tamarind paste
- 1 tablespoon Asian chile oil
- 5 dried red chiles, pounded well
- 5 cloves garlic, finely chopped
- 1 tablespoon minced fresh ginger
- 4 tablespoons dark soy sauce
- 1 tablespoon oyster sauce
- 1 tablespoon superfine (caster) sugar
- 6 curry leaves (optional)
- 6 cups (1.5 liters) chicken broth or stock (see page 56)
- 2 boneless, skinless chicken breasts, cut into thin strips
- 2 medium carrots, finely chopped
- 1 cup (125 g) mung bean sprouts
- 6–8 baby corn (sweet corn)
- ½ cup (125 g) chopped green bell peppers (capsicums)
- ½ cup (125 g) chopped red bell peppers (capsicums)
- 6 ounces (180 g) rice vermicelli
- Salt
- Handful of chopped fresh cilantro (coriander) leaves, to garnish

Mix the tamarind, chile oil, chiles, garlic, ginger, and soy and oyster sauces in a large wok.

Warm the wok over medium heat. Add the superfine sugar and curry leaves, if using, and pour in the broth. Bring to a boil, stirring constantly. Simmer for about 5 minutes.

Add the chicken and simmer for another 5 minutes, stirring well. Stir in the carrots, sprouts, baby corn, bell peppers, and rice noodles. and simmer until the chicken and vegetables are tender, about 10 minutes.

Season with salt to taste. Garnish with the cilantro and serve hot.

Serves: 4–6 • Prep: 30 min • Cooking: 30 min

Tomato Noodle Soup

The cumin seeds add a touch of the East to this tomato and noodle soup. Add them if you like cumin, or leave them out. If you like spicy dishes, add crumbled dried chile peppers along with the onion and garlic.

- 2 tablespoons extra-virgin olive oil
- 1 large white onion, finely chopped
- 4 cloves garlic, finely chopped
- ½ teaspoon cumin seeds, freshly ground (optional)
- 2 (14-ounce/400-g) cans whole tomatoes, with juice, chopped
- 3 cups (750 ml) chicken broth or stock (see page 56)
- Salt and freshly ground white pepper
- 4 (3-ounce) packages ramen noodles (350 g instant noodles), flavor packet discarded, soaked in boiling water for 10 minutes (or according to instructions on the package), then drained
- 1–2 tablespoons finely chopped fresh basil or cilantro (coriander), to garnish (optional)

Heat the oil in a large soup pot over medium-high heat. Add the onion, garlic, and cumin, if using, and sauté until the onion is softened, about 5 minutes.

Add the tomatoes and 2 cups (500 ml) of the broth. Season with salt and white pepper. Reduce the heat to low, partially cover the pot, and simmer for 30 minutes.

Add the remaining 1 cup (250 ml) of broth and the soaked noodles. Raise the heat to medium and bring to a boil. Remove from the heat, garnish with the basil or cilantro, if using, and serve hot.

Serves: 4 • Prep: 15 min • Cooking: 40 min

Beef Soup with Chiles and Tamarind

BEEF AND BARLEY SOUP

- 3 tablespoons extra-virgin olive oil
- 1 large onion, finely chopped
- 1 pound (500 g) boneless beef or lamb, cut into small pieces
- 1 tablespoon finely chopped fresh parsley
- 1 teaspoon ground cinnamon

- 5 cups (1.25 liters) water
- 2 tablespoons tomato paste (purée)
  Salt
- 1 cup (100 g) pearl barley
- 2 tablespoons fresh lemon juice
- 2 tablespoons finely chopped fresh cilantro (coriander), to garnish

Heat the oil in a medium soup pot over medium heat. Add the onion and beef and sauté until lightly browned, 8–10 minutes. Add the parsley and cinnamon.

Pour in the water, tomato paste, and salt. Bring to a boil and cook over low heat for 10 minutes.

Stir in the barley. Raise the heat until the soup returns to a boil. Lower the heat again, cover, and simmer until the barley is tender, 40–45 minutes.

Add the lemon juice and cilantro and serve hot.

Serves: 4 • Prep: 20 min • Cooking: about 1 hr

SPICY BEEF SOUP

- 2 tablespoons extra-virgin olive oil
- 1 large white onion, finely chopped
- 2 cloves garlic, finely chopped
- 1 carrot, finely chopped
- 1 stalk celery, finely chopped
- 1 fresh red chile pepper, finely sliced
- 2 tablespoons finely chopped fresh parsley
- 12 ounces (350 g) ground (minced) beef

- 2 (14-ounce/400-g) cans whole tomatoes, chopped, with juice
- 2–3 large potatoes, peeled and diced
- 4 cups (1 liter) beef broth or stock (see page 28)
  Salt and freshly ground black pepper
- 2 tablespoons finely chopped cilantro (coriander), to garnish, optional

Heat the oil in a large soup pot over medium-high heat. Add the onion, garlic, carrot, celery, chile, and parsley and sauté until the onion is softened, about 5 minutes. Add the beef and sauté until nicely browned, about 5 minutes.

Add the tomatoes, potatoes, beef broth, salt, and pepper. Partially cover the pan and simmer over medium-low heat until the potatoes are tender, 15–20 minutes.

Garnish with the cilantro, if desired, and serve hot.

Serves: 4–6 • Prep: 15 min • Cooking: 30 min

TUSCAN MEAT AND VEGETABLE SOUP

- ½ cup (125 ml) extra-virgin olive oil
- 4 scallions (spring onions), trimmed and thinly sliced
- 2 ounces (60 g) cubed pancetta or bacon
- 4 ounces (125 g) ground (minced) beef
- 4 ounces (125 g) fresh or frozen fava (broad) beans
- 1 cup (150 g) fresh or frozen peas

- 2 artichokes, cleaned and sliced
- 4 ounces (125 g) asparagus tips
  Salt and freshly ground black pepper
- 6 cups (1.5 liters) beef broth or stock (see page 28)
- 2 tablespoons finely chopped fresh rosemary
- 4 thick slices firm-textured bread, cut into cubes

Heat 4 tablespoons of the oil in a large soup pot over medium heat. Sauté the scallions until softened, about 5 minutes. Add the pancetta and sauté until browned, about 5 minutes. Add the beef and sauté until browned, about 5 minutes.

Add the fava beans, peas, artichokes, and asparagus. Season with salt and pepper. Sauté for 10–15 minutes, or until the meat is cooked.

Pour in the broth and simmer for 20 minutes more.

Heat the remaining 4 tablespoons of oil in a frying pan with the rosemary and sauté the cubes of bread until pale and golden brown. Season with salt and pepper.

Ladle the soup into individual soup bowls and top with the cubes of fried bread.

Serves: 4 • Prep: 15 min • Cooking: 45–50 min

SOUTHERN ITALIAN EASTER SOUP

- 12 ounces (350 g) lean ground (minced) pork
- 4 large eggs
- 5 tablespoons freshly grated aged pecorino cheese
- 2 cloves garlic, finely chopped
- 1 tablespoon finely chopped fresh parsley
- ¼ teaspoon freshly grated nutmeg

- Salt
- 6 cups (1.5 liters) beef broth or stock (see page 28)
- 10 ounces (300 g) soft fresh ricotta cheese
- 4 tablespoons fine, dry bread crumbs
- 2 tablespoons golden raisins (sultanas)

Place the pork in a large bowl and mix in 1 of the eggs, the pecorino, garlic, parsley, nutmeg, and salt.

Shape heaping teaspoonfuls of the mixture into small meatballs.

Bring the broth to a boil in a large soup pot. Drop in the meatballs and simmer until cooked, about 10 minutes.

Beat the remaining 3 eggs and combine with the ricotta, bread crumbs, and golden raisins to make a creamy mixture. Season with salt.

Pour the egg mixture into the hot broth and stir with a fork for about 1 minute, or until the egg sets into tiny shreds. Serve immediately.

Serves: 4–6 • Prep: 15 min • Cooking: 15 min

GARLIC

This strongly flavored member of the onion family is loved—and loathed—the world over for its pungent odor and taste. Its use in cooking dates from the earliest times; it has been found in Egyptian tombs, where it was placed as a food offering, and is even mentioned in the Bible (Numbers 11:5). Its health benefits have also been lauded for thousands of years, although only in recent times has modern medical science confirmed its medicinal properties as an antibacterial, antifungal, and antithrombotic (preventing blood from clotting). It is rich in sulfur and vitamins B1 and C and contains trace minerals such as phosphorus, iron, and calcium.

HEARTY LEBANESE BEEF AND SPINACH SOUP

- 3 tablespoons sunflower oil
- 8 ounces (250 g) lean beef, cut into thin strips
- 1 large eggplant (aubergine), peeled and diced
- 2 potatoes, peeled and cut into cubes
- 2 carrots, diced
- 2 green bell peppers (capsicums), seeded and diced
- 1 leek, white and tender green parts, finely chopped
- 4 cups (1 liter) beef broth or stock (see page 28), boiling
- 2 teaspoons fresh pomegranate seeds (optional)
- ¼ teaspoon saffron threads
- 3 ears corn, cut into thirds
  Salt and freshly ground black pepper
- 3 ounces (90 g) spinach, finely shredded
- 1 ounce (30 g) dill, finely chopped
- 1 cup (100 g) canned garbanzo beans (chick peas), rinsed and drained

Heat the oil in a large soup pot over medium heat. Add the beef and sauté until the meat is browned, 8–10 minutes.

Add the eggplant, potatoes, carrots, bell peppers, leek, broth, pomegranate seeds, if using, saffron, and corn. Cook over medium heat, stirring constantly, until well mixed.

Bring to a boil. Simmer over medium heat for 20 minutes.

Season with salt and pepper. Add the spinach, dill, and garbanzo beans. Cook for 10 minutes more.

Serve hot.

Serves: 4 • Prep: 10 min • Cooking: 40 min

MIDDLE EASTERN MEATBALL SOUP

Meatballs
- 1 pound (500 g) ground (minced) lamb
- 2 teaspoons minced fresh ginger
- 2 cloves garlic, finely chopped
- 1 teaspoon ground turmeric
  Juice of ½ lemon
- 1 teaspoon salt
- 2 tablespoons ground coriander
- ½ teaspoon garam masala
- 2 tablespoons finely chopped fresh cilantro (coriander)
- ½ teaspoon crushed red pepper flakes (optional)

Soup
- 2 tablespoons extra-virgin olive oil
- 2 tablespoons butter
- 1 onion, finely chopped
- 1 cup (250 ml) crushed tomatoes (passata)

- 1 large stalk celery, diced
- 1 red bell pepper (capsicum), seeded and diced
- 2 dried bird's-eye chiles, seeded and finely chopped
- 1 tablespoon ground coriander
- 1 teaspoon sweet paprika
- 1 teaspoon garam masala
- ½ teaspoon salt
- ¼ teaspoon ground turmeric
- 1 vegetable bouillon (stock) cube dissolved in 4 cups (1 liter) boiling water
- 2 tablespoons finely chopped fresh parsley
  Juice of ½ lime
- 1 (14-ounce/400-g) can garbanzo beans (chick peas), rinsed and drained

Meatballs: Place all the ingredients in a bowl and mix well. Dampen your hands and shape the mixture into meatballs the size of walnuts. Set aside.

Soup: Heat the oil and butter in a large soup pot over medium heat. Add the onion and sauté until the onion is softened, about 5 minutes.

Add the tomatoes, celery, bell pepper, chiles, coriander, paprika, garam masala, salt, and turmeric. Stir well. Sauté until all the moisture has evaporated and the oil has begun to seep to the top, 15–20 minutes.

Remove the pan from the heat. Blend the ingredients together with a handheld blender until smooth.

Add the meatballs and return to the heat. Cook over low heat, stirring occasionally, for 10 minutes more.

Pour in the dissolved bouillon. Cook until the soup has thickened slightly, 15 minutes more.

Add the parsley, lime juice, and the garbanzo beans. Boil for 2 minutes. Stir well and serve hot.

Serves: 4–6 • Prep: 15 min • Cooking: 50 min

NORTH AFRICAN SOUP

1 pound (500 g) lamb or mutton, cut into small chunks
2 tablespoons clarified butter (ghee)
2 onions, finely chopped
1 stalk celery, finely chopped
3 teaspoons finely chopped fresh flat-leaf parsley
1 tablespoon finely chopped fresh cilantro (coriander)
1 small stick cinnamon
4 saffron threads, crumbled
¼ teaspoon ground ginger
Salt and freshly ground black pepper
3½ quarts (3.5 liters) cold water
2 cups (400 g) dried garbanzo beans (chickpeas), soaked overnight and drained
2½ cups (250 g) brown lentils
2 pounds (1 kg) firm-ripe tomatoes, coarsely chopped
½ cup (100 g) short-grain rice
3 tablespoons all-purpose (plain) flour
2 tablespoons fresh lemon juice

Combine the lamb, butter, onions, celery, 1½ teaspoons of the parsley, 1½ teaspoons of the cilantro, cinnamon, saffron, and ginger in a large soup pot. Season with salt and pepper. Stir over medium heat until the butter has melted.

Pour in 4 cups (1 liter) of the cold water. Bring to a boil and simmer for 25–30 minutes, or until reduced by half.

Stir in the garbanzo beans and lentils and the remaining water. Simmer over medium heat until the lentils and beans are tender, about 75 minutes.

Stir in the tomatoes and the remaining 1½ teaspoons parsley and 1½ teaspoons cilantro. Bring to a boil, lower the heat, and simmer for 10 minutes.

Add the rice.

Mix the flour to a smooth paste with a little cold water in a small bowl.

Remove the soup from the heat and add the flour mixture, stirring constantly.

Return to the heat and cook for 10 minutes, stirring constantly. The soup should not be too thick.

Stir in the lemon juice and serve hot.

Serves: 8–10 • Prep: 20 min + 12 hr to soak beans • Cooking: 2 hr 25 min

CALDO GALLEGO

Vegetables may vary in this spicy Galician soup, but chorizo (a spicy pork and pimiento sausage), garbanzo beans, and tomatoes are constants.

⅓ cup (80 ml) extra-virgin olive oil
2 large Spanish onions, finely chopped
4 cloves garlic, finely chopped
Salt
1½ teaspoons smoked Spanish paprika (pimentòn)
8 ounces (250 g) chorizo sausage, thinly sliced
8 ounces (250 g) roasted pork loin, cut into cubes
2 medium potatoes, peeled and cut into small cubes
1 red bell pepper (capsicum), seeded and diced
1 green bell pepper (capsicum), seeded and diced
1 (14-ounce/400-g) can garbanzo beans (chickpeas), rinsed and drained
10 tomatoes, peeled and finely chopped
6 cups (1.5 liters) cold water
2 bay leaves
2 teaspoons finely chopped fresh sage
Freshly ground black pepper
3 tablespoons finely chopped fresh flat-leaf parsley

Heat the oil in a large soup pot over medium heat. Add the onions and garlic and season with salt. Sauté until the onions are softened, about 5 minutes.

Stir in the paprika, chorizo, and pork. Sauté until lightly browned.

Add the potatoes, bell peppers, beans, and tomatoes. Season with salt.

Pour in the water and add the bay leaves and sage. Bring to a boil. Simmer over low heat until the potatoes and tomatoes are tender, about 30 minutes.

Season with salt and pepper to taste. Remove the bay leaves. Stir in the parsley. Serve hot.

Serves: 4–6 • Prep: 15 min • Cooking: 50 min

North African Soup

TUSCAN MINESTRONE WITH ITALIAN SAUSAGE

- 1 cup (200 g) thickly sliced Italian sausage
- 3 cloves garlic, finely chopped
- 1 onion, coarsely chopped
- 4 stalks celery, thinly sliced
- 2 potatoes, unpeeled and diced
- 2 carrots, diced
- 2 tomatoes, diced
- 1 cup (100 g) sliced green beans
- 1 cup (100 g) fresh or frozen shell beans (lima beans, cranberry/ borlotti beans, etc.)
- 2 tablespoons coarsely chopped fresh flat-leaf parsley
- 3 leaves fresh sage, coarsely chopped

- 1 tablespoon finely chopped fresh rosemary leaves
- 6 cups (1.5) liters boiling water
- 1 small bunch Scotch kale or Italian kale (cavolo nero), or cabbage, coarsely chopped
- ½ cup (75 g) fresh or frozen peas
- 4 thick slices oven-toasted dense-grain bread (rubbed with garlic)
  Salt and freshly ground black pepper
- 4 tablespoons extra-virgin olive oil (preferably peppery Tuscan oil)
- ½ cup (60 g) freshly grated Parmesan cheese

Combine the sausage, garlic, onion, celery, potatoes, carrots, tomatoes, green beans, shell beans, parsley, sage, and rosemary in a large soup pot. Pour in the water, cover, and simmer over low heat for 90 minutes.

Add the kale and peas. Cook for 30 minutes more.

Preheat the oven to 400°F (200°C/gas 6). Toast the bread in the oven until dried and golden brown, about 10 minutes.

Place the toast in individual serving bowls and ladle the soup over the top. Season the soup with salt and pepper and a drizzle of Tuscan oil.

Sprinkle with the Parmesan and serve hot.

Serves: 4–6 • Prep: 30 min • Cooking: 2 hr

QUICK MINESTRONE WITH ITALIAN SAUSAGE

- 4 large sweet Italian sausages, quartered, well pricked with a fork
- 6 cups (1.5 liters) beef broth or stock (see page 28)
- 1 (14-ounce/400-g) can whole tomatoes, chopped, with juice
- 2 large potatoes, peeled and diced

- 1 (10-ounce/300-g) package mixed frozen vegetables
  Salt and freshly ground black pepper
- 4 tablespoons freshly grated Parmesan cheese

Place the sausages in a large soup pot over medium-high heat and sauté until well browned, 6–8 minutes. Drain off the fat in the pan.

Pour in the broth, tomatoes, potatoes, and mixed vegetables. Season with salt and pepper. Bring to a boil. Partially cover the pot and simmer over low heat until the potatoes and vegetables are tender, about 15 minutes.

Sprinkle with the Parmesan and serve hot.

Serves: 4–6 • Prep: 10 min • Cooking: 25 min

GERMAN PEA SOUP WITH BACON AND HAM SAUSAGE

- 2 tablespoons sunflower oil
- 1 large onion, finely chopped
  8-ounce (250 g) piece lean bacon
- 1 potato, finely chopped
- 1 small carrot, finely chopped
- 2½ cups (250 g) green split peas
- 6 cups (1.5 liters) chicken broth or stock (see page 56)

- ½ teaspoon dried marjoram
  Salt and freshly ground black pepper
- 4 ounces (100 g) German ham sausage, skinned and chopped
- 1 tablespoon finely chopped fresh parsley

Heat the oil in a large soup pot over medium heat. Add the onion and sauté until softened, about 5 minutes.

Add the bacon, potato, and carrot and cook for 5 minutes.

Add the split peas, broth, and marjoram and bring to a boil. Boil for 2 minutes, skimming off any froth. Partially cover and simmer for 35–45 minutes, or until the soup has thickened and the peas have softened.

Remove the bacon from the soup, trim off any fat, and cut into small cubes. Return the cubes to the soup and stir in the sausage and parsley.

Reheat the soup and season with salt and pepper. Simmer for 5 minutes more. Serve hot.

Serves: 4–6 • Prep: 15 min • Cooking: 1 ¼ hr

BAVARIAN POTATO SOUP WITH FRANKFURTERS

Frankfurters originated in the German city of Frankfurt in the mid-17th century. In 1904, a Frankfurt butcher moved to Vienna, where he made similar smoked sausages. These became known as Wiener Würstel (Vienna sausages) and were sometimes called wieners in the United States.

- 4 ounces (125 g) bacon, cut into small pieces
- 2 onions, finely chopped
- 2 large carrots, finely chopped
- 1 large leek, trimmed and thinly sliced
- ½ celery root (celeriac), peeled and cut into small pieces
- 6 medium potatoes, (about 1½ pounds/750 g), peeled and cubed
- 1 clove garlic, finely chopped
- ½ teaspoon sweet paprika
- ½ teaspoon dried marjoram, or 1 tablespoon finely chopped fresh marjoram
  Salt
- 6–8 cups (1.5–2 liters) beef or chicken broth or stock (see pages 28 or 56)
- 4–6 frankfurters, thinly sliced
- 2 tablespoons finely chopped fresh flat-leaf parsley

Sauté the bacon in a large soup pot over medium heat until the fat has melted, about 4 minutes.

Add the onions, carrots, leek, and celery root and sauté for 5 minutes, stirring constantly.

Stir in the potatoes and add the garlic, paprika, marjoram, and ½ teaspoon salt. Pour in 6 cups (1.5 liters) of the broth and bring to a boil. Partially cover the pan and simmer over low heat until the vegetables have softened, 20–30 minutes, stirring occasionally. Add more stock if the soup begins to thicken in the early stages of the cooking time.

Stir in the frankfurters and 1 tablespoon of the parsley. Simmer for 4 minutes more, without letting the soup come to a boil. Remove from the heat and season with salt and white pepper. Garnish with the remaining 1 tablespoon of parsley and serve hot.

Serves: 6 • Prep: 25 min • Cooking: 40 min

SALAMI AND CABBAGE SOUP

- ⅓ cup (80 ml) extra-virgin olive oil
- 2 cloves garlic, finely chopped
- 1 onion, finely chopped
- 1 savoy cabbage, finely shredded
  Salt and freshly ground black pepper
- 6 cups (1.5 liters) water
- 4 ounces (150 g) salami, diced
- 2 cups (400 g) short-grain rice
- 2 tablespoons finely chopped fresh parsley
- 1 cup (125 g) freshly grated Parmesan cheese

Heat the oil in a large soup pot over medium heat. Add the garlic and onion and sauté until softened, about 5 minutes.

Add the cabbage and season with salt and pepper. Cook over medium heat for 15 minutes.

Pour in the water and bring to a boil. Add the salami and rice and simmer over low heat until the rice is tender, about 15 minutes.

Sprinkle with the parsley and Parmesan and serve hot.

Serves: 4–6 • Prep: 10 min • Cooking: 35 min

CHICKEN AND MILK SOUP

This protein-rich soup is simple to make. Its unusual combination of milk and chicken is nutritious and warming on a winter's day or when recovering from any ailment.

- ⅓ cup (80 g) butter
- 1 large onion, finely chopped
- 2 boneless, skinless chicken breasts, diced
- 1 cup (100 g) fresh or frozen corn (sweet corn) kernels
- 1 cup (250 g) creamed corn (sweet corn)
- 6 cups (1.5 liters) whole milk
- 1 cup (250 ml) heavy (double) cream
- 1 teaspoon freshly ground white pepper
- 2 chicken bouillon (stock) cubes, crumbled
- 2 tablespoons cornstarch (cornflour)
- ½ cup (60 ml) warm water
  Salt

Melt the butter in a large soup pot over medium heat. Add the onion and chicken and sauté until the onion is softened and the chicken is white, about 10 minutes.

Add the corn kernels and creamed corn, milk, cream, pepper, and bouillon cubes. Partially cover and simmer over low heat until the liquid has reduced by about a quarter, about 40 minutes.

Stir together the cornstarch and water and stir into the soup. Cook, stirring often, until the soup has thickened slightly, about 10 minutes. Season with salt. Serve hot.

Serves: 4–6 • Prep: 10 min • Cooking: 1 hr

Bavarian Potato Soup with Frankfurters

CHILE CORN SOUP

1 tablespoon extra-virgin olive oil

1 boneless, skinless chicken breast, cut into small chunks

4 cups (1 liter) milk

1 large onion, finely chopped

12 ounces (350 g) potatoes, peeled and diced

2 tablespoons finely chopped fresh cilantro (coriander)

3 fresh red bird's-eye chiles, seeded and finely chopped

1 pound (500 g) frozen or canned corn (sweet corn)

1 tablespoon cornstarch (cornflour) mixed with 3 tablespoons cold water

Salt and freshly ground black pepper

½ cup (125 ml) light (single) cream

3 tablespoons snipped fresh chives

Heat the oil in a medium soup pot over high heat. Add the chicken and sauté until white, 7–8 minutes. Transfer to a bowl and set aside.

Pour the milk into the pan and add the onion and potatoes. Bring just to a boil over medium heat.

Lower the heat and add the cilantro, chiles, and half the corn. Continue stirring for 3 minutes. Simmer over very low heat for 10 minutes, stirring occasionally to make sure the milk does not burn.

Remove the pan from the heat. Blend with a handheld blender until smooth. Mix in the cornstarch paste.

Return the soup to the heat and reheat gently until the soup has thickened. Bring to a boil again and add the remaining corn. Simmer until the corn is cooked, about 3 minutes. Remove from the heat and season with salt and pepper to taste.

Stir in the cream and keep stirring for 3 minutes. Stir in the chives and chicken. Serve hot.

Serves: 4–6 • Prep: 15 min • Cooking: 30 min

CURRIED CHICKEN SOUP WITH CORN

2½ tablespoons Asian sesame oil

2 boneless, skinless chicken breasts (about 1 pound/500 g), cut into long, thin strips

2 cloves garlic, finely chopped

5 cups (1.25 liters) chicken broth or stock (see page 56)

1 (14-ounce/400-g) can corn (sweet corn) kernels, drained

1 tablespoon curry powder

3 tablespoons rice wine

1 teaspoon sugar

Salt

1 large egg

2 tablespoons chopped scallions (green onions)

Heat 2 tablespoons of the sesame oil in a large soup pot over medium-high heat. Add the chicken and garlic and sauté until the chicken is white, 7–8 minutes. Remove the chicken and set aside.

Pour in the chicken broth and corn. Bring to a boil and simmer for 10 minutes.

Stir together the curry powder and rice wine in a small bowl until smooth. Stir into the simmering soup. Add the sugar and season with salt to taste. Simmer for another 5 minutes.

In a small bowl, beat together the egg and remaining ½ tablespoon of sesame oil.

Return the cooked chicken to the soup. Stir well and return to a gentle simmer. Slowly pour the egg and sesame oil into the soup, stirring constantly.

Remove from the heat. Garnish with the scallions and serve hot.

Serves: 4 • Prep: 15 min • Cooking: 25 min

PENNSYLVANIA CHICKEN AND CORN SOUP

1 small chicken, about 1½ pounds (750 g), cut into 8 pieces
4 cups (1 liter) water
1 large onion, finely chopped
2 stalks celery, finely chopped
2 teaspoons salt
1 teaspoon freshly ground white pepper

1 (15-ounce/400 g) can creamed corn (sweet corn)
1 (14-ounce/400-g) can cream of celery soup
½ cup (125 ml) light (single) cream
Handful of chives, snipped, to garnish

Place the chicken in a large soup pot with the water, onion, celery, salt, and white pepper. Bring to a boil over medium heat. Simmer over low heat for 2 hours, or until the chicken is cooked through.

Remove the pan from the heat and take the chicken out. Remove all the bones, skin, and any fat that has accumulated. Cut the chicken meat into rough pieces.

Blend the vegetables in the pan with a handheld blender until partially smooth.

Return the chicken meat to the soup. Stir in the corn, creamed corn, and celery soup. Simmer over low heat, stirring constantly, until the corn is cooked, about 10 minutes more.

Remove from the heat and mix in the cream. Garnish with the chives and serve hot.

Serves: 4–6 • Prep: 15 min • Cooking: 2¼ hr

CORN

Corn, or sweet corn in British English, is one of the world's staple cereal crops. Originally from Central and South America, it is now cultivated around the world and is the basic ingredient in many much-loved dishes, including a whole range of corn breads, popcorn, hush puppies, tamales, tortillas, and polenta, to name a few. Nutritionally, corn is a useful source of protein and fiber and contains beta-carotene and small amounts of B vitamins and vitamin C. When buying fresh corn, always choose fresh-looking, tight, green husks. Strip back a part of the husk and check that the kernels are plump; pop one between your thumb and index finger—a milky liquid should spurt out.

Borscht

2 tablespoons extra-virgin olive oil
1 large onion, chopped
2 large stalks celery, chopped
1 large carrot, chopped
  Pinch of crushed red pepper flakes
1 teaspoon caraway seeds
1 bay leaf
2 tablespoons finely chopped fresh parsley
3 cloves garlic, finely chopped
  Handful of chopped fresh dill
1 pound (500 g) green (white) cabbage, chopped

2 pounds (1 kg) potatoes, peeled and cut into cubes
1 pound (500 g) beets (beetroot), peeled and coarsely chopped
1 teaspoon salt
1 teaspoon freshly ground black pepper
6 cups (1.5 liters) beef broth or stock (see below)
1 (14-ounce/400-g) can whole tomatoes, with juice
  Sour cream, to garnish
  Few sprigs of fresh dill, to garnish

Heat the oil in a large soup pot over medium heat. Add the onion, celery, carrot, red pepper flakes, and caraway seeds and sauté until the vegetables are softened but not browned, about 10 minutes.

Add the bay leaf, parsley, garlic, dill, and cabbage. Sauté until the cabbage is wilted and half its original bulk, about 5 minutes.

Add the potatoes, beets, salt, pepper, and broth. Bring to a boil, cover, and simmer for 30 minutes.

Add the tomatoes, crushing them between your fingers as you add them. Partially cover the pan and simmer on low heat for 30 more minutes.

Discard the bay leaf. In a blender, puree the soup in batches, blending until the borscht is free of lumps, but still has a bit of texture. You do not want it to be completely smooth. Taste for salt and pepper.

Serve hot with a dollop of sour cream and a small piece of fresh dill on top.

Serves: 6–8 • Prep: 15 min • Cooking: 1 ¼ hr

Beef Stock

Beef stock is a basic ingredient in so many recipes—from soups and sauces, to risottos and meat and vegetable dishes—that it really is worth taking the time to make it at home. It freezes well, so it can be made in large quantities and frozen for later use.

1 large onion, cut into quarters
1 large carrot, cut in half
1 leek
2 stalks celery, including leaves
4 whole cloves (optional)
  Small bunch parsley
2 bay leaves

2 cloves garlic, peeled
2 very ripe tomatoes
1 tablespoon coarse sea salt
3 pounds (1.5 kg) boiling beef
2 pounds (1 kg) beef bones
  About 5 quarts (5 liters) cold water

Rinse and peel or scrape the vegetables. If using cloves, stick them into the onion quarters.

Place all the ingredients in a large soup pot and cover with the water. Over medium-low heat, bring the mixture to a boil.

Simmer over low heat for 3 hours. Skim the stock during cooking to remove the scum that will rise to the surface, at first abundantly but then tapering off.

Strain the stock into a large bowl, discarding the vegetables. Let the stock cool. (The meat can be served as a main course or used in the recipe on page 104.)

When the stock is completely cool, place in the refrigerator. If you wish to remove the fat, it will solidify on the top and can be lifted off and discarded.

Makes: about 3 quarts (3 liters) • Prep: 15 min • Cooking: 3–4 hr

GREEK FISH SOUP

- 4 tablespoons extra-virgin olive oil
- 2 medium onions, coarsely chopped
- 4 cloves garlic, finely chopped
- 2 tablespoons finely chopped fresh parsley
- 2 pounds (1 kg) potatoes, scrubbed and cubed
- 1 (14-ounce/400-g) can tomatoes, chopped, with juice
- 2 pounds (1 kg) scorpion fish or dogfish fillets (or, in North America, halibut, cod, or grouper fillets; in Australia, flathead, snapper, or dory fillets)
  Water
  Salt and freshly ground white pepper

Heat 3 tablespoons of the oil in a large soup pot. Add the onions, 3 cloves of the garlic, and the parsley and sauté until lightly browned, 7–8 minutes.

Add the potatoes and sauté for 5 minutes. Add the tomatoes and bring to a boil.

Add the fish and enough water to cover. Partially cover the pan and cook for 20–30 minutes, until the fish is very tender.

Season with salt and white pepper. Stir in the remaining 1 tablespoon of oil and 1 clove garlic and let stand for 5 minutes before serving.

Serves: 4 • Prep: 20 min • Cooking: 40 min

FISH SOUP WITH BULGUR

You can substitute short-grain rice for the bulgur for an equally delicious soup.

- 3 pounds (1.5 kg) mixed firm-textured fish, cleaned, boned, and cut into chunks
- 4 tablespoons fresh lemon juice
- 8 saffron threads, crumbled
- ½ teaspoon salt
- 3 large red bell peppers (capsicums), seeded and cut into strips
- 6 tablespoons extra-virgin olive oil
- 2 onions, chopped
- 4 cloves garlic, chopped
- 6 large ripe tomatoes, chopped
- 1 stalk celery, chopped
- 1 carrot, chopped
- 4 sprigs wild or common fennel
- 1 bay leaf
  Grated zest of 1 orange
- 1 teaspoon cumin seeds
- 8 cups (2 liters) water
- 1 cup (200 g) bulgur
- 1 tablespoon salted capers, rinsed

Place the fish in a large bowl and drizzle with the lemon juice. Add half the saffron and sprinkle with the salt. Stir well and set aside for 15 minutes.

Heat the oil in a large soup pot over medium heat. Add the bell peppers and sauté until slightly softened, about 10 minutes. Transfer to a plate with a slotted spoon and set aside.

In the same pan, sauté the onions, garlic, tomatoes, celery, carrot, fennel, bay leaf, orange zest, and cumin for 5 minutes.

Pour in the water and bring to a boil. Add the fish and simmer until the fish is cooked but not crumbly, about 10 minutes.

Remove the fish from the pan and cover with a serving plate to keep warm.

Return the soup to a boil and add the bulgur. Simmer until the bulgur is tender, 15–20 minutes.

Turn off the heat and stir in the fish, capers, bell peppers, and remaining saffron. Let rest for 5 minutes. Remove the bay leaf. Serve hot.

Serves: 6–8 • Prep: 30 min + 15 min to marinate • Cooking: 50 min

FRENCH FISH SOUP

Serve this striking red soup with rouille au safran *(a Provençal saffron and garlic sauce). The recipe is provided below.*

⅓ cup (80 ml) extra-virgin olive oil
2 leeks, trimmed and finely chopped
1 onion, finely chopped
4 tomatoes, peeled and finely chopped
1 tablespoon tomato paste (concentrate)
2 cloves garlic, finely chopped
¼ teaspoon fennel seeds

1 bay leaf
1 (½-inch/1-cm) piece of orange zest
Salt and freshly ground black pepper
8 cups (2 liters) water
2 pounds (1 kg) boneless fish (red snapper, halibut, cod, sea bass, flathead, dory), cleaned and cut into chunks

Heat the oil in a large soup pot over medium heat. Add the leeks and onion and sauté until lightly browned, about 7 minutes.

Add the tomatoes. Lower the heat and cook for 2–3 minutes, until the tomatoes have softened.

Stir in the tomato paste, garlic, fennel, bay leaf, and orange zest. Season with salt and pepper. Pour in the water. Add the fish, bring to a boil, and cook for 20 minutes.

Discard the bay leaf and orange zest. Transfer to a food processor and process until smooth.

Add the saffron and return to medium heat for 2–3 minutes, or until heated through, stirring often. Serve hot.

Serves: 4–6 • Prep: 20 min • Cooking: 30 min

BOUILLABAISSE

½ cup (125 ml) extra-virgin olive oil
2 medium onions, finely chopped
2 leeks, trimmed and finely sliced
1 pound (500 g) tomatoes, peeled, seeded, and finely chopped
6 small potatoes, peeled
2 cups (500 ml) dry white wine
6 cloves garlic, finely chopped, + 2 cloves, peeled and left whole
1 small bunch wild fennel, finely chopped
2 bay leaves

½ teaspoon crumbled saffron threads
Salt and freshly ground black pepper
6 cups (1.5 liters) fish stock (see page 98) or water
24 small clams, in shell
2 pounds (1 kg) mixed shellfish
2 pounds (1 kg) fish fillets or boneless steaks, such as halibut, cod, sea bass, red snapper, or grouper, cut into chunks
6–8 thick slices firm-textured bread

Heat ¼ cup (60 ml) of the oil in a large soup pot over low heat. Add the onions and leeks and sauté until lightly browned, 7–8 minutes.

Add the tomatoes, potatoes, wine, chopped garlic, fennel, bay leaves, saffron, and remaining ¼ cup (60 ml) of oil. Season with salt and pepper. Add the stock and simmer for 10 minutes.

Add the clams and cook until they begin to open, 5 minutes. Discard any that do not open. Add the remaining shellfish and the chunks of fish and simmer gently until the fish begins to flake, 10–15 minutes.

Preheat the oven to 400°F (200°C/gas 6). Toast the bread in the oven until it dries out, 5–7 minutes. Rub each piece of toast with the whole garlic and set aside.

Place pieces of toast in individual soup bowls and ladle the fish stock and pieces of fish and seafood over the top. Serve hot.

Serves: 6–8 • Prep: 30 min • Cooking: 40 min

SAFFRON ROUILLE

This Provençal sauce contains raw eggs; you may prefer to use pasteurized eggs. Place the rouille in a small bowl with a serving spoon in the center of the table and allow your guests to help themselves.

6 cloves garlic, peeled
½ teaspoon salt
Freshly ground white pepper

½ teaspoon crumbled saffron threads
2 large egg yolks
1 cup (250 ml) extra-virgin olive oil

Crush the garlic with the salt, preferably using a mortar and pestle. Place in a small bowl and stir in the pepper, saffron, and egg yolks.

Let stand for 5 minutes, then add the oil in a thin, steady trickle, stirring constantly, until smooth and creamy.

Makes: about 1 cup (250 ml) • Prep: 15 min

BOURRIDE

- 2 leeks, white part only, thinly sliced
- 1 shallot, finely sliced
- 1 pound (500 g) potatoes, peeled and thinly sliced
- 2 cloves garlic, crushed (optional)
- 2 pounds (1 kg) firm-textured white fish, such as cod, brill, turbot, or monkfish, filleted, skinned, and cut into large pieces
- 4 cups (1 liter) fish stock (see page 98)
- 2/3 cup (150 ml) dry white wine
- 2 cups (500 ml) aïoli (see recipe below)
  Salt and freshly ground black pepper
- 4–6 slices French bread, toasted
- 2 tablespoons finely chopped fresh flat-leaf parsley, to garnish

Place the leeks, shallot, and potatoes in layers in a large soup pot with the garlic (if using). Lay the pieces of fish on top and pour in the stock and wine.

Poach gently (do not boil) until the fish is just cooked, 10–15 minutes. Use a slotted spoon to transfer the fish to a serving dish and keep warm.

Bring the cooking liquid to a boil and simmer over high heat until reduced to half of its original volume. Remove the potatoes when tender and keep warm.

Warm 1¼ cups (310 ml) of the aïoli in a saucepan over low heat. Strain the reduced stock and gradually pour it into the aïoli, whisking constantly.

Bring the soup to a simmer. Do not boil. It should be thick, pale, and creamy. Season with salt and pepper.

Place a slice of toast in individual serving bowls and arrange the fish and potato on top. Ladle the soup over the top. Spoon the remaining aïoli on top and sprinkle with the parsley. Serve hot.

Serves: 4 • Prep: 20 min • Cooking: 30 min

MUSSEL SOUP

- 3 pounds (1.5 kg) fresh mussels, in shell
- ¼ cup (60 ml) extra-virgin olive oil
- 4 large tomatoes, peeled and chopped
- 3 tablespoons finely chopped fresh parsley
- 4 cloves garlic, finely chopped
  Salt and freshly ground black pepper
- 2 cups (500 ml) fish stock (see page 98)
- 4 large, thick slices of bread, toasted and, if desired, rubbed

Soak the mussels in cold water for 1 hour. Scrub well.

Heat the oil in a large soup pot over medium heat. Add the tomatoes, 2 tablespoons of the parsley, and 2 cloves of garlic. Cook for 5 minutes. Add the mussels and cook until they are all open, about 5 minutes. Discard any that do not open.

Sprinkle with the remaining 1 tablespoon of parsley and 2 cloves of garlic. Add the fish stock. Season with salt and pepper and cook for 4–5 minutes more.

Arrange the toasted bread in individual serving dishes and spoon the mussels and the cooking juices over the top. Serve hot.

Serves: 4 • Prep: 15 min + 1 hr to soak mussels • Cooking: 15 min

AIOLI

Another classic Provençal sauce. Use it in the recipe above or serve with fish soups, or boiled or baked fish and meats. It contains raw eggs; you may prefer to use pasteurized eggs.

- 6 cloves garlic, peeled
- 2 large egg yolks
- 1 tablespoon white wine vinegar
- 2 cups (500 ml) extra-virgin olive oil
- Salt and freshly ground white pepper
- 1 tablespoon lemon juice

Crush the garlic, preferably using a pestle and mortar.

Place in a medium bowl and stir in the egg yolks and vinegar. Add the oil in a thin, steady trickle, stirring constantly until smooth and creamy. Season with salt and white pepper and drizzle with the lemon juice.

Makes: about 2 cups (500 ml) • Prep: 15 min

FINNAN CHOWDER

This Scottish fish soup is made with finnan haddie, or smoked haddock named after Findon, a fishing village near Aberdeen. It is best made with skinned, undyed smoked haddock.

¼ cup (60 g) butter
2 medium onions, thinly sliced
2 stalks celery, finely chopped
2 carrots, one thinly sliced and one finely grated
1 leek, trimmed and finely chopped
4 ounces (125 g) bacon, diced
  Salt and freshly ground black pepper
5 cups (1.25 liters) fish stock (see page 98)

About 1½ cups (350 g) leftover mashed potatoes
2 smoked haddocks, weighing about 1 pound (500 g) total, cut into 1-inch (2.5-cm) cubes
1¼ cups (310 ml) light (single) cream
1 tablespoon finely chopped fresh flat-leaf parsley, to garnish

Melt the butter in a large soup pot over low heat. Add the onions, celery, sliced carrot, and leek and sauté until softened, about 10 minutes. Remove and set aside.

Add the bacon and sauté until lightly browned, about 5 minutes.

Return the vegetables to the pan with the bacon. Season with salt and pepper. Pour in the fish stock and bring to a boil. Stir in the mashed potatoes, grated carrot, bacon, and haddock. Gently stir the mixture and simmer for 5 minutes.

Stir in the cream and heat gently. Season with salt and pepper and garnish with the parsley. Serve hot.

Serves: 4–6 • Prep: 15 min • Cooking: 25 min

NEW ENGLAND CLAM CHOWDER

Clam chowder is a traditional shellfish soup in New England and in Newfoundland. Chowder probably comes from the French chaudière, *an iron cooking pot that settlers brought with them. The Native Americans cooked their clams with hot stones placed in water in a hollowed-out tree trunk. The settlers' pots came in handy for all clam lovers. Various versions of clam chowder exist, some with diced salt pork and no potatoes. Manhattan clam chowder even incorporates tomatoes (and is red).*

3 pounds (1.5 kg) fresh clams (about 30 clams) or one 10-ounce (300-g) can or 12 ounces (350 g) frozen clam meat
1¼ cups (310 ml) water or bottled clam juice, if using canned clams
1 teaspoon + 4 tablespoons butter
1 onion, finely chopped
1 stalk celery, finely chopped
2 cloves garlic, finely chopped
  Salt

2 tablespoons all-purpose (plain) flour
⅔ cup (150 ml) dry white wine
3 medium potatoes, diced
1 bay leaf
2 allspice berries
1½ cups (375 ml) heavy (double) cream
1 cup (100 g) frozen corn kernels or kernels from 1 ear fresh corn
  Freshly ground black pepper
  Fresh flat-leaf parsley, to garnish

Wash the fresh clams and place in a large soup pot with the water or clam juice and 1 teaspoon of the butter. Simmer until the clams have opened up, 8–10 minutes.

Strain the clams through a large strainer into a large bowl. Reserve the stock. Discard any unopened shells. Remove the meat from the rest. Chop the larger clams and leave the small ones whole.

If you are using canned clams, drain the juices and add them to the water or clam juice. If you are using frozen clams, defrost them first.

Melt the remaining 4 tablespoons of butter in the same soup pot over medium heat. Add the onion, celery, garlic, and ¼ teaspoon salt and sauté over medium heat until softened, about 5 minutes.

Mix in the flour and stir in the clam stock (or fish stock) and the wine. Add the potatoes, bay leaf, and allspice. Simmer until the potatoes are tender, about 10 minutes. Add the corn and cook for 5 minutes more.

Remove from the heat and discard the bay leaf and allspice berries. Stir in the cream and clams. Cook for 3 minutes more, but do not bring to a boil.

Season with salt and pepper to taste. Garnish with the parsley and serve hot.

Serves: 4 • Prep: 30 min • Cooking: 30 min + 8–10 min extra for fresh clams

New England Clam Chowder

CORN CHOWDER WITH NEW POTATOES, BELL PEPPERS, AND BASIL

You can make this soup with frozen corn, but it's best when made with fresh cobs. Scrape the cob downward with a sharp knife to remove all the kernels.

- 3 tablespoons extra-virgin olive oil
- 2 small onions, finely chopped
- 2 cloves garlic, finely chopped
- 1 mild red or green chile, seeded and finely chopped
- 1 stalk celery, thinly sliced
- 1 carrot, thinly sliced
- 1 teaspoon salt
- 1 tablespoon cornstarch/cornflour, dissolved in ¼ cup (60 ml) cold water
- 1 pound (500 g) new potatoes, thinly sliced
- Kernels from 4 ears corn (sweet corn), or 1 pound (500 g) frozen corn (sweet corn) kernels

- 1 teaspoon tomato paste (concentrate)
- 8 cups (2 liters) chicken broth or stock (see page 56)
- 2 red bell peppers (capsicums), seeded and diced
- 2 tablespoons finely chopped fresh basil
- 1 tablespoon finely chopped fresh flat-leaf parsley
- 6 tablespoons heavy (double) cream (optional)

Heat the oil in a large soup pot over medium heat. Add the onions, garlic, chile, celery, and carrot and sauté for 5 minutes.

Add the salt. Cover and cook until the vegetables have softened, 5–10 minutes.

Stir in the cornstarch mixture and mix until blended. Add the potatoes and corn.

Dissolve the tomato paste in 4 cups (1 liter) of the broth. Whisk the mixture into the vegetables.

Bring to a boil and simmer until the potatoes are just tender, but not mushy, 8–10 minutes.

For a thick soup, break the vegetables up a little in the pot with a potato masher.

Add the bell peppers and pour in the remaining 4 cups (1 liter) of broth. Return to a gentle boil. Stir in the basil, parsley, and cream, if using, and serve hot.

Serves: 6–8 • Prep: 25 min • Cooking: 25 min

CORN AND SWEET POTATO CHOWDER

- 4 ounces (100 g) smoked bacon, diced
- 2 leeks, white and pale green part only, finely chopped
- 3 shallots, finely chopped
- 2 stalks celery, finely chopped
- 2 tablespoons butter
- 1 bay leaf
- 2 cloves garlic, finely chopped
- 3 medium potatoes, weighing about 12 ounces (350 g), peeled and cut into 1-inch (2.5-cm) cubes
- 1 pound (500 g) sweet potatoes, peeled and cut into 1-inch (2.5-cm) cubes
- 2 cups (300 g) fresh, canned, or frozen corn (sweet corn) kernels

- 6 tablespoons dry white wine
- 3 tablespoons dry sherry
- 3 tablespoons finely chopped fresh flat-leaf parsley
- 1 tablespoon finely chopped fresh thyme
- ½ teaspoon salt + more as needed
- 1 teaspoon freshly ground black pepper
- ⅛ teaspoon cayenne pepper
- 5 cups (1.25 liters) beef broth or stock (see page 28)
- 4 tablespoons heavy (double) cream
- Chopped fresh parsley, to garnish

Sauté the bacon in a large soup pot over medium heat until it turns brown and has released its fat, about 5 minutes.

Add the leeks, shallots, celery, and butter. Sauté gently for 5–10 minutes, reducing the heat if the leeks and shallots threaten to brown.

Add the bay leaf, garlic, potatoes, sweet potatoes, and corn. Stir well. Cook for 5–10 minutes, stirring frequently.

Pour in the wine and sherry. Cook over medium heat until the liquid is reduced, 3–5 minutes. Add the parsley, thyme, salt, pepper, cayenne, and broth. Bring to a boil and then reduce the heat to low. Partially cover and simmer over low heat until the potatoes are tender and easily pierced with a fork but still hold their shape, about 1 hour.

Stir in the cream. Taste for salt and seasoning. Remove the bay leaf. Serve hot with a sprinkle of parsley on top.

Serves: 6–8 • Prep: 45 min • Cooking:1 ½ hr

LEEK AND POTATO SOUP

¼ cup (60 ml) extra-virgin olive oil

6 leeks, trimmed and thinly sliced

1 large onion, finely chopped

1 clove garlic, finely chopped

1 carrot, finely chopped

1 stalk celery, finely chopped

1 small bunch parsley, finely chopped

6 large potatoes, peeled and diced

4 cups (1 liter) cold water
   Salt and freshly ground black pepper

Heat the oil in a large soup pot over medium heat. Add the leeks, onion, garlic, carrot, celery, and parsley and sauté until the vegetables are almost tender, about 15 minutes.

Add the potatoes and pour in the water. Season with salt and pepper. Cook over medium heat until the potatoes are tender, about 15 minutes.

Remove the pan from the heat and let cool slightly.

Blend with a handheld blender until smooth. Return the pan to the heat and reheat gently. Serve hot.

Serves: 4–6 • Prep: 15 min • Cooking: 30 min

LEEK, POTATO, AND PEARL BARLEY SOUP

   White of 1 leek, trimmed and finely chopped

8 cups (2 liters) vegetable broth or stock (see page 112)

1 pound (500 g) baking (floury) potatoes, peeled and cut into small cubes

½ cup (100 g) pearl barley

2 tablespoons butter

4 tablespoons freshly grated Parmesan cheese

1 tablespoon finely chopped fresh flat-leaf parsley

¼ teaspoon freshly grated nutmeg

Combine the leek and broth in a large soup pot over medium heat. Bring to a boil and simmer for 10 minutes.

Add the potatoes and cook for 15 minutes.

Add the barley, stirring constantly, and simmer until the barley is tender, about 45 minutes.

Stir in the butter. Sprinkle with the Parmesan, parsley, and nutmeg. Serve hot.

Serves: 6 • Prep: 25 min • Cooking: 1¼ hr

MINESTRONE WITH PEARL BARLEY

1 large carrot, sliced

1 medium turnip, peeled and diced

1 zucchini (courgette), sliced

1 large potato, diced

1 leek, white part only, sliced

2 small celery hearts, sliced

1 medium onion, coarsely chopped

1 cup (50 g) coarsely chopped spinach

1 tablespoon finely chopped fresh parsley

3 ounces (90 g) pancetta, diced

8 cups (2 liters) beef broth or stock (see page 28), boiling

1 cup (200 g) pearl barley
   Salt and freshly ground black pepper

4 tablespoons extra-virgin olive oil

Combine the carrot, turnip, zucchini, potato, leek, celery, onion, spinach, parsley, and pancetta in a large soup pot over medium-high heat.

Add the broth and bring to a boil. Stir in the barley. Cover, turn the heat down to low, and simmer for 1½ hours, stirring occasionally.

Season with salt and pepper, stir in the oil, and serve.

Serves: 4–6 • Prep: 30 min • Cooking: 1 ½ hr

RICE AND POTATO SOUP

2 ounces (60 g) lean pancetta, finely chopped

1 medium onion, finely chopped

1 tablespoon fresh rosemary leaves, finely chopped

4 medium potatoes, peeled and sliced

6 cups (1.5 liters) beef broth or stock (see page 28)

1 cup (200 g) short-grain rice
   Salt

1 tablespoon coarsely chopped fresh parsley

6 tablespoons freshly grated Parmesan cheese

Combine the pancetta, onion, and rosemary in a large soup pot over medium heat and sauté until the onion and pancetta are lightly browned, 7–8 minutes.

Add the potatoes and broth. Raise the heat to high and bring to a boil. Stir in the rice and simmer until the rice is tender, about 15 minutes. Taste for salt. Sprinkle with the parsley and Parmesan and serve hot.

Serves: 4 • Prep: 20 min • Cooking: 25 min

Rice and Pea Soup

4 tablespoons butter
3 tablespoons extra-virgin olive oil
1 onion, finely chopped
1 clove garlic, finely chopped
1 tablespoon finely chopped fresh parsley
2 cups (300 g) frozen peas

4 cups (1 liter) beef broth or stock (see page 28)
1¼ cups (250 g) short-grain rice
Salt
4 tablespoons freshly grated Parmesan cheese

Melt 2 tablespoons of the butter with the oil in a soup pot over medium-high heat. Add the onion and sauté until softened, 5 minutes.

Add the garlic and parsley and sauté until the garlic is pale gold, 2–3 minutes.

Add the peas and a few tablespoons of the broth, cover, and cook over low heat until the peas are almost tender, 8–10 minutes.

Stir in the remaining stock and the rice and cook until the rice is almost tender, 13–14 minutes. Season with salt.

Add the remaining 2 tablespoons of butter and cook until the rice is completely tender. This will take another 2–3 minutes, depending on the rice.

Add the Parmesan, mix well, and serve.

Serves: 4 • Prep: 15 min • Cooking: 30 min

Hearty Cabbage and Rice Soup

2 large carrots, finely sliced
2 stalks celery, sliced
1 small savoy cabbage, shredded
6 cups (1.5 liters) beef broth or stock (see page 28)
1¼ cups (250 g) short-grain rice

Salt and freshly ground black pepper
3 tablespoons extra-virgin olive oil
6 tablespoons freshly grated Parmesan cheese

Combine the carrots, celery, and cabbage with the broth in a large soup pot and bring to a boil. Lower the heat, cover, and simmer until the vegetables are tender, 25–30 minutes.

Add the rice and cook until tender, about 15 minutes. Season with salt, pepper, oil, and Parmesan and serve hot.

Serves: 4–6 • Prep: 15 min • Cooking: 45–50 min

Beef, Rice, and Spinach Soup

6 tablespoons extra-virgin olive oil
2 onions, finely chopped
4 cloves garlic, finely chopped
1 small carrot, sliced
1½ pounds (750 g) stewing beef, cut into small chunks
12 cups (3 liters) cold water
2 tomatoes, chopped
¾ cup (150 g) long-grain rice

2 pounds (1 kg) fresh spinach, tough stems removed, or 1 pound (500 g) frozen spinach
1 teaspoon ground cinnamon
Salt and freshly ground black pepper
6 tablespoons finely chopped fresh flat-leaf parsley

Heat 4 tablespoons of the oil in a large soup pot over medium heat. Add the onions, garlic, and carrot and sauté until lightly browned, 8–10 minutes.

Add the beef and sauté until browned, 8–10 minutes.

Pour in the water and tomatoes. Lower the heat, cover, and cook over low heat until the beef is tender, 1½ hours.

Stir in the rice and cook for 15 minutes more.

Add the spinach and cinnamon. Season with salt and pepper. Cook for 10 minutes more.

Add the parsley and remaining 2 tablespoons of oil just before serving.

Serves: 6–8 • Prep: 30 min • Cooking: 2 hr

Beef, Rice, and Spinach Soup

MINESTRONE

- 4 tablespoons extra-virgin olive oil
- 1 cup (120 g) diced pancetta
- 3 cloves garlic, finely chopped
- 1 onion, coarsely chopped
- 4 stalks celery, sliced
- 3 tablespoons finely chopped fresh flat-leaf parsley
- 3 sage leaves, coarsely chopped
- 1 tablespoon finely chopped fresh rosemary leaves
- 1 large potato, peeled and diced
- 2 large carrots, diced
- 2 large zucchini, diced
- 2 large tomatoes, peeled and coarsely chopped
- 1 cup fresh red kidney or other shell beans
- 8 cups (2 liters) boiling water
- ½ savoy cabbage, coarsely chopped
- ½ cup (75 g) fresh or frozen peas
  Salt and freshly ground black pepper
- 1 cup (200 g) short-grain rice
- ½ cup (60 g) freshly grated Parmesan cheese

Heat 2 tablespoons of the oil in a large soup pot over medium-high heat. Add the pancetta, garlic, onion, celery, 2 tablespoons of the parsley, sage, and rosemary and sauté until the onions are pale golden brown, about 8 minutes.

Add the potato, carrots, zucchini, tomatoes, beans, and water. Cover and simmer over low heat for 75 minutes.

Add the cabbage and peas. Cover and simmer for 25 more minutes.

Season with salt and pepper. Add the rice, cover, and simmer until tender, about 20 minutes.

Drizzle with the remaining 2 tablespoons of oil. Sprinkle with the Parmesan and remaining 1 tablespoon of parsley and serve hot.

Serves: 4–6 • Prep: 30 min • Cooking: 2 hr

RIBOLLITA

This thick Tuscan soup is a kind of minestrone that is "re-boiled" (hence the Italian name) with dense-textured saltless peasant bread. If you have never eaten this soup, it may not sound very appetizing; but when made with care and drizzled with high-quality extra-virgin Tuscan olive oil, it is a memorable dish.

- 1 pound (500 g) fresh shell beans or 1¼ cups (275 g) dried cannellini beans, soaked overnight and drained
- 3 cherry tomatoes (pricked with a fork)
- 2 cloves garlic
- 6 leaves fresh sage
  Water
  Salt
- 7 tablespoons extra-virgin olive oil, + extra for serving
- 1 onion, thinly sliced
- 1 leek, trimmed and thinly sliced
- 2 medium carrots, diced
- 8 ounces (250 g) Tuscan kale or Swiss chard (silver beet), shredded
- ½ small savoy cabbage, shredded
- 1 (14-ounce/400-g) can tomatoes, chopped, with juice
  About 3 cups (500 g) sliced vegetables (potatoes, peas, zucchini, carrots, etc)
- 2 tablespoons finely chopped fresh flat-leaf parsley
  Small sprig of thyme
- 4 cups (1 liter) beef broth or stock + more as needed (see page 28)
- 10 ounces (300 g) firm-textured white or whole-wheat (wholemeal) bread, sliced about ½ inch (1 cm) thick
  Freshly ground black pepper

Combine the beans in a large soup pot with the cherry tomatoes, garlic, and sage. Cover with cold water. If using fresh beans, add salt to taste.

Bring slowly to a boil, cover, and simmer for about 25 minutes for fresh beans or about 1 hour for dried beans. If using dried beans, add salt when they are almost cooked.

Discard the garlic and sage and blend briefly with a handheld blender until smooth.

Spoon the beans onto a plate and set aside.

Clean the pot and heat 4 tablespoons of the oil over medium heat. Add the onion, leek, carrots, kale, cabbage, tomatoes, sliced vegetables, parsley, and thyme and sauté until softened, about 10 minutes.

Add the beans, followed by the broth. Add the bread and season lightly with salt and pepper. Cover and simmer over very low heat for about 3 hours, adding more broth if the soup becomes too thick.

Season generously with freshly ground black pepper. Drizzle with the remaining 3 tablespoons of oil and serve hot.

Serves: 6–8 • Prep: 45 min + 12 hr soaking if using dried beans
Cooking: 3 ½–4 hr

SUMMER MINESTRONE

- 4 tablespoons extra-virgin olive oil
- 2 leeks, trimmed and finely chopped
- 2 potatoes, diced
- 2 carrots, diced
- 1 stalk celery, diced
- 1¼ cups (150 g) fresh or frozen peas
- 8 cups (2 liters) vegetable broth or stock (see page 112)
- 1 red bell pepper (capsicum), seeded and diced
- 1 yellow bell pepper (capsicum), seeded and diced
- 2 zucchini (courgettes), diced
- 2 tomatoes, peeled and coarsely chopped
- 1 sprig basil, torn
- 1 sprig marjoram, finely chopped
- 1 sprig parsley, finely chopped
  Salt and freshly ground black pepper
- 2 ounces (60 g) Parmesan cheese, shaved

Heat the oil in a large soup pot over medium heat. Add the leeks and sauté until softened, about 5 minutes.

Add the potatoes, carrots, celery, and peas. Sauté over high heat for 5 minutes.

Pour in the broth and bring to a boil. Simmer over low heat for 30 minutes.

Add the bell peppers, zucchini, and tomatoes and cook for 20 minutes. Add the basil, marjoram, and parsley, and season with salt and pepper.

Sprinkle with the Parmesan. Serve hot or at room temperature.

Serves: 4–6 • Prep: 20 min • Cooking: 1 hr

VEGETABLE SOUP WITH BASIL SAUCE

Different versions of this soup are made in Liguria (in northeastern Italy) and neighboring Provence (in France). Known as pesto *in Italy and the United States and* pistou *in France—the basil sauce is very similar in both regions.*

- 2 cups (200 g) fresh red kidney or other shell beans
- 2 cups (200 g) fresh white kidney or other shell beans
- 1⅓ cups (125 g) green beans, cut into 1-inch (2.5-cm) lengths
- 2–3 medium potatoes, peeled and cut into cubes
- 2–3 medium carrots, sliced
- 2–3 zucchini (courgettes), sliced
- 3 tomatoes, finely chopped
- 1 medium onion, finely chopped
- 4 quarts (4 liters) water
  Salt and freshly ground black pepper
- 8 ounces (250 g) small soup pasta
- 1½ cups (375 ml) pesto (see below)
- 6–8 tablespoons freshly grated Parmesan cheese

Combine the kidney beans, green beans, potatoes, carrots, zucchini, tomatoes, and onion in a large soup pot with the water. Season with salt and pepper.

Bring to a boil, decrease the heat, and simmer, stirring often, for 1 hour.

Add the pasta and cook for 15 minutes more.

Ladle the soup into individual serving bowls. Spoon 2–3 tablespoons of the pesto onto each portion of soup.

Sprinkle with Parmesan and serve hot.

Serves: 6–8 • Prep: 20 min • Cooking: 1 ¼ hr

PESTO (BASIL SAUCE)

Pesto is a wonderful pasta sauce that originated in Italy. If you wish to serve it with pasta, this quantity is enough for a one pound (500 g) package, which is usually sufficient for 4–6 people.

- 1 large bunch fresh basil leaves
- 4 cloves garlic, peeled
- 2 tablespoons pine nuts
- ½ cup (60 g) freshly grated Parmesan cheese
- 1 cup (250 ml) extra-virgin olive oil
  Salt

Combine the basil, garlic, and pine nuts in a food processor and chop finely.

Transfer the sauce to a small bowl and stir in the Parmesan. Gradually stir in the oil. Taste and season with salt.

Makes: About 1 ½ cups (375 ml) • Prep: 10 min

Spelt and Vegetable Minestrone

Spelt has been grown in Italy for thousands of years. It has become popular again in recent years as healthier eating habits have gained popularity. If you buy rolled and flaked spelt rather than the whole grains or presoaked whole spelt berries (it will say on the package), you can skip the soaking step. Look for spelt in Italian food stores, or replace it with equal quantities of pearl barley.

- 12 ounces (350 g) dried red kidney, cranberry (borlotti), or white beans, soaked overnight and drained
- 4 fresh sage leaves
  Water
- 3 ounces (90 g) pancetta, diced
- 1 small leek, sliced
- 1 stalk celery, sliced
- 1 carrot, trimmed and sliced
- 8 ounces (250 g) Swiss chard (silver beet), coarsely

- ½ teaspoon crushed red pepper flakes
- 1 clove garlic, crushed
- 6 cups (1.5 liters) beef broth or stock (see page 28)
- 1 cup (200 g) whole spelt berries, soaked in cold water for 2–4 hours, drained
- ½ cup (125 ml) extra-virgin olive oil
  Salt and freshly ground white or black pepper
  Pinch of nutmeg

Place the beans in a large soup pot with the sage and enough cold water to cover by 2 inches (5 cm). Cover and simmer until tender, 45–60 minutes.

Discard the sage. Purée half the beans and their liquid in a food processor with as much of the cooking water as needed to make a fairly dense cream. Leave the remaining whole beans in the soup pot with their cooking liquid.

Add the pancetta, leek, celery, carrot, Swiss chard, red pepper flakes, and garlic to the soup pot with the whole beans. Add the broth, bring to a boil, and cook over medium-low heat for 15 minutes.

Add the spelt and half the oil and cook for 20 minutes.

Add the puréed beans and cook for another 20 minutes.

Season with salt, pepper, and nutmeg. Drizzle with the remaining oil just before serving.

Serves: 4–6 • Prep: 20 min + soaking time • Cooking: about 2–2 ½ hr

Spelt

Spelt is an ancient strain of wheat that was cultivated by early farmers thousands of years ago. Although it has always been popular, especially in Europe (where it is known as *farro* in Italy and *dinkel* in Germany), it has really come back into its own in recent years as its health benefits have become more widely known. Spelt has a delicious nutty flavor and is high in fiber. It contains significantly more protein than regular wheat and is also richer in B vitamins and both simple and complex carbohydrates. Spelt is also of interest to those with wheat intolerance because it contains a more digestible form of gluten. Whole spelt berries benefit from soaking before use, although presoaked versions are now widely

Acqua Cotta

Another Italian soup—its name in Italian means "cooked water"—from the cattle-raising Maremma region on the southern coast of Tuscany, where it was traditionally made by the local cowboys.

5 tablespoons extra-virgin olive oil
2 onions, thinly sliced
2½ cups (300 g) fresh or frozen peas
1¾ cups (200 g) freshly shelled (hulled) fava (broad) beans
1 medium carrot, sliced
1 stalk celery, thinly sliced
1 dried chile, crumbled
Salt and freshly ground black pepper
12 ounces (300 g) trimmed young

Swiss chard (silver beet) or spinach leaves, washed and finely shredded
1¼ cups (310 g) firm-ripe tomatoes, peeled and coarsely chopped
6 cups (1.5 liters) boiling water
4 large eggs, lightly beaten
½ cup (60 g) freshly grated Parmesan cheese
4 slices firm-textured white bread, 2 days old, toasted

Heat the oil in a large soup pot over medium heat. Add the onions, peas, fava beans, carrot, celery, chile pepper, and ¼ teaspoon of salt and sauté until the vegetables are tender and lightly browned, about 10 minutes.

Add the Swiss chard and tomatoes and cook over low heat for 15 minutes.

Pour in the water and simmer over low heat for 40 minutes. Season with salt and pepper to taste.

Add the eggs and Parmesan and cook for 3 minutes, beating often.

Place a slice of toast in individual soup bowls and ladle over the soup. Serve immediately.

Serves: 4 • Prep: 30 min • Cooking: 70 min

Pappa al Pomodoro

This delicious thick soup comes from Tuscany, where yesterday's bread is never wasted. If preferred, add red pepper flakes at the end of the cooking time or garnish with thinly sliced fresh green chile.

5 tablespoons extra-virgin olive oil + extra to serve
3 cloves garlic, finely chopped
8–10 leaves fresh basil, torn + extra to garnish
14 ounces (400 g) firm-textured white or brown bread, 2 days old, diced

2 pounds (1 kg) firm-ripe tomatoes, peeled, seeded, and finely chopped
Salt and freshly ground black pepper
1¼ cups (310 ml) water + extra as required

Heat the oil in a large soup pot over low heat. Add the garlic and basil and sauté for 2 minutes.

Add the bread and cook over medium heat, stirring constantly, for 2 minutes.

Add the tomatoes and 1 cup (250 ml) of the water. Simmer for 15 minutes, stirring often. Season with salt and pepper to taste and add more liquid if the soup begins to stick to the bottom of the pan. The consistency of the soup should be very thick.

Drizzle with the extra olive oil, garnish with the extra basil, and serve hot.

Serves: 4 • Prep: 15 min • Cooking: 20 min

French Onion Soup

4 tablespoons extra-virgin olive oil
4 large onions, finely chopped
2 tablespoons all-purpose (plain) flour
6 cups (1.5 liters) water
Salt and freshly ground black pepper

4 slices firm-textured bread, toasted
4 ounces (125 g) freshly grated firm-textured cheese (Gruyère, cheddar, Emmentaler)

Heat the oil in a large soup pot over medium heat. Add the onions and sauté until lightly browned, 7–8 minutes.

Sprinkle with flour and continue cooking, stirring often, for 5 minutes. Pour in the water and season with salt and pepper. Bring to a boil and simmer for 20 minutes.

Ladle the soup into ovenproof soup bowls and top each one with a slice of toast. Sprinkle with the grated cheese. Place under a preheated broiler (grill) until the cheese is lightly browned, about 5 minutes. Serve hot.

Serves: 4 • Prep: 20 min • Cooking: 40 min

WATERCRESS, BEAN, AND POTATO SOUP

This soup is thickened with potatoes and beans.

1 tablespoon extra-virgin olive oil

1 tablespoon butter

1 large onion, finely chopped

1 clove garlic, finely chopped

3 medium baking (floury) potatoes, peeled and finely chopped

2 large bunches watercress, about 7 ounces (200 g) total weight

1⅔ cups (400 g) canned lima or butter beans, drained and rinsed

6 cups (1.5 liters) chicken or vegetable broth or stock (see pages 56 or 112)

1 cup (250 ml) milk (optional)

Salt and freshly ground black pepper

1 teaspoon fresh lemon juice

⅓ cup (80 ml) sour cream (optional)

Heat the oil and butter in a large soup pot over medium heat. Add the onion and garlic and sauté until softened, about 5 minutes. Add the potatoes, cover, and cook for 5 minutes, stirring occasionally.

Strip the watercress leaves from the stems and chop the stems coarsely. Stir the stems and the beans into the pan. Pour in the broth. Bring to a boil, partially cover, and simmer until the potatoes and stems are tender, about 15 minutes.

Stir in the watercress leaves, reserving a few to garnish. Cook for 1 minute. Remove the pan from the heat and blend with a handheld blender until smooth. Return the pan to the heat and reheat gently. If the soup is too thick, thin with the milk. Season with salt and pepper and add the lemon juice.

Ladle into individual bowls and swirl in the sour cream, if using. Garnish with the reserved watercress. Serve hot.

Serves: 6 • Prep: 10 min • Cooking: 30 min

ITALIAN LENTIL SOUP

You can make a smooth cream of lentil soup by puréeing the cooked soup in a blender until smooth. Return the soup to the pot for 2–3 minutes over medium heat before serving.

1½ cups (300 g) dried red lentils, picked over for stones and rinsed

1 medium onion, finely chopped

2 small carrots, diced

2 stalks celery, thinly sliced

1 bay leaf

2 cloves garlic, whole or finely chopped (optional)

Water

3 fresh sage leaves, finely chopped

2 tablespoons fresh rosemary, finely chopped

Salt and freshly ground white or black pepper

4 tablespoons extra-virgin olive oil

Combine the lentils in a soup pot with the onion, carrots, celery, bay leaf, and garlic. Add enough cold water to cover by about 2 inches (5 cm). Cover and cook over low heat until the lentils are tender, about 45 minutes.

Discard the bay leaf, add the sage and rosemary, and continue cooking, still covered and over low heat, for 5–10 minutes. At this point the lentils should be very soft and will begin to disintegrate.

Add salt and pepper to taste, drizzle with the oil, and serve hot.

Serves: 4–6 • Prep: 15 min • Cooking: 1 hr

QUICK BUTTER BEAN AND PESTO SOUP

3 tablespoons extra-virgin olive oil

1 onion, finely chopped

14 ounces (400 g) frozen butter beans or lima beans

8 ounces (250 g) potatoes, peeled and cut into small cubes

4 cups (1 liter) chicken or vegetable broth or stock (see pages 56 or 112)

4 tablespoons pesto (see page 46)

Salt and freshly ground black pepper

1 tablespoon torn fresh basil

Heat the oil in a large soup pot over medium heat. Add the onion and sauté until softened, about 5 minutes. Add the butter beans, potatoes, and broth and bring to a boil.

Simmer over low heat for 20 minutes, or until the beans and potatoes are tender. Stir in the pesto. Remove the pan from the heat and blend with a handheld blender until smooth. Return the pan to the heat and reheat.

Season with salt and pepper and garnish with the basil.

Serves: 4 • Prep: 10 min • Cooking: 25 min

Aduki Bean Soup

Aduki beans have a nutty flavor and are known as the "king of beans" in China and Japan. They are used as a traditional medicine to treat kidney disorders, as well as for making a hearty soup.

¼ cup (60 ml) sunflower oil
2 onions, finely chopped
2 stalks celery, finely chopped
3 carrots, finely chopped
2 cloves garlic, finely chopped
1 tablespoon finely chopped fresh thyme leaves, or 1 teaspoon dried
2 bay leaves
7 cups (1.75 liters) chicken or vegetable broth or stock (see pages 56, 112)

1¼ cups (200 g) dried aduki beans, soaked overnight and drained
1 (14-ounce/400-g) can tomatoes, chopped, with juice
1 tablespoon tomato paste (concentrate)
Salt and freshly ground black pepper
2 tablespoons finely chopped fresh flat-leaf parsley

Heat the oil in a large soup pot over medium heat. Add the onions, celery, carrots, garlic, thyme, and bay leaves and sauté until the onion is softened, about 5 minutes.

Pour in the broth and add the aduki beans. Bring to a boil and simmer over low heat until the beans are tender, about 1 hour.

Stir in the tomatoes and tomato paste and simmer for 20 minutes. Remove the bay leaves.

Season with salt and pepper and stir in 1 tablespoon of the parsley. Garnish with the remaining parsley and serve hot.

Serves: 6 • Prep: 20 min • Cooking: 1 hr 20 min

Herbed Bean Soup

For extra flavor, use fresh beans (cannellini, borlotti, white kidney), which are available in spring and early summer. If using fresh beans, eliminate the soaking time and reduce the cooking time to 25–30 minutes.

⅓ cup (80 ml) extra-virgin olive oil + extra to drizzle
1 onion, finely chopped
1 carrot, finely chopped
1 stalk celery, finely chopped
2 cups (250 g) dried cannellini, white kidney, or cranberry (borlotti) beans, soaked overnight and drained
Handful of parsley stems, finely chopped
3 leaves fresh sage, finely chopped
2 cloves garlic, finely chopped

5 ripe cherry tomatoes
8 cups (2 liters) vegetable broth or stock (see page 112)
Salt and freshly ground black pepper
2 sprigs rosemary
5 ounces (150 g) green beans or snow peas (mangetout), trimmed and halved
Handful of fresh basil
Handful of celery leaves
1 tablespoon finely chopped fresh parsley

Heat the oil in a large soup pot over medium heat. Add the onion, carrot, and celery and sauté until softened, 7–10 minutes.

Stir in the beans, parsley stems, sage, garlic, tomatoes, and broth. Season with pepper. Bring to a boil and add the rosemary. Simmer over very low heat until the beans are tender but not mushy, 60–90 minutes.

Discard the rosemary. Add the green beans and basil. Simmer until the green beans are tender but still crunchy, 5–7 minutes.

Season with salt and pepper to taste. Stir in the celery leaves. Garnish with parsley and drizzle with olive oil. Serve hot.

Serves: 4 • Prep: 15 min + 12 hr to soak the beans • Cooking: 1 ¾ hr

Moroccan Fava Bean Soup

2 pounds (1 kg) dried fava (broad) beans, soaked overnight and drained
1 pound (500 g) potatoes, peeled and cubed
2 cloves garlic, chopped
10 cups (2.5 liters) cold water

Salt
Paprika
2 teaspoons harissa
2 teaspoons ground cumin
2 tablespoons fresh lemon juice
6 tablespoons extra-virgin olive oil

Combine the fava beans, potatoes, and garlic in a large soup pot with the water. Bring to a boil over medium heat. Lower the heat and simmer, covered, for 50–60 minutes, or until the beans are very tender. Season with salt and paprika.

Purée the beans with their liquid in a blender. Cook over low heat for 15–20 minutes, until the soup is thick.

Stir in the harissa, cumin, and lemon juice. Drizzle with the oil. Serve hot or at room temperature.

Serves: 6–8 • Prep: 15 min + 12 hr to soak beans • Cooking: 1 ¼ hr

Moroccan Fava Bean Soup

RED LENTIL SOUP WITH LIME

- 3 tablespoons sunflower oil
- 1 large onion, finely chopped
- 1 stalk celery, finely chopped
- 1 carrot, finely chopped
- 1 clove garlic, finely chopped
- ½ teaspoon dried marjoram
- 2 soft stems lemon thyme, or ½ teaspoon dried thyme
- 1 teaspoon cumin seeds, toasted and ground
- 1¼ cups (350 g) red lentils, picked over for stones and rinsed
- 8 cups (2 liters) chicken or

- vegetable broth or stock (see pages 56 or 112)
- Grated zest of ¼ lime
- 1 bay leaf
- 2 tablespoons fresh lime juice
- Water (optional)
- Salt and freshly ground black pepper
- 2 tablespoons finely chopped fresh flat-leaf parsley

Heat the oil in a large soup pot over medium heat. Add the onion, celery, and carrot and sauté until softened, 7–10 minutes.

Stir in the garlic, marjoram, thyme, and cumin. Add the lentils, broth, lime zest, and bay leaf, and bring to a boil. Cover and simmer for 25 minutes, or until the lentils are soft.

Discard the bay leaf and add 1 tablespoon of the lime juice. Remove from the heat and let cool slightly. Blend with a handheld blender until smooth.

Return the pan to the heat and reheat gently. If the soup is too thick, add a little water. Season with salt and pepper and add more lime juice to taste. Garnish with the parsley and serve hot.

Serves: 6–8 • Prep: 20 min • Cooking: 40 min

RED LENTIL SOUP WITH MANGO

This unusual yet delicious and colorful lentil soup has a slight tangy flavor from the addition of the chopped mango. Ideal for a cold winter's day.

- 1 cup (100 g) red lentils, picked over for stones and rinsed
- 1 tablespoon extra-virgin olive oil
- ½ onion, finely sliced
- 2 cloves garlic, finely chopped
- 3 tablespoons chopped dried mango
- 2 potatoes, peeled and diced
- 3 cups (750 ml) chicken broth or stock (see page 56)

- 1½ cups (375 g) peeled and chopped canned tomatoes
- ¼ teaspoon ground cumin
- ¼ teaspoon ground red chile
- ¼ teaspoon sweet paprika
- ¼ teaspoon dried thyme
- Salt and freshly ground black pepper
- 2 tablespoons fresh lemon juice
- Sesame seed bread, toasted and buttered, to serve

Cover the lentils with cold water in a large pot and bring to a boil. Simmer until tender, 30–35 minutes. Drain and set aside.

Heat the oil over low heat in the same pot. Add the onion, garlic, and mango and sauté until softened, about 5 minutes.

Add the lentils and potatoes and pour in the broth. Bring to a boil and simmer over low heat for 30 minutes. Stir in the tomatoes, cumin, ground red chile, paprika, and thyme. Season with salt and pepper.

Simmer for 10 minutes. Stir in the lemon juice. Remove from the heat and blend with a handheld blender until partially smooth. Return to the heat and reheat gently. Serve hot with the toast.

Serves: 4–6 • Prep: 20 min • Cooking: 75 min

BLACK-EYED PEA SOUP

- 2 tablespoons extra-virgin olive oil
- 4 shallots, finely chopped
- 4 stalks celery, coarsely chopped
- 4 cloves garlic, finely chopped
- 1 fresh red or green chile, seeded and finely chopped
- 8 cups (2 liters) chicken or vegetable broth or stock (see pages 56 or 112)
- 1½ cups (150 g) black-eyed peas,

- soaked overnight and drained
- ¼ teaspoon cayenne pepper
- Salt and freshly ground black pepper
- 5 tomatoes, peeled and coarsely chopped
- Juice of 2 limes
- 2 tablespoons finely chopped fresh cilantro (coriander)

Heat the oil in a large soup pot over medium heat. Add the shallots, celery, garlic, and chile, and sauté until softened, about 7 minutes.

Pour in the broth and add the peas. Bring to a boil. Cover and simmer over low heat, until the black-eyed peas are almost soft, 30–50 minutes.

Add the cayenne and season with salt and pepper. Add the tomatoes and simmer until tender, 20 minutes.

Stir in the lime juice and 1 tablespoon of the cilantro. Garnish with the remaining cilantro and serve hot.

Serves: 6 • Prep: 15 min + 12 hr to soak peas • Cooking: 60–80 min

Garbanzo Bean Soup

If desired, rub each slice of toasted bread with a little fresh garlic just before you ladle the soup over the top.

- 8 cups (2 liters) cold water
- 8 ounces (250 g) young Swiss chard (silver beet), sliced
- 4 tablespoons extra-virgin olive oil
- 1 onion, finely chopped
- 1–2 cloves garlic, lightly crushed
- 3–4 anchovy fillets in oil
- 2 cups (300 g) dried garbanzo beans (chickpeas), soaked overnight and drained

- 6 plum tomatoes, peeled and chopped
  Salt and freshly ground black pepper
- 4–6 large slices dense-grain, home-style bread, toasted
- 6 tablespoons freshly grated pecorino cheese

Heat 2 cups (500 ml) of the water in a large soup pot over high heat. Add the Swiss chard, cover, and cook for 5 minutes. Drain, reserving the cooking liquid, and set aside.

Heat the oil in the same pot. Add the onion and garlic and sauté until the onion is softened, 5 minutes.

Add the anchovy fillets with the oil, mashing them with a fork as you stir. Add the garbanzo beans to the pot, together with the chard, the liquid it was cooked in, and the tomatoes. Season with salt and pepper, stir, and add the remaining 6 cups (1.5 liters) of water. Bring to a boil. Cover the pot and simmer over medium heat for at least 3 hours. The garbanzo beans should be very tender.

Arrange the toast in individual soup bowls and ladle the soup over the top. Sprinkle with the pecorino and serve.

Serves: 4–6 • Prep: 30 min + 12 hours to soak the beans
• Cooking: 3 ¹/₂ hr

Lime

Limes are an acidic citrus fruit believed to have originated in Southeast Asia. Usually slightly smaller than the lemon and of similar shape, limes have green skins and a more acidic flavor. There are several different types of limes available commercially, and they vary in size, skin color, and acidity. In many Asian cuisines, the lime occupies the place that the lemon fills in Mediterranean and other Western cuisines. Introduced to the Americas by the Spanish, limes grow well in the hot climates of Mexico and Central America and are of major importance in those cuisines. Nutritionally, limes are an excellent source of vitamin C.

BUTTERNUT SQUASH SOUP

2 tablespoons butter
2 small onions, finely chopped
1 clove garlic, finely chopped
1 teaspoon salt
½ teaspoon ground cumin
½ teaspoon ground coriander
¼ teaspoon dry mustard powder
2 medium butternut squash, peeled, seeded, and cut into 1-inch (2.5-cm) cubes
1 sweet potato or white potato, cubed
1 teaspoon honey
1 green chile, seeded and finely chopped

1-inch (2.5-cm) piece fresh ginger, peeled and finely chopped
6 cups (1.5 liters) chicken broth or stock (see page 56)
2 cups (400 g) canned garbanzo beans (chick peas), drained and rinsed
Juice of 2 lemons
Salt and freshly ground black pepper
¼ teaspoon cayenne pepper
½ cup (125 ml) plain yogurt
2 tablespoons diced red bell pepper (capsicum)

Melt the butter in a large soup pot over medium heat. Add the onions, garlic, salt, cumin, coriander, and mustard and sauté until the onions are tender, about 5 minutes.

Add the squash, potato, honey, chile, and ginger. Pour in 4 cups (1 liter) of the broth and bring to a boil over low heat. Cover and simmer until the vegetables have softened, about 15 minutes.

Add the beans, remaining 2 cups (500 ml) of broth, and half the lemon juice. Simmer for 5 minutes.

Remove from the heat and let cool slightly. Blend with a handheld blender until smooth.

Return the pan to the heat and reheat gently, adding the remaining lemon juice and more broth if needed.

Season with salt, pepper, and cayenne. Swirl in the yogurt and garnish with the diced red bell pepper.

Serves: 6 • Prep: 20 min • Cooking: 30 min

CHICKEN STOCK

Soups based on homemade stock are so much better than those made with bouillon cubes that it really is worthwhile taking the time to prepare stock at home. Luckily, stock freezes well, so you can make it in large quantities and then freeze it in portion-size containers. To freeze, cool the stock to room temperature then pour into small containers and place in the freezer.

3 pounds (1.5 kg) chicken wings, backs and necks or one whole 3-pound (1.5-kg) boiling chicken
About 5 quarts (5 liters) cold water
2 medium onions, cut into quarters

2 medium carrots, halved
2 stalks celery, cut into thirds
Small bunch parsley
2 bay leaves
2 tablespoons coarse sea salt

Place the chicken pieces or whole chicken in a large stockpot. Add enough of the water to cover the chicken and bring to a gentle simmer over medium heat.

Skim off and discard any scum that forms on the surface. Add the onions, carrots, celery, parsley, bay leaves, and salt and return to a gentle simmer.

Reduce the heat and simmer for 3–4 hours. Never allow the water to boil; just keep it gently simmering. Add boiling water if the water evaporates to the level of the ingredients.

Turn off the heat, remove the chicken and vegetables, and let the stock cool. Strain through a fine sieve or a double thickness of cheesecloth. Refrigerate the stock until the fat hardens on the surface. Discard the fat.

Makes: about 3 quarts (3 liters) • Prep: 15 min • Cooking: 3–4 hr

CREAM OF POTATO SOUP

4 tablespoons butter
1 medium onion, finely chopped
2 ounces (60 g) bacon, coarsely chopped
1 fresh red chile, seeded and finely chopped
1½ pounds (750 g) potatoes, peeled and cut into small cubes
1 teaspoon ground allspice
1 tablespoon finely chopped fresh marjoram

1 bay leaf
  Salt and freshly ground black pepper
1 tablespoon all-purpose (plain) flour
4 cups (1 liter) water
1 tablespoon finely chopped fresh parsley
2 cloves garlic, finely chopped
1 teaspoon white wine vinegar

Melt the butter in a large soup pot over medium heat. Sauté the onion and bacon until lightly browned, 7–9 minutes.

Add the chile, potatoes, allspice, marjoram, and bay leaf. Season with salt and pepper. Add the flour, stirring well, followed by the water. Cook for 15–20 minutes, or until the potatoes are tender.

Remove the bay leaf. Transfer the soup to a food processor and process until smooth.

Return the soup to the soup pot. Add the parsley, garlic, and vinegar and bring to a boil. Serve hot.

Serves: 4 • Prep: 15 min • Cooking: 30 min

CREAMY CAULIFLOWER SOUP

2 tablespoons butter
1 large onion, finely chopped
2 cups (500 ml) water
3 medium potatoes, (about 12 ounces/350 g), peeled and diced
2 stalks celery, finely chopped
1 small head cauliflower, (about 1 pound/500 g), broken up in florets
1½ tablespoons fresh dill or 2 teaspoons dried
1 tablespoon fresh lemon juice
1 teaspoon dry mustard powder

½ teaspoon salt
½ teaspoon freshly ground white pepper
¼ teaspoon caraway seeds
¼ teaspoon ground fennel seeds
2 cups (500 ml) buttermilk
⅔ cup (150 ml) sour cream or crème fraîche (optional)
⅛ teaspoon ground nutmeg or mace
2 tablespoons snipped chives, to garnish

Melt the butter in a large soup pot over medium heat. Add the onion and sauté until softened, about 5 minutes.

Add the water, potatoes, and celery and bring to a boil. Simmer over low heat for 10 minutes.

Stir in the cauliflower, dill, lemon juice, mustard, salt, pepper, caraway seeds, and fennel seeds. Simmer until the potatoes and cauliflower are very tender, 10–15 minutes.

Remove the pan from the heat and let cool slightly. Blend with a handheld blender until smooth.

Gradually pour in the buttermilk, as you are puréeing, until the soup is smooth and creamy. For a richer soup, add the sour cream or crème fraîche.

Return the pan to the heat and reheat gently. Dust with the nutmeg. Sprinkle with the chives and serve hot.

Serves: 4 • Prep: 10 min • Cooking: 35 min

BROCCOLI SOUP WITH CHEESE CROUTONS

1 large head broccoli
(about 2 pounds/1 kg)

4 tablespoons extra-virgin olive oil

2–3 cloves garlic, finely chopped

1 large potato, peeled and diced

6 cups (1.5 liters) chicken broth or
stock (see page 56)
Salt and freshly ground white
pepper

1 small loaf French bread, sliced
and toasted

½ cup (60 g) freshly grated
Emmentaler cheese

1–2 tablespoons diced red bell pepper
(capsicum)

Separate the broccoli into florets. Chop the stalk into small dice and coarsely chop the leaves.

Heat 2 tablespoons of the oil in a large soup pot over high heat. Add the garlic and sauté until soft, 2–3 minutes.

Add the broccoli (leaves, florets, and stalks), potato, and broth. Season with salt and white pepper. Partially cover and cook over low heat for 20 minutes, or until the broccoli is tender. Remove from the heat and purée in a food processor until smooth.

Ladle the soup into individual serving bowls. Sprinkle the toasted bread with cheese and diced bell pepper. Garnish the soup with the croutons and drizzle with the remaining oil.

Serves: 4 • Prep: 20 min • Cooking: 25 min

WILD MUSHROOM SOUP WITH KASHA

4 tablespoons extra-virgin olive oil

1 medium onion, finely chopped

6 ounces (180 g) mixed wild
mushrooms, thinly sliced

2 cloves garlic, finely chopped

4 ounces (125 g) kasha (buckwheat
groats)

1 bay leaf

5 cups (1.25 liters) water
Salt and freshly ground black
pepper

4 tablespoons sour cream,
to garnish

1 tablespoon finely chopped thyme,
to garnish

Heat the oil in a large soup pot over medium heat. Add the onion and sauté until softened, about 5 minutes.

Stir in the mushrooms and garlic. Sauté until the mushrooms have softened slightly, about 5 minutes.

Add the kasha and bay leaf. Pour in the water. Bring to a boil, lower the heat, and simmer until the kasha is tender and the mushrooms are cooked, about 20 minutes. Remove the bay leaf.

Season with salt and pepper. Swirl in the sour cream and garnish with the thyme. Serve hot.

Serves: 4 • Prep: 20 min • Cooking: 30 min

FENNEL MISO

2 tablespoons extra-virgin olive oil

1 pound (500 g) fennel bulbs, cut
into wedges and finely sliced

1 carrot, cut into very thin strips
Whites of 2 leeks, trimmed and
cut into ½-inch (1-cm) rounds

2 potatoes, peeled and cut into
small cubes

1-inch (2.5-cm) piece fresh ginger,
peeled and finely chopped

1 clove garlic, finely chopped

½ small green chile, seeded and
finely chopped

1 small fresh red chile, seeded and
finely chopped

1 teaspoon fennel seeds

3 tablespoons barley miso
Salt

6 cups (1.5 liters) boiling water

4 ounces (125 g) watercress, stems
removed and coarsely chopped,
reserving some leaves to garnish

5 snow peas (mangetout), broken in
half (optional)

1 tablespoon fresh lemon juice

1 tablespoon finely chopped fresh
flat-leaf parsley

Heat the oil in a large soup pot over medium heat. Add the fennel, carrot, leeks, and potatoes and sauté until the vegetables are softened, 8–10 minutes.

Stir in the ginger, garlic, chiles, and fennel seeds. Season with salt and sauté over low heat for 10 minutes more.

Dissolve the miso in ½ cup (125 ml) of the boiling water. Stir the miso mixture and remaining water into the soup. Simmer until the potatoes are tender, 15–20 minutes.

Add the watercress, snow peas, and lemon juice. Simmer for 3 minutes more.

Garnish with the parsley and reserved watercress leaves. Serve hot.

Serves: 4–6 • Prep: 20 min • Cooking: 45 min

FARMHOUSE CABBAGE SOUP

8 ounces (250 g) bacon, chopped
1 teaspoon butter
1 large onion, finely chopped
1 large waxy potato, cut into small cubes
1 teaspoon sweet paprika
1 tablespoon finely chopped fresh marjoram or dill
1 green or savoy cabbage, weighing about 1½ pounds (750 g), finely shredded

6 cups (1.5 liters) water
  Salt and freshly ground white pepper
⅔ cup (150 ml) sour cream
4 ounces (100 g) spicy, smoked sausage, thinly sliced (optional)
2 tablespoons finely chopped parsley, to garnish

Sauté the bacon in a large soup pot over medium heat until the fat has melted, about 5 minutes.

Stir in the butter and onion and sauté until the onion is softened, about 5 minutes.

Add the potato, ¼ teaspoon of the paprika, and marjoram. Sauté over low heat until the potato has almost softened, for 8–10 minutes.

Keep stirring the mixture. Add the cabbage and pour in the broth. Bring to a boil and simmer for 4–8 minutes, depending on how finely the cabbage was shredded— it should retain some crispness. Season with salt and pepper.

Stir in the sour cream, and add the sausage, if using. Return to a gentle boil.

Garnish with the parsley and dust with the remaining paprika. Serve hot.

Serves: 6 • Prep: 20 min • Cooking: 30 min

FENNEL

Fennel is a member of the parsley family and comes in several forms: bitter fennel, sweet fennel, wild fennel, and Florence fennel (also known by its Italian name *finocchio*). The first two types are used as seeds; the wild fennel is a herb; and Florence fennel—as shown in the photograph—is a bulbous vegetable. Bitter fennel is native to southern Europe and its seeds have a distinctive bitter taste. The seeds are now rare outside of Eastern Europe, and if a recipe calls for them, celery seed is the best substitute. Sweet fennel seeds are not bitter at all and have a mild anise flavor. Crisp Florence fennel, or fennel bulbs, also have a delicate anise flavor and are best used in salads or lightly steamed.

FRY POT

STIR-FRIES, SAUTÉS, RISOTTOS, AND PAELLAS

Some deeply delicious dishes can be made in a simple frying pan or wok placed over a flame. We have included a host of risotto dishes from Italy, some paellas from Spain, and many crisp stir-fries from the East, among others. Most of the recipes in this chapter are simple and quick, although many do require the cook's full attention during the brief cooking. For those unfamiliar with Asian cooking methods, stir-frying is very similar to sautéing food. The speed with which the food is cooked ensures a minimum loss of texture, vitamins, and color.

Paella, Valencia-Style

This is a traditional recipe from the coastal regions of southeastern Spain. Paella lends itself to an endless array of variations and many authentic recipes will include rabbit, eel, and snails. We have substituted chicken, clams, and tuna for those ingredients, but feel free to reinstate them. Short-grain Valencia rice is a good choice for making perfect paella.

1 pound (500 g) clams, in shell

1 pound (500 g) mussels, in shell

4 tablespoons extra-virgin olive oil

3 cloves garlic, lightly crushed

1 spring chicken, weighing about 1½ pounds (750 g), boned and cut into small chunks

3 cups (600 g) short-grain rice

6 cups (1.5 liters) boiling water

1 pound (500 g) tuna, cleaned and chopped

8 ounces (250 g) shrimp (prawns), shelled and deveined

2 artichoke hearts, cleaned and chopped

8 ounces (250 g) green beans, cut into short lengths

1½ cups (225 g) fresh or frozen peas
Salt and freshly ground black pepper

1 bay leaf

10 threads saffron, crumbled

Soak the clams and mussels in cold water for 1 hour. Preheat the oven to 400°F (200°C/gas 6).

Heat the oil in a paella pan or large ovenproof frying pan about 18 inches (45 cm) in diameter over medium heat. Add the garlic and sauté until pale gold, 2–3 minutes. Discard the garlic.

Sauté the chicken in the same pan until white, 7–9 minutes.

Add the rice and stir until well coated with oil. Pour in the water and bring to a boil. Add the clams, mussels, tuna, shrimp, artichokes, green beans, and peas. Season with salt and pepper. Add the bay leaf and saffron.

Continue cooking over medium heat until the liquid has almost all been absorbed, about 15 minutes. Stir often during cooking. Discard any clams or mussels that do not open. The rice grains still should be slightly crunchy.

Bake in the oven, uncovered, for 10 minutes.

Cover the pan with foil or parchment paper and let stand for 10 minutes. Remove the bay leaf before serving.

Serves: 6–8 • Prep: 30 min + 10 min to stand + 1 hr to soak shellfish • Cooking: 40 min

Vegetarian Paella

⅓ cup (80 ml) extra-virgin olive oil

½ teaspoon saffron threads, infused in ½ cup (125 ml) boiling water for 15 minutes

2 onions, thinly sliced

2 tablespoons pine nuts

3 cloves garlic, finely chopped

1 dried red chile, crumbled

8 ounces (250 g) tomatoes, peeled and chopped

1 large green bell pepper (capsicum), seeded and thinly sliced

1¼ cups (250 g) arborio rice
Salt and freshly ground black pepper

1 teaspoon sweet paprika

2¾ cups (700 ml) vegetable broth or stock (see page 112)

¾ cup (90 g) fresh or frozen peas

1 pound (500 g) spinach, tough stems removed, coarsely chopped

2 Spanish piquillo peppers (or chiles), sliced

Heat the oil in a paella pan or large frying pan about 18 inches (45 cm) in diameter over medium heat. Add the onions and garlic and sauté until softened, about 5 minutes.

Add the pine nuts and chile and sauté for 2 minutes.

Lower the heat and add the tomatoes and bell pepper. Sauté for 6 minutes, stirring constantly.

Add the rice and sauté for 2 minutes. Season with salt and pepper.

Add the paprika, saffron and water, and enough broth to cover the rice by about 1 inch (2.5 cm). Bring to a boil, cover, and simmer gently until the rice is tender and almost all the liquid has evaporated, about 15 minutes. Stir occasionally to prevent the rice from sticking to the pan.

Add the spinach and peas and mix well. Cook for 5 minutes more, or until the peas are cooked.

Remove from the heat, cover, and let rest for 5 minutes. Garnish with the piquillo peppers and serve.

Serves: 4 • Prep: 20 min + 15 min to infuse saffron • Cooking: 40 min

SPICY LAMB AND PORK PAELLA

- 1 pound (500 g) boned lamb, cut into thin strips
  Salt and freshly ground black pepper
- 4 tablespoons extra-virgin olive oil
- 8 ounces (250 g) pork loin, cut into thin strips
- 1 red bell pepper (capsicum), sliced into thin strips
- 8 ounces (250 g) green beans, trimmed
- 4 ounces (125 g) spicy salami, thinly sliced

- 1 tablespoon cayenne pepper
- 1 teaspoon finely chopped fresh red chile pepper
- 2 cups (400 g) short-grain rice
- 4 firm-ripe tomatoes, peeled and chopped
- 6 saffron threads, crumbled, dissolved in 1 tablespoon hot water
- 3 cups (750 ml) boiling chicken broth or stock (see page 56)
- 1 tablespoon finely chopped fresh rosemary

Season the lamb with salt and pepper.

Heat the oil in a paella pan or large frying pan about 18 inches (45 cm) in diameter over medium heat. Add the lamb and sauté until browned, about 5 minutes. Remove the lamb from the pan and keep warm.

Brown the pork in the same oil, about 8 minutes. Remove from the pan and keep warm.

Sauté the bell pepper and beans over medium heat for 3 minutes. Increase the heat and add the salami, cayenne pepper, and chile. Sauté for 30 seconds. Add the rice and cook for 3 minutes, stirring constantly. Stir in the tomatoes and cook for 3 minutes.

Add the pork and its cooking juices, the saffron mixture, broth, salt, and pepper. Add the lamb and rosemary and bring to a boil. Cover and simmer over medium-low heat for 20 minutes without stirring, shaking the pan every so often to keep the rice from sticking.

When the rice is tender, remove from the heat and allow the paella to rest for 5 minutes before serving.

Serves: 4–6 • Prep: 20 min • Cooking: 40 min + 5 min to rest

SPANISH CHICKEN WITH RICE

This is a delicious variation on arroz con pollo, *an old Spanish chicken and rice classic.*

- 4 pounds (2 kg) chicken pieces, with skin and bones
  Salt and freshly ground black pepper
- 4 tablespoons extra-virgin olive oil
- 2 large white onions, coarsely chopped
- 3 cloves garlic, finely chopped
- 1 red bell pepper (capsicum), seeded and diced
- ½ cup (125 g) diced ham
- 2 cups (400 g) long-grain rice

- 3 cups (750 ml) chicken broth or stock (see page 56)
- ½ teaspoon saffron threads
- 1 cup (150 g) frozen mixed vegetables
- 1 small green chile, seeded and finely chopped (optional)
- ½ cup (60 g) small black olives
- 1 tablespoon finely chopped fresh cilantro (coriander)
- 1 tablespoon finely chopped fresh parsley

Place the chicken in a large dish and season generously with salt and pepper. Rub the seasoning into the chicken.

Heat 3 tablespoons of the oil in a large frying pan over medium-high heat. Add the chicken pieces in a single layer and sauté until well-browned, 8–10 minutes. Remove the chicken from the pan and set aside, leaving the oil and cooking juices in the pan.

Add the onions, 2 cloves of the garlic, bell pepper, and ham. Sauté until the onions are softened, about 5 minutes.

Add the rice and broth and bring to a boil, stirring often. Return the chicken to the pan. Add the saffron. Mix, then cover and cook over low heat for 20 minutes.

Stir in the mixed vegetables, olives, and half the chile, if using. Cover and continue cooking until the rice is tender, about 10 minutes.

Stir in the remaining 1 clove garlic, chile, cilantro, and parsley. Drizzle with the remaining 1 tablespoon of oil, stirring gently over high heat for 30 seconds. Just warm the oil and herbs, don't cook them; they should retain their clean, fresh aromas, adding a scrumptious "lift" to the final flavors of the dish.

Serves: 4–6 • Prep: 25 min • Cooking: 45 min

Spanish Chicken with Rice

RISOTTO WITH TRUFFLES

- 4 tablespoons (60 g) butter
- 2 tablespoons very finely chopped onion
- 1¾ cups (350 g) Italian risotto rice
- ½ cup (125 ml) dry white wine
- 4 cups (1 liter) chicken broth or stock
- ¾ cup (90 g) freshly grated Parmesan cheese
- Salt and freshly ground white pepper
- 3 tablespoons cooking juices from roast meat or poultry (optional)
- Fresh white truffles, very thinly sliced

Melt 2 tablespoons of the butter in a large frying pan over medium heat. Add the onion and sauté until softened, about 5 minutes.

Add the rice and toast for 2 minutes, stirring to coat the grains. Pour in the wine and cook until the alcohol has evaporated, about 4 minutes.

Begin stirring in the broth, ½ cup (125 ml) at a time. Cook and stir until each addition has been absorbed and the rice is tender, 15–18 minutes.

Stir in half the Parmesan and season with salt and white pepper. Turn off the heat. Cover tightly and let stand for about 2 minutes. Add the remaining butter and Parmesan. Add the roast meat juices, if using, and stir again. Top with the truffles and serve.

Serves: 4 • Prep: 25 min • Cooking: 30 min

RISOTTO WITH ITALIAN SAUSAGES AND SAVOY CABBAGE

- 4 tablespoons butter
- 12 ounces (350 g) savoy cabbage, thinly sliced
- Salt and freshly ground black pepper
- ¼ teaspoon freshly grated nutmeg
- 1 onion, finely chopped
- 12 ounces (350 g) Italian sausages, cut into small chunks
- 2 cups (400 g) Italian risotto rice
- 1 tablespoon dry white wine
- 4 cups (1 liter) beef broth or stock, boiling (see page 28)
- ½ cup (60 g) freshly grated Parmesan cheese

Melt 2 tablespoons of the butter in a large frying pan over high heat. Add the cabbage and sauté until wilted, 3 minutes. Season with salt, pepper, and nutmeg. Set aside.

Melt the remaining 2 tablespoons of butter in the same pan over medium heat. Add the onion and sauté until softened, about 5 minutes.

Add the sausage and cook until browned all over, about 5 minutes. Add the rice and stir until the grains are well coated, 2 minutes. Pour in the wine and cook until the alcohol evaporates, about 4 minutes.

Begin stirring in the broth, ½ cup (125 ml) at a time. Cook and stir until each addition has been absorbed, and the rice is tender, 15–18 minutes. Stir the cabbage into the risotto and cook until heated through. Sprinkle with the Parmesan and serve hot.

Serves: 4 • Prep: 30 min • Cooking: 35 min

PROSCIUTTO AND MASCARPONE RISOTTO

- 5 tablespoons butter
- 1 small white onion, finely chopped
- 2 cups (400 g) Italian risotto rice
- 1 cup (250 ml) dry white wine
- 4 cups (1 liter) beef broth or stock (see page 28)
- 1 cup (120 g) diced prosciutto (Parma ham)
- ⅔ cup (150 g) mascarpone cheese
- Salt and freshly ground black pepper

Melt the butter in a large frying pan over medium heat. Add the onion and sauté until softened, about 5 minutes.

Add the rice and stir until the grains are well coated, 2 minutes. Pour in the wine and cook until the alcohol evaporates, about 4 minutes.

Begin stirring in the broth, ½ cup (125 ml) at a time. Cook and stir until each addition has been absorbed and the rice is tender, 15–18 minutes. Stir in the prosciutto and mascarpone. Season with salt and pepper. Serve hot.

Serves: 4–6 • Prep: 15 min • Cooking: 25 min

Pea and Pancetta Risotto

- 4 cups (1 liter) vegetable broth or stock (see page 112)
- 1¼ pounds (650 g) fresh or frozen peas
- 4 tablespoons extra-virgin olive oil
- ½ cup (125 g) finely diced pancetta
- 1 medium white onion, finely chopped

- 2 cups (400 g) Italian risotto rice
  Salt and freshly ground black pepper
- ½ cup (60 g) freshly grated Parmesan cheese and 1 ounce (30 g) Parmesan cheese, in flakes

Pour the broth into a large frying pan and add half the peas. Bring to a boil, then simmer for 10 minutes. Transfer to a food processor and process until smooth.

Heat the oil in the same pan over medium heat and add the pancetta. Sauté over medium heat until the pancetta begins to crispen, about 5 minutes.

Add the onion and sauté until softened, about 5 minutes. Add the rice and remaining peas and stir until the grains are coated, 2 minutes.

Begin stirring in the pea stock, ½ cup (125 ml) at a time. Cook and stir until each addition has been absorbed and the rice is tender, 15–18 minutes.

Season with salt and pepper and stir in the grated Parmesan. Scatter the flakes of Parmesan over the top. Cover the pan and let stand for 2 minutes. Serve hot.

Serves: 4–6 • Prep: 20 min • Cooking: 35 min

Risotto Rice

A good risotto should have a creamy consistency, but the kernels of rice should still be *al dente* (an Italian term meaning "firm to the bite"). This is not as easy as it sounds, and making risotto requires the cook's constant attention in carefully stirring and adding broth or stock until the rice is perfectly cooked. The choice of rice is also very important; the ideal rice releases its starch gradually during the prolonged cooking-and-stirring process to obtain the desired consistency. Traditionally, Italian short-grain *superfino* rice varieties are used, especially arborio and carnaroli. Of the two, the carnaroli is the easiest to manage if you are not expert, since it will hold its firmness a little longer than the arborio. In the region around Venice, another type of rice, called vialone nano, is used with fabulous results.

RISOTTO WITH GRAPES AND PANCETTA

- 4 tablespoons butter
- 1 onion, finely chopped
- 4 ounces (125 g) pancetta, diced
- 2 cups (400 g) Italian risotto rice
- 1 cup (250 ml) dry white wine
- 4 cups (1 liter) chicken broth or stock (see page 56), boiling
- 12 ounces (350 g) fresh white or green grapes, peeled
- Small bunch chives, chopped
- 2 tablespoons finely chopped fresh flat-leaf parsley
- Salt and freshly ground white pepper
- 1 cup (125 g) freshly grated Parmesan cheese

Melt the butter in a large frying pan over medium heat. Add the onion and pancetta and sauté until the onion is softened and the pancetta is lightly browned, about 5 minutes.

Add the rice and stir for 2 minutes, until the grains are well coated. Pour in the wine and cook until the alcohol has evaporated, about 4 minutes.

Begin stirring in the broth, $1/2$ cup (125 ml) at a time. Cook and stir until each addition has been absorbed and the rice is tender, 15–18 minutes.

Add the grapes, chives, and parsley. Season with salt and white pepper. Sprinkle with the Parmesan and serve hot.

Serves: 4 • Prep: 15 min • Cooking: 30 min

PUMPKIN RISOTTO

- $1/4$ cup (60 ml) extra-virgin olive oil
- $1/2$ cup (80 g) butter
- 2 pounds (1 kg) orange-fleshed pumpkin or winter squash, seeds and fibers removed, cut into small dice
- 2 cups (400 g) Italian risotto rice
- $1/2$ cup (125 ml) dry white wine
- Salt and freshly ground black pepper
- 3 cups (750 ml) beef broth or stock (see page 28), boiling
- $1/2$ cup (60 g) freshly grated Parmesan cheese

Heat the oil with $1/4$ cup (60 g) of the butter in a large, deep frying pan over medium heat. Add the pumpkin. Cover and cook over low heat for about 20 minutes, or until almost tender.

Add the rice and stir well. Pour in the wine and cook until the alcohol has evaporated, about 4 minutes. Season with salt and pepper.

Begin stirring in the broth, $1/2$ cup (125 ml) at a time. Cook and stir until each addition has been absorbed and the rice is tender, 15–18 minutes.

Stir in the remaining $1/4$ cup (60 g) butter and the Parmesan. Serve hot.

Serves: 4–6 • Prep: 15 min • Cooking: 45 min

CHICKEN RISOTTO

- 4 tablespoons extra-virgin olive oil
- $1/3$ cup (80 g) butter
- 1 onion, finely chopped
- 1 carrot, finely chopped
- 1 stalk celery, finely chopped
- 1 chicken, weighing about $2 1/4$ pounds (1.2 kg), cut into 6 pieces
- 8 cups (2 liters) chicken broth or stock (see page 56), boiling
- 2 cups (400 g) Italian risotto rice
- $1/2$ cup (125 ml) dry white wine
- Salt and freshly ground black pepper
- $1/2$ cup (60 g) freshly grated Parmesan cheese

Heat the oil and $1/4$ cup (60 g) of the butter in a large, deep frying pan over medium heat. Add the onion, carrot, and celery and sauté until lightly browned, about 7 minutes.

Add the chicken and brown all over, 6–8 minutes. Add $1/2$ cup (125 ml) of the broth, partly cover the pan, and cook until the chicken is almost tender, about 30 minutes.

Add the rice and stir well. Pour in the wine and cook until evaporated. Begin adding more broth, $1/2$ cup (125 ml) at a time. Cook and stir until each addition is absorbed and the rice is tender, 15–18 minutes.

Stir in the remaining $1/2$ cup butter and season with salt and pepper. Sprinkle with the Parmesan and serve hot.

Serves: 4 • Prep: 20 min • Cooking: 1 hr

Chicken Risotto

RISOTTO WITH PEARS AND SAGE

This is a truly superb risotto—the Marsala wine and cheeses meld into the full flavor of the pears (do try to use Williams pears) to create a refined yet intoxicating mix. A word about Stracchino: This is a fresh, delicately flavored, buttery cheese from Lombardy, in the north of Italy. It is almost identical to Crescenza cheese. Some small cheesemakers in America do make these cheeses. They are readily available in Australia. If you can't get either, substitute 6 ounces (180 g) of cream cheese and 2 tablespoons of sour cream.

- 3 tablespoons butter
- 2 large ripe pears, peeled and cored; 1 thinly sliced, 1 cut into small cubes
- 12 leaves fresh sage, coarsely chopped
- 1/3 cup (90 ml) dry Marsala wine Freshly ground black pepper Freshly grated nutmeg (optional)
- 1 medium white onion, finely chopped

- 4 cups (1 liter) vegetable broth or stock (see page 112)
- 2 cups (400 g) Italian risotto rice
- 1/3 cup (90 ml) dry white wine
- 8 ounces (200 g) fresh, creamy Stracchino cheese
- 6 tablespoons freshly grated Parmesan cheese Salt

Melt 1½ tablespoons of the butter in a large frying pan over medium heat and add the sliced pear and about 8 sage leaves. Pour in the Marsala and season generously with pepper and nutmeg, if using. Simmer until the pear softens, 2–3 minutes, then pour the mixture into a small bowl and set aside.

Melt the remaining 1½ tablespoons butter in the same pan and add the onion, 1/2 cup (125 ml) of the broth, and the remaining sage leaves. Cook over medium-low heat until the onion is soft, about 5 minutes.

Increase the heat to medium-high, add the rice, and stir constantly for 2 minutes.

Decrease the heat to medium and add the cubes of pear and the wine. Continue stirring gently until the wine has evaporated, about 4 minutes. Add 1/2 cup (125 ml) of the broth and cook and stir until it has been absorbed. Continue stirring and adding stock, a little at a time, until the rice is cooked, 15–18 minutes.

Add the Stracchino and Parmesan and taste for salt. Stir in the reserved pear-and-sage mixture. Serve hot.

Serves: 4–6 • Prep: 15 min • Cooking: 30 min

ASPARAGUS RISOTTO WITH MINT

- 4 tablespoons (60 g) butter, cut up
- 1¼ pounds (625 g) asparagus, trimmed and chopped into short lengths
- 5 cups (1.25 liters) vegetable broth or stock (see page 112), boiling
- 1 onion, finely chopped
- 2 cups (400 g) Italian risotto rice

- 1/3 cup (80 ml) dry white wine
- 1/4 cup (60 ml) heavy (double) cream
- 1/2 cup (60 g) freshly grated Parmesan cheese Freshly ground white pepper
- 1 small bunch mint, finely chopped

Melt 2 tablespoons of the butter in a large frying pan over medium heat. Add the chopped asparagus and sauté for 3 minutes. Pour in 1 cup (250 ml) of the broth and bring to a boil. Reduce the heat and simmer until the asparagus is very tender, about 15 minutes.

Transfer to a bowl and blend with a handheld blender until smooth. Set aside.

Wipe the pan clean. Melt the remaining 2 tablespoons of butter in the frying pan over medium heat. Add the onion and sauté until softened, about 5 minutes.

Stir in the rice and toast for 2 minutes, stirring to coat the grains. Stir in the wine and cook until the alcohol has evaporated, about 4 minutes.

Begin adding the remaining broth, 1/2 cup (125 ml) at a time. Cook and stir until each addition is absorbed. After about 10 minutes, add the asparagus purée and tips. Add more broth and cook and stir until all the broth has been absorbed and the rice is tender, 15–18 minutes.

Add the cream and Parmesan and season with white pepper. Sprinkle with the mint and serve hot.

Serves: 4–6 • Prep: 30 min • Cooking: 1 hr

Risotto with Pears and Sage

ORANGE RISOTTO WITH FONTINA CHEESE

- 6 tablespoons butter
- 1 small onion, finely chopped
- 2 cups (400 g) Italian risotto rice
- ½ cup (125 ml) dry white wine
- 6 cups (1.5 liters) chicken broth or stock (see page 56), boiling

- 5 ounces (150 g) Fontina cheese, diced
- Salt and freshly ground white pepper
- 2 large oranges, zest chopped into tiny dice, juice squeezed

Melt the butter in a large frying pan over medium heat. Add the onion and sauté until softened, about 5 minutes.

Add the rice and stir until the grains are coated, 2 minutes. Pour in the wine and stir until the alcohol has evaporated. Begin stirring in the broth, ½ cup (125 ml) at a time. Cook and stir until each addition has been absorbed and the rice is tender, 15–18 minutes. Add the Fontina 5 minutes before the rice is cooked.

Season with salt and white pepper and add the orange juice and zest. Stir well and serve.

Serves: 4–6 • Prep: 15 min • Cooking: 25 min

SAFFRON RISOTTO WITH SHRIMP AND ZUCCHINI FLOWERS

- 4 tablespoons extra-virgin olive oil
- 20 shrimp (prawns), shelled
- 3 zucchini (courgettes), sliced
- 12 zucchini (courgette) flowers
- Salt and freshly ground black pepper
- 1 onion, finely chopped

- 1¾ cups (350 g) Italian risotto rice
- ½ cup (125 ml) dry white wine
- 4 saffron threads, crumbled
- 4 cups (1 liter) boiling vegetable broth or fish stock (see pages 98 or 112)
- 2 tablespoons butter

Heat 2 tablespoons of oil in a large frying pan over high heat. Add the shrimp and zucchini and sauté for 5 minutes. Add the zucchini flowers, season with salt and pepper, and cook for 2 minutes. Set aside.

Heat the remaining 2 tablespoons of oil in the same frying pan and sauté the onion until softened. Add the rice and cook for 2 minutes, stirring constantly. Pour in the wine and let it evaporate.

Dissolve the saffron in ½ cup (125 ml) of the broth and stir until absorbed. Continue stirring and adding stock, a little at a time, until the rice is cooked, 15–18 minutes. Stir in the zucchini mixture and butter and serve hot.

Serves: 4 • Prep: 25 min • Cooking: 40 min

PEARL BARLEY RISOTTO

- 3 tablespoons extra-virgin olive oil
- 1 small onion, finely chopped
- 2 cloves garlic, finely chopped
- 1½ cups (300 g) pearl barley
- 1 cup (250 ml) dry white wine
- 6 cups (1.5 liters) beef or vegetable broth or stock (see pages 28 or 112)
- 2 tablespoons butter
- ½ cup (60 g) freshly grated Parmesan cheese

- Salt and freshly ground black pepper
- 1 tablespoon finely chopped fresh parsley
- 1 tablespoon finely chopped fresh basil
- 1 tablespoon finely chopped fresh cilantro (coriander)
- 2 tablespoons fresh lemon juice

Heat the oil in a large frying pan over medium heat. Add the onion and garlic and sauté until softened, about 5 minutes. Turn the heat up to high and add the barley. Stir rapidly for 1–2 minutes to coat the grains.

Add half the wine and cook until almost absorbed. Add the rest of the wine and cook and stir until absorbed.

Add 2 cups (500 ml) of the broth, cover the pan, and cook until almost all absorbed. Uncover and begin adding the broth ½ cup (125 ml) at a time, stirring until each addition is absorbed. Cook and stir, adding more broth, until the barley is tender, about 40 minutes.

Add the butter and cheese and season with salt and pepper. Stir in the parsley, basil, cilantro, and lemon juice and serve hot.

Serves 4 • Prep: 20 min • Cooking: 50 min

Orange Risotto with Fontina Cheese

SEAFOOD RICE

- 3 pounds (1.5 kg) mussels or clams, in shell
- 4 tablespoons extra-virgin olive oil
- 1 onion, finely chopped
- 2 cloves garlic, finely chopped
- 1 fresh red chile pepper, seeded and sliced
- 1 pound (500 g) small squid, cleaned and cut into rings
- 6 tomatoes, peeled and cut into cubes
  Salt and freshly ground white pepper
- 2 cups (400 g) short-grain rice
- 4 tablespoons white wine
- 6 cups (1.5 liters) fish stock (see page 98), boiling
- 1¾ pounds (800 g) medium shrimp (prawns), shelled (reserve the shells for the stock)
- 2 tablespoons butter
- 2 tablespoons finely chopped fresh flat-leaf parsley

Place 2 tablespoons of water in a large frying pan over medium-high heat and add the mussels. Cover and cook, shaking the pan from time to time, until the mussels are open, about 10 minutes. Discard any that have not opened. Set aside.

Heat 2 tablespoons of the oil in the same frying pan over high heat. Add the onion and sauté until pale golden brown, 7–8 minutes.

Add the garlic and chile. Add the squid and sauté until tender, 5–7 minutes. Add the tomatoes, season with salt and white pepper, and cook over medium heat for 10 minutes. Remove from the pan and set aside.

Heat the remaining 2 tablespoons of oil over medium heat in the same frying pan. Add the rice and sauté for 1 minute. Return the squid mixture to the pan. Pour in the wine and cook until it has evaporated.

Pour in enough stock to cover the rice. Lower the heat, cover, and cook until the rice is tender, 10–15 minutes. Add the shrimp and mussels and cook until heated through, about 3 minutes. Add the butter and garnish with the parsley. Serve hot.

Serves: 4–6 • Prep: 25 min • Cooking: 45 min

SMOKED SAUSAGE WITH RICE

- 2 tablespoons butter
- 2 tablespoons finely chopped fresh parsley
- 1 (10-ounce/300-ml) can cream of celery soup
- 1 cup (250 ml) water
- ½ cup (125 ml) milk
- 1½ pounds (750 g) smoked sausage (kielbasa or other), sliced
- 1½ cups (300 g) short-grain rice
- 2 cups (300 g) frozen peas, thawed
- 5 ounces (150 g) white mushrooms, thinly sliced
- 1 cup (180 g) freshly grated cheddar cheese

Melt the butter in a large frying pan over medium heat. Add the parsley, soup, water, and milk and bring to a boil. Stir in the sausage and rice and simmer until the rice is almost tender, about 15 minutes.

Add the peas and mushrooms and cook until they are tender, about 15 minutes.

Sprinkle with the cheese and remove from the heat. Cover the pan and let stand until the cheese is melted, about 5 minutes. Serve at once.

Serves: 4–6 • Prep: 20 min • Cooking: 30 min

RICE WITH CHORIZO SAUSAGE

- 4 tablespoons extra-virgin olive oil
- 1 small onion, finely chopped
- 1 pound (500 g) Spanish chorizo sausage,
- 1 cup (200 g) short-grain rice
  Salt and freshly ground black pepper
- 2 cups (500 ml) beef broth or stock (see page 28)
- 2 cups (300 g) frozen peas
- 2 cups (500 g) peeled and chopped tomatoes
- ⅓ cup (30 g) Kalamata olives
- 2 tablespoons finely chopped fresh parsley

Heat the oil in a large frying pan over medium heat. Add the onion and sauté until softened, about 5 minutes.

Add the sausage and sauté until browned, 5–7 minutes. Add the rice and stir over high heat until lightly toasted, 2–3 minutes. Season with salt and pepper.

Pour in the stock and add the peas. Bring to a boil and simmer, covered, for 15 minutes.

Stir in the tomatoes, olives, and parsley. Cover and cook for 5–7 minutes, until the rice is tender. Serve hot.

Serves 4 • Prep: 15 min • Cooking: 30–40 min

LAMB AND MUSHROOM PILAF

1½ pounds (750 g) boneless lamb, cut into bite-sized pieces

1 (14-ounce/400-g) can tomatoes, chopped and drained, reserving the juice

5 tablespoons extra-virgin olive oil

4 tablespoons fresh lemon juice

2 tablespoons firmly packed brown sugar

2 cloves garlic, finely chopped

1 fresh red chile, sliced

½ teaspoon cumin seeds

Salt and freshly ground black pepper

1 pound (500 g) white button mushrooms, sliced

1 cup (200 g) brown rice

2 cups (500 ml) chicken broth or stock (see page 56)

1 tablespoon finely chopped fresh mint or cilantro (coriander), to garnish (optional)

1 tablespoon finely grated lemon zest, to garnish (optional)

Place the lamb in a large stainless steel or glass bowl with the tomato juice, 4 tablespoons of the oil, lemon juice, brown sugar, garlic, chile, cumin, salt, and pepper. Stir gently so that the lamb is well coated with the marinade. Refrigerate for 4 hours.

Heat the remaining 1 tablespoon of oil in a large frying pan over medium-high heat.

Carefully remove the pieces of lamb from the marinade, reserving the marinade.

Sauté the lamb, in two separate batches, in the pan with the oil until browned, 7–9 minutes each. Remove the lamb and set aside.

Add 2 tablespoons of marinade to the pan and sauté the mushrooms until tender, about 10 minutes.

Return the lamb to the pan and add the rice, tomatoes, remaining marinade, and the broth. Cover, decrease the heat to low, and simmer until the lamb and rice are very tender, 75–80 minutes.

If desired, stir in the fresh herbs and lemon zest just before serving.

Serves: 4 • Prep: 30 min + 4 hr to marinate • Cooking: about 2 hr

BROWN RICE

Brown rice is not a variety of rice; it is a less refined version of any long- or short-grain rice. To obtain white rice, the outer husk, bran, and most of the germ are removed from the grains during the milling process. For brown rice, only the outer husk is removed. Not only does this make brown rice prettier, with its matte, browny green flecks and mottles, it also makes it much healthier and more flavorful. Nutritionally, it is rich in fiber and B vitamins, and contains useful amounts of trace minerals. Brown rice has a deep, nutty flavor and a chewy texture. It also takes longer to cook, usually about 30 to 40 minutes, as opposed to 15 to 20 minutes for white rice.

Seared Shrimp with Couscous

- 4 tablespoons extra-virgin olive oil
- 1½ pounds (750 g) medium shrimp (prawns), peeled and deveined
- Salt and freshly ground black pepper
- 1 teaspoon mustard seeds
- ½ teaspoon cumin seeds
- 4 cloves garlic, finely chopped
- 2 medium white onions, thinly sliced
- 2 carrots, shredded
- 1½ cups (350 g) instant couscous
- 1 cup (150 g) frozen peas
- 3 cups (750 ml) boiling water
- 1 tablespoon finely chopped fresh cilantro (coriander)

Heat 2 tablespoons of the oil in a large frying pan over medium-high heat. Add the shrimp and season with salt and pepper. Sauté the shrimp until pink, about 4 minutes. Remove from the pan and set aside.

Heat the remaining 2 tablespoons of oil in the same pan over medium heat. Add the mustard and cumin seeds and toast until the mustard seeds begin to pop, about 1 minute.

Add the garlic, onions, and carrots and sauté until softened, 5–7 minutes. Add the couscous, peas, and water and cook, stirring constantly for 3–4 minutes, until the peas are heated through.

Remove from the heat and cover the pan with a lid. Let stand until the couscous is tender, about 5 minutes.

Stir in the shrimp and cilantro. Check the seasoning, adding more salt and pepper to taste. Serve hot.

Serves: 4–6 • Prep: 30 min • Cooking: 20 min

Shrimp Goa-style

The Portuguese-influenced port of Goa, on the west coast of India, has an abundance of fish and seafood, and this recipe takes its inspiration from that region. Cooking with coconuts and tomatoes draws out the sweetness of the succulent shrimp. The sweet and spicy addition of tamarind paste makes this dish absolutely delicious.

- ¼ cup (60 ml) peanut or other vegetable oil
- 2 medium onions, thinly sliced
- 1 teaspoon cumin seeds
- ½ teaspoon mustard seeds
- 4 cloves garlic, finely chopped
- 2 teaspoons red curry paste (see below)
- 4 curry leaves (optional)
- 1 pound (500 g) jumbo shrimp (king or tiger prawns), deveined
- ½ teaspoon ground turmeric
- ¼ teaspoon salt
- 2 medium tomatoes, chopped
- 2 teaspoons tamarind paste
- ¼ cup (60 ml) coconut milk
- Handful of finely chopped fresh cilantro (coriander)
- Freshly cooked long-grain rice or naan bread, to serve

Heat the oil in a large wok or frying pan over medium heat. Add the onions, cumin and mustard seeds and sauté until lightly golden, 7–8 minutes.

Add the garlic, red curry paste, and curry leaves, if using, and stir until a wonderful aroma escapes, 2 minutes.

Add the shrimp, turmeric, and salt and stir everything together. Cook, stirring occasionally, until the shrimp are pink, about 5 minutes.

Stir in the tomatoes and tamarind paste. Cover and simmer over low heat for 5 minutes.

Pour in the coconut milk and stir over high heat for 2 minutes. Garnish with the cilantro. Serve with rice or fresh naan bread.

Serves: 4–6 • Prep: 10 min • Cooking: 25 min

Curry Paste

 Red or green curry paste can be bought at Asian supermarkets, but it can also be made at home.

- 16 cloves garlic, chopped
- 1 teaspoon salt
- 2 tablespoons fresh cilantro (coriander stems), minced
- 1 tablespoon ground coriander
- 2 teaspoons cumin seeds
- 1 teaspoon cayenne pepper
- 10 fresh red or green chiles, chopped
- 2 tablespoons minced fresh ginger
- 3 stalks lemongrass, minced
- 1 tablespoon finely grated lime zest
- 1 teaspoon anchovy paste
- 2 tablespoons peanut oil

Chop all the ingredients in a food processor, pulsing intermittently and using a spatula to push the ingredients down, until a smooth paste forms.

Place in a glass jar. Cover and store in the refrigerator for up to 1 month.

Makes: about 1 cup • Prep: 20 min

TROPICAL SHRIMP STIR-FRY

1 pound (500 g) shrimp (prawns), peeled and deveined

2 tablespoons fresh lime juice

2 teaspoons minced fresh garlic

¼ teaspoon sweet paprika

¼ teaspoon cayenne pepper

2 tablespoons Asian sesame oil

2 tablespoons peanut oil

1 green bell pepper (capsicum), seeded and thinly sliced

4 scallions (green onions), white and tender green parts only, trimmed and finely sliced

8 ounces (250 g) sugar snap peas

4 ounces (125 g) snow peas (mangetout)

3 tablespoons light soy sauce

2 tablespoons cornstarch (cornflour) dissolved in ¾ cup (180 ml) vegetable broth or stock (see page 112)

½ teaspoon salt

2 cups (400 g) cooked long-grain rice

Stir the shrimp, lime juice, garlic, paprika, and cayenne pepper with the sesame and peanut oils in a large wok or frying pan until the flavors are well combined. Place the pan over medium-high heat and stir-fry for 8 minutes.

Add the bell pepper and scallions. Stir-fry until the bell pepper has softened slightly, 4 minutes.

Add the sugar snap peas, snow peas, soy sauce, cornstarch mixture, and salt. Stir-fry until the liquid has thickened and the vegetables are cooked, 4–5 minutes.

Stir in the rice until heated through. Serve hot.

Serves: 4–6 • Prep: 15 min • Cooking: 20 min

SHRIMP STIR-FRY WITH BELL PEPPERS AND MANGO

2 tablespoons peanut or other vegetable oil

1¼ cups (125 g) walnuts, coarsely chopped

1 pound (500 g) shrimp (prawns), peeled and deveined

4 cloves garlic, finely chopped

4 carrots, thinly sliced

2 medium zucchini (courgettes), sliced

1 green bell pepper (capsicum), seeded and cut into thin strips

¼ cup (60 g) chunky mango chutney

1 (8-ounce/250-g) can pineapple chunks, drained

2 tablespoons dark soy sauce

Freshly cooked basmati or Thai rice, to serve

Heat a wok or large frying pan over medium-high heat and add the oil. Add the walnuts, shrimp, and garlic. Stir-fry until the shrimp turn pink, about 3 minutes. Remove with a slotted spoon and set aside.

Add the carrots, zucchini, and bell pepper and stir-fry until tender-crisp, about 5 minutes.

Mix in the mango chutney and simmer for 2 minutes.

Return the shrimp and walnuts to the wok, along with the pineapple and soy sauce. Stir-fry over high heat for 1 minute. Serve hot with the freshly cooked rice.

Serves: 4 • Prep: 10 min • Cooking: 15 min •

CHILE SHRIMP

Sambal is a very spicy chile-based Indonesian sauce. It is used to flavor stir-fries or as a dipping sauce for spring rolls and other Asian dishes. You can find small jars of it in the Asian section of your supermarket or in Asian food stores. If you prefer, substitute 2–3 minced fresh jalapeño peppers for the sambal in this recipe. Rice vinegar has a sweet mild flavor and is available in Asian food stores and many supermarkets. You can substitute with cider vinegar or leave it out.

2 tablespoons peanut oil

6 scallions (green onions), trimmed and sliced

4 cloves garlic, finely chopped

1 tablespoon minced fresh ginger

1½ pounds (750 g) shrimp (prawn), shelled and deveined

1 (14-ounce/400-g) can whole tomatoes, drained and chopped

2 teaspoons cornstarch (cornflour)

1 tablespoon rice vinegar

1 tablespoon sambal (spicy chile sauce)

1 tablespoon dark brown sugar

2 tablespoons Chinese rice wine or dry sherry

1 pound (500 g) rice noodles, soaked in boiling water for 5 minutes or prepared according to the directions on the package

Finely chopped scallions (green onions), to garnish

Heat the wok over high heat. Add the peanut oil and swirl quickly to coat the sides. Add the sliced scallions, garlic, and ginger and stir-fry for 1 minute.

Add the shrimp and stir-fry until just pink, about 3 minutes. Remove and set aside in a warm place.

Add the tomatoes to the wok and stir over high heat until smooth and reduced, about 5 minutes.

Dissolve the cornstarch in the rice vinegar. Add the sambal, brown sugar, rice wine, and vinegar mixture and cook until the sauce thickens slightly, about 2 minutes.

Return the shrimp to the pan and cook until heated through. Serve hot over the noodles and garnish with the finely chopped scallions.

Serves: 4–6 • Prep: 15 min • Cooking: 10 min

Shrimp Stir-Fry with Bell Peppers and Mango

CHICKEN STIR-FRY WITH CASHEW NUTS AND MANGO

3 tablespoons peanut or other vegetable oil
1 medium red onion, finely sliced
1 red bell pepper (capsicum), seeded and thinly sliced
1 green bell pepper (capsicum), seeded and thinly sliced
3 carrots, julienned
1 (4-ounce/90-g) can bamboo shoots, drained
1 pound (500 g) boneless, skinless chicken breasts, cut into small cubes

1 medium mango, peeled and cut into small pieces
2 tablespoons fresh lime juice
1 tablespoon cornstarch (cornflour)
1 tablespoon dark soy sauce
1 tablespoon orange-flower water
  Handful of finely chopped fresh cilantro (coriander)
1 cup (100 g) roasted cashew nuts
  Freshly cooked basmati rice, to serve

Heat a wok or large frying pan over medium-high and add the oil. Add the onion, bell peppers, carrots, and bamboo shoots. Stir-fry until the vegetables are softened, about 5 minutes.

Add the chicken and stir-fry until it turns white, about 5 minutes. Add the mango and stir-fry gently for 2 minutes.

Mix the lime juice, cornstarch, soy sauce, and orange-flower water in a cup and pour it into the pan. Cook until the liquid has thickened.

Garnish with the cilantro and cashew nuts. Serve hot with the rice.

Serves: 4 • Prep: 10 min • Cooking: 15 min

CANTONESE SWEET AND SOUR SHRIMP

16 large shrimp (prawns), shelled and deveined
1 large egg, lightly beaten
½ cup (75 g) cornstarch (cornflour)
5 tablespoons peanut or other vegetable oil
1 medium onion, finely chopped
1 red bell pepper (capsicum), seeded and coarsely chopped

3 tablespoons light soy sauce
2 tablespoons tomato ketchup
2 tablespoons water
1 tablespoon superfine (caster) sugar
1 tablespoon rice vinegar
¼ teaspoon salt
  Freshly cooked basmati rice, to serve

Dip the shrimp in the egg, followed by the cornstarch.

Heat a wok or large frying pan over medium heat and add the oil. Add the shrimp and stir-fry until golden brown and crispy, about 5 minutes. Use a slotted spoon to remove the shrimp and set aside.

Add the onion and bell pepper and stir-fry for 3 minutes.

Add the soy sauce, ketchup, water, sugar, rice vinegar, and salt. Stir constantly until the sauce thickens. Return the shrimp to the pan and reheat gently.

Serve hot, over the rice.

Serves: 4 • Prep: 15 min • Cooking: 10 min

THAI VEGETABLE FRIED RICE

A delicious dish that can be made in minutes using leftover rice.

2 tablespoons peanut or other vegetable oil
4 cloves garlic, finely chopped
8 ounces (250 g) firm tofu, diced
2 cups (400 g) cooked long-grain rice
2 scallions (green onions), white and green tender parts only, finely chopped + ½ bunch scallions (green onions), cut on the diagonal, to garnish

2 tablespoons light soy sauce
1 tablespoon oyster sauce
1 teaspoon ground coriander
¼ teaspoon ground turmeric
½ bunch cilantro (coriander) leaves, finely chopped
1 cup (150 g) fresh or canned pineapple chunks (optional)

Heat a wok or large frying pan over medium-high heat and add the oil.

Add the garlic and stir-fry for 1 minute. Add the tofu and stir-fry for 3 minutes.

Stir in the rice, chopped scallions, soy and oyster sauces, coriander, and turmeric. Stir-fry for 5 minutes.

Garnish with the cilantro, scallions, and pineapple, if using. Serve hot.

Serves: 2–4 • Prep: 5 min • Cooking: 10 min

Chicken Stir-Fry with Cashew Nuts and Mango

NASI GORENG

- 6 tablespoons (80 ml) peanut or other vegetable oil
- 2 cloves garlic, finely chopped
- 1 small slice fresh ginger
- 4 scallions (spring onions), tender green white parts only, finely sliced
- 2 carrots, cut into thin strips
- 8 ounces (200 g) bok choy, finely shredded
- 3 cups (600 g) cooked long-grain rice
- 3 tablespoons dark soy sauce
- 1 teaspoon Chinese chili paste
  Salt and freshly ground black pepper
- 1 cup (100 g) mung bean sprouts
- 4 large eggs

Heat a wok or large frying pan over medium heat and add 4 tablespoons (60 ml) of the oil. Stir-fry the garlic and ginger for 30 seconds.

Add the scallions, carrots, and bok choy and stir-fry for 2 minutes. Add the rice and stir-fry for 2 minutes.

Stir in the soy sauce and chili paste. Season with salt and pepper. Add the bean sprouts. Stir-fry for 2 minutes.

Spoon the rice onto individual plates. Add the remaining 2 tablespoons oil and fry the eggs until cooked through. Place a fried egg on each serving.

Serves: 4 • Prep: 15 min • Cooking: 15 min

COCONUT CHICKEN AND PINEAPPLE

- 2 tablespoons peanut or other vegetable oil
- 1 medium onion, finely chopped
- ½ red bell pepper (capsicum), seeded and finely sliced
- 2 teaspoons red curry paste
- 4 cloves garlic, minced
- 1 teaspoon minced fresh ginger
- 1 teaspoon sweet paprika
- ½ teaspoon ground turmeric
- ½ cup (50 g) cashews
- 2 tablespoons pineapple juice
- 6 curry leaves
- 2 bay leaves
- 1 tablespoon dark soy sauce
- 1 teaspoon dark brown sugar
- 3½ cups (900 ml) unsweetened coconut milk
- 4 boneless, skinless chicken breasts, cut into thin strips
- 8 ounces (250 g) sliced bamboo shoots
- 10 cherry tomatoes
  Freshly cooked basmati rice, to serve
  Juice of ½ lime
- 1 (7-ounce/200-g) can pineapple cubes, drained
  Generous handful of freshly chopped fresh cilantro (coriander)
  Salt

Heat a wok or large frying pan over low heat and add the oil. Add the onion, bell pepper, curry paste, garlic, ginger, paprika, turmeric, and cashews. Stir-fry until aromatic, 2 minutes.

Remove from heat and stir in the pineapple juice. Return to low heat and add the curry leaves, bay leaves, soy sauce, and brown sugar. Pour in the coconut milk. Bring to a boil. Simmer for 15 minutes, or until the sauce has reduced by one-third of its original volume.

Remove from the heat and remove the curry leaves and curry leaves. Blend with a handheld blender until smooth. Add the chicken, bamboo shoots, and tomatoes. Return to the heat and simmer until the chicken is cooked, about 15 minutes. Transfer to a serving plate with a bed of basmati rice.

Add the lime juice, pineapple cubes, and cilantro to the sauce. Season with salt and spoon over the chicken. Serve hot.

Serves: 4–6 • Prep: 5 min • Cooking: 35 min

INDO-CHINESE SHRIMP STIR-FRY

If you like spicy food, add a finely sliced fresh red or green chile to the pan with the turmeric and garlic.

- 3 tablespoons peanut oil
- 1 pound (500 g) medium shelled and deveined shrimp (prawns)
- ½ teaspoon ground turmeric
- 2 cloves garlic finely chopped
  Salt
- 6 cherry tomatoes, halved
- 4 ounces (125 g) snow peas (mangetout)
- 1 small red bell pepper (capsicum), seeded and thinly sliced
- 1 green bell pepper (capsicum), seeded and thinly sliced
- 1 cup (100 g) mung bean sprouts
- ⅓ cup (60 g) canned water chestnuts, cut into quarters
- ¼ cup (60 ml) dark soy sauce
- 1 tablespoon oyster sauce
- 2 (3-ounce) packages (180 g) ramen noodles, (flavor package discarded) or instant Chinese-style egg noodles, cooked
- 4 scallions (green onions), white and tender green parts, sliced

Heat a wok or large frying pan over high heat and add the oil. Add the shrimp and stir-fry for 3 minutes.

Add the turmeric and garlic and season with salt.

Stir-fry until the water from the shrimp has evaporated, then add the tomatoes, snow peas, and bell peppers. Stir-fry for 2 minutes.

Add the bean sprouts, water chestnuts, soy sauce, and oyster sauce. Stir-fry for 2 minutes. Add the well-drained noodles and stir well. Add the scallions and serve immediately.

Serves: 4 • Prep: 15 min • Cooking: 10 min

CAMBODIAN RICE

5	tablespoons peanut or other vegetable oil
1	onion, finely chopped
2	cloves garlic, finely chopped
12	ounces (350 g) pork, cut into small pieces
4	ounces (125 g) boneless, skinless chicken breast, cut into small pieces
4	ounces (125 g) shrimp (prawns), peeled and cut in half lengthwise
1¼	cups (250 g) basmati rice

4	cups (1 liter) fish stock (see page 98)
2	tablespoons white wine vinegar Pinch of aniseed
1	teaspoon grated fresh ginger
½	teaspoon ground cinnamon Salt and freshly ground black pepper
2	large eggs
2	fresh green chiles, seeded and finely sliced

Heat 4 tablespoons of the oil in a large frying pan over medium heat. Add the onion and garlic and sauté until pale gold, 7–8 minutes.

Add the pork and chicken and sauté until browned all over, about 10 minutes. Add the shrimp and sauté 2 minutes.

Add the rice and cook for 3 minutes, stirring constantly.

Pour in the stock, vinegar, aniseed, ginger, and cinnamon. Season with salt and pepper. Cover and cook over low heat until the rice is tender, about 20 minutes.

Beat the eggs with a pinch of salt. Heat the remaining 1 tablespoon of oil in a frying pan and fry the eggs until firm. Cut into strips.

Gently mix the fried egg into the rice. Garnish with chile pepper. Serve hot.

Serves: 4–6 • Prep: 20 min • Cooking: 30 min

LONG-GRAIN RICE

Rice is one of our oldest crops and is a staple food even today for more than half the people in the world. There are thousands of different kinds of rice and many different ways of growing it. In the kitchen, rice is often divided into three main groups depending on the size and length of the grain. Generally speaking, long-grain rice comes from Asia. Two of the best-known types of long-grain rice are basmati (from India, Pakistan, and the Middle East) and jasmine, or Thai, rice (from Thailand). These are both fragrant with mouthwatering floral overtones that will fill your house during cooking. As a food, rice is easy to digest and full of energy-giving starches. White rice is stripped of its vitamin-rich substances during milling, although it does still contain useful amounts of protein. This protein is incomplete but when eaten with beans, fish, or meat, it becomes a complete protein.

BEEF AND SPINACH STIR-FRY

This delicious stir-fry has some interesting ingredients and looks extremely appealing, with the green spinach and the red-orange of the papaya, or pawpaw as some people call it. Papaya is high in vitamins and acts very efficiently as a meat tenderizer.

- 2 pounds (1 kg) beef tenderloin, cut into thin strips
- 5 tablespoons dark soy sauce
- 5 tablespoons apple juice
- 1 teaspoon finely chopped dried red bird's-eye chile
- 2 cloves garlic, finely chopped
- 1 medium papaya or pawpaw, peeled and cut into small cubes
- 10 cherry tomatoes, halved
- 3 tablespoons peanut oil
- 2 stalks celery, cut into thin strips
- 2 tablespoons minced fresh ginger
- 3 bunches leaf spinach, tough stems removed, finely shredded
- 8 ounces (250 g) thin rice noodles, cooked

Combine the beef with the soy sauce, apple juice, chile, garlic, papaya, and tomatoes in a large nonreactive bowl. Use your hands to mix the ingredients for about 10 minutes to ensure all the spices are well absorbed. The heat from your hands will aid the tenderizing process. Let marinate for 2 hours.

Heat a wok or large frying pan over high heat and add the oil. Stir-fry the celery and ginger until aromatic, 1 minute.

Add the beef and the marinade. Stir occasionally until all the liquid has evaporated and the meat is tender, about 5 minutes.

Add the spinach and noodles. Stir-fry for another 2 minutes. Serve hot.

Serves: 4–6 • Prep: 10 min + 2 hr to marinate • Cooking: 15 min

CHICKEN, SPINACH, AND PINEAPPLE STIR-FRY

- 4 (3-ounce) packages ramen noodles (350 g instant noodles), flavor packet discarded
- 4 tablespoons peanut or other vegetable oil
- 2 whole boneless, skinless chicken breasts, cut into thin strips
- 1 tablespoon finely minced fresh ginger
- 2 cloves garlic, finely chopped
- 2 cups (200 g) cubed fresh pineapple
- 3 tablespoons molasses (treacle)
- 5 cups (200 g) fresh young spinach leaves (or chopped cabbage)
- 8 shiitake mushrooms, caps quartered and stems diced
- 2 tablespoons fresh lemon juice
- 1 teaspoon Tabasco
- ½ teaspoon crushed red pepper flakes
- 4 tablespoons toasted sesame seeds

Soak the noodles in boiling water for 10 minutes to soften (or follow the instructions on the package).

Heat 2 tablespoons of oil in a wok or large frying pan over medium-high heat. Add the chicken, ginger, and garlic and stir-fry until the chicken is white, 6–8 minutes. Remove with a slotted spoon and set aside.

Add the pineapple and molasses to the same pan. Stir-fry until the pineapple is brown and tender, about 2 minutes. Remove with a slotted spoon and place over the chicken.

Heat the remaining 2 tablespoons of oil in the same wok and add the spinach, noodles, and mushrooms. Stir in the lemon juice, Tabasco, and red pepper flakes. Stir-fry until the spinach is just wilted and the mushrooms are tender, about 5 minutes.

Return the chicken and pineapple to the wok and stir-fry over high heat until everything is warmed through, 2 minutes. Sprinkle with the sesame seeds and serve.

Serves: 4 • Prep: 20 min • Cooking: 20 min

CARIBBEAN RICE

- 3 cups (750 ml) water
- 1½ cups (300 g) long-grain rice
- 1 teaspoon salt
- 2 cups (300 g) canned red kidney beans, rinsed and drained
- 1 cup (100 g) canned pineapple chunks, drained
- ½ cup (60 g) slivered nuts
- 1 large onion, finely chopped
- 2 cloves garlic, finely chopped
- 1 teaspoon hot pepper sauce

Bring the water to a boil in a large saucepan. Add the rice and salt. Mix well. Cover and cook over low heat until the rice is tender, about 20 minutes.

Stir in the beans, pineapple, nuts, onion, garlic, and pepper sauce. Cook over high heat until heated through and well mixed, about 2 minutes. Serve hot.

Serves: 4 • Prep: 5 min • Cooking: 25 min

Chicken, Spinach, and Pineapple Stir-Fry

SICHUAN CHICKEN STIR-FRY

2 eggs, lightly beaten

3 tablespoons dark soy sauce

1 tablespoon light soy sauce

3 tablespoons fresh lemon juice

4 tablespoons peanut oil

2 pounds (1 kg) boneless, skinless chicken breasts, cut into small pieces

1 white onion, finely sliced

8 ounces (250 g) canned water chestnuts, sliced

2 fresh green chiles, seeded and finely chopped

3 scallions (green onions), finely chopped

8 ounces (250 g) snow peas (mangetout)

2 cloves garlic, finely chopped

1 teaspoon brown sugar

1 teaspoon cornstarch (cornflour) dissolved in 2 teaspoons water

Freshly cooked long-grain rice, to serve

1 small bunch chives, chopped, to garnish

Mix the eggs, soy sauces, and lemon juice in a cup.

Heat the oil in a large wok or frying pan over medium heat. Add the chicken in small batches and stir-fry until the meat is white, 4–5 minutes. Remove and set aside.

Add the onion, water chestnuts, chiles, scallions, snow peas, garlic, and brown sugar. Stir-fry for 5 minutes.

Pour in the cornstarch mixture. Stir-fry over high heat until the mixture is almost dry, about 4 minutes.

Add the chicken and mix well.

Spoon the mixture over the freshly cooked rice. Garnish with the chives and serve hot.

Serves: 4 • Prep: 10 min • Cooking: 15 min

WALNUT AND CHICKEN STIR-FRY

2 tablespoons peanut oil

1 cup (150 g) coarsely chopped walnuts

1½ pounds (750 g) boneless, skinless chicken breasts, cut into small chunks

4 cloves garlic, thinly sliced

1 teaspoon Chinese chili paste (red chile paste)

8 ounces (250 g) green beans, trimmed and cut into short lengths

4 ounces (125 g) water chestnuts, finely chopped

1 green bell pepper (capsicum), seeded and finely sliced

1 cup (250 ml) chicken broth or stock

2 tablespoons fresh lime juice

1 tablespoon light soy sauce

2 tablespoons peanut butter mixed with 2 tablespoons boiling water

Freshly cooked long-grain rice or instant noodles, to serve

Heat the oil in a large wok or frying pan over medium-high heat. Stir-fry the walnuts until toasted and brown, about 5 minutes. Remove with a slotted spoon and set aside on paper towels.

Add the chicken and garlic and stir-fry until the chicken is lightly browned, 6–8 minutes.

Add the chili paste, green beans, water chestnuts, and bell pepper. Stir-fry for 5 minutes.

Add the chicken broth, lime juice, and soy sauce. Mix over medium-low heat until the ingredients are blended.

Stir in the peanut butter mixture and sprinkle with the walnuts. Serve hot with rice or noodles.

Serves: 4 • Prep: 5 min • Cooking: 20 min

CHICKEN AND HAM FRICASSÉE

⅓ cup (80 ml) extra-virgin olive oil

1 leek, trimmed and thinly sliced

1 pound (500 g) boneless, skinless chicken breasts, cut into bite-size chunks

8 ounces (200 g) zucchini (courgettes), diced

8 ounces (200 g) eggplants (aubergines), peeled and diced

1 large red bell pepper (capsicum), seeded and diced

Salt and freshly ground black pepper

⅓ cup (80 ml) chicken broth or stock (see page 56)

3 large egg yolks, lightly beaten

Juice of 1 lemon

1 small bunch fresh basil, torn

¼ teaspoon dried oregano

2 firm-ripe tomatoes, finely chopped

4 ounces (125 g) roast ham, diced

Heat the oil in a large frying pan over medium heat. Add the leek and sauté until softened, about 5 minutes.

Add the chicken and sauté over high heat until it turns white, 6–8 minutes.

Add the zucchini, eggplants, and bell pepper. Sauté over medium heat for 5 minutes.

Season with salt and pepper and drizzle in the broth. Cook over medium heat for 5 minutes.

Mix in the egg yolks, lemon juice, basil, and oregano and stir over high heat for 3 minutes. Stir in the tomatoes and ham. Serve hot.

Serves: 4 • Prep: 15 min • Cooking: 25 min

SPICY LAMB AND VEGETABLE STIR-FRY

This recipe is a fusion of Chinese method and ingredients with Indian spices. Serve it hot, straight from the wok, over a bed of steaming basmati rice.

- 3 tablespoons Asian chili oil
- 2 tablespoons peanut or other vegetable oil
- 1½ pounds (750 g) lamb (sirloin or leg), cut into thin strips
- ¼ teaspoon ground turmeric
- 1 teaspoon ground red chile powder
- 1 teaspoon ground coriander
- ½ teaspoon finely chopped fresh ginger
- 2 cloves garlic, finely chopped
- ¼ teaspoon garam masala
  Salt
- 1 small yellow bell pepper (capsicum), seeded and thinly
  sliced
- 1 small green bell pepper, seeded and thinly sliced
- 1 small red bell pepper, seeded and thinly sliced
- 2 carrots, cut into thin sticks
- 1 rutabaga (swede), peeled and cut into thin sticks
- 4 canned water chestnuts, cut into eighths
- 2 tablespoons light soy sauce
- 2 tablespoons oyster sauce
  Freshly cooked basmati rice, to serve
  Green chiles, sliced, to garnish

Heat the oils in a large wok or frying pan over medium-high heat. Add the lamb and sauté until lightly browned, about 8 minutes.

Add the turmeric, red chile powder, coriander, ginger, garlic, garam masala, and salt to taste. Stir-fry to combine all the flavors and finish cooking the lamb, about 5 minutes. Remove the lamb with a slotted spoon and set aside.

Add the bell peppers, carrots, rutabaga, and water chestnuts to the same wok over medium-high heat, and stir-fry until the vegetables are just cooked (they should still be a little crisp), about 8 minutes.

Return the lamb to the wok and add the soy and oyster sauces. Continue stirring until the dish begins to bubble. Serve hot with the rice and the green chile peppers.

Serves: 4 • Prep: 15 min • Cooking: 20 min

SPICY VEGETARIAN STIR-FRY

Paneer, also known as surati, is a soft Indian cheese made from buffalo's milk

- 2 tablespoons Asian chili oil
- 1 red onion, finely sliced
- 2 large cloves garlic, finely chopped
- 1 teaspoon finely grated fresh ginger
- 6 ounces (180 g) paneer, cut into small cubes
- 4 ounces (125 g) shiitake mushrooms, thinly sliced
- 2 red bird's-eye chiles, snipped
- 1 large eggplant (aubergine), unpeeled and cut into small cubes
- 4 ounces (125 g) baby carrots, halved lengthwise
- 4 ounces (125 g) baby corn, halved
- 4 ounces (125 g) snow peas (mangetout), trimmed and halved
- 4 ounces (125 g) mung bean sprouts
- 2 scallions (spring onions), trimmed and very finely chopped
- 2 tablespoons fresh lemon juice
- 2 tablespoons light soy sauce
- 2 tablespoons finely chopped fresh cilantro (coriander)
  Freshly cooked basmati rice, to serve

Heat the oil in a wok over high heat. Add the onion, garlic , ginger, and paneer. Stir-fry for 2 minutes.

Add the mushrooms and chiles and stir-fry over medium-high heat for 3 minutes.

Add the eggplant, carrots, corn, snow peas, bean sprouts, and scallions and stir-fry until the vegetables are all cooked but still firm, 7–10 minutes.

Stir in the lemon juice and soy sauce. Garnish with the cilantro and serve with the rice.

Serves: 4–6 • Prep: 15 min • Cooking: 15 min

ASPARAGUS AND SHRIMP STIR-FRY

- 3 tablespoons Asian sesame oil
- 2–3 slices fresh ginger root, peeled
- 2 cloves garlic, finely chopped
- 2 tablespoons toasted sesame seeds
- 1 teaspoon mustard seeds
- 2 pounds (1 kg) asparagus, trimmed and cut diagonally into 1½-inch (4-cm) pieces
- 1 pound (500 g) small shrimp (prawns), shelled and deveined
- 1 tablespoon sugar, dissolved in 3 tablespoons soy sauce
- 4 scallions (spring onions), white and tender green parts, sliced
- 2–3 fresh red chiles, sliced
  Freshly cooked basmati rice, to serve

Heat a wok or large frying pan over medium-high heat and add the oil. Add the ginger, garlic, and the sesame and mustard seeds. Stir-fry for 30 seconds.

Add the asparagus and stir-fry until tender but still crunchy, about 4 minutes.

Add the shrimp and stir-fry until pink, 3 minutes.

Turn down the heat slightly and add the soy sauce and sugar. Stir until everything is coated well. Sprinkle with the scallions and chiles. Serve hot over the rice.

Serves: 4 • Prep: 10 min • Cooking: 10 min

Spicy Lamb and Vegetable Stir-Fry

SPICY BEEF NOODLE STIR-FRY

- 1 pound (500 g) lean beef fillet, cut into thin strips
- 2 tablespoons Asian chili oil
- 6 tablespoons fresh lemon juice
- 1 tablespoon soy sauce
- 2 cloves garlic, finely chopped
- 1 teaspoon minced fresh ginger
- 1 teaspoon Tabasco
- 2 tablespoons peanut oil
- 1 red onion, finely sliced
- 1 medium red bell pepper (capsicum), seeded and sliced
- 1 medium green bell pepper (capsicum), seeded and sliced
- 6 ounces (180 g) snow peas (mangetout), trimmed and chopped
- 1 cup (100 g) fresh or frozen corn kernels
- 1 red chile, seeded and finely chopped
- 2 teaspoons crushed red pepper flakes
- 2 scallions (green onions), white and tender green parts only, sliced
- 4 (3-ounce) packages ramen noodles (350 g instant noodles), flavor packet discarded, cooked

Marinate the beef strips in the chili oil, 3 tablespoons of the lemon juice, soy sauce, garlic, ginger, and Tabasco for 15 minutes.

Heat the oil in a wok or large frying pan over medium-high heat. Add the onion and stir-fry until softened, about 5 minutes.

Add the beef and its marinade and stir-fry until the beef is lightly browned, about 6 minutes.

Add the bell peppers, snow peas, corn, chile pepper, red pepper flakes, and remaining 3 tablespoons lemon juice. Stir-fry until the vegetables are tender-crisp, 6–8 minutes.

Add the scallions and noodles and stir-fry over high heat until well combined. Serve hot.

Serves: 4 • Prep: 10 min + 15 min to marinate • Cooking: 20 min

QUICK VEGETARIAN NOODLE STIR-FRY

- 2 tablespoons sesame oil
- 4 tablespoons peanut or other vegetable oil
- 1 large white onion, thinly sliced
- 3 medium carrots, very thinly sliced
- 4 ounces (125 g) shiitake (or plain white) mushrooms, sliced
- 1 small yellow bell pepper (capsicum), seeded and thinly sliced
- 1 small red bell pepper (capsicum), seeded and thinly sliced
- 4 (3-ounce) packages ramen noodles (350 g instant Chinese-style egg noodles), flavor packet discarded, cooked
- 4 ounces (125 g) baby corn (sweet corn)
- 3 tablespoons dark soy sauce
- 1 tablespoon Chinese bean sauce
- 4 ounces (125 g) bean sprouts
- ½ cup (50 g) coarsely chopped cashew nuts
- 2 tablespoons finely chopped chives

Heat the sesame and olive oils in a wok or large frying pan over medium heat. Add the onion, carrots, mushrooms, and bell peppers and sauté until just tender, about 10 minutes.

Add the noodles, baby corn, soy sauce, and bean sauce. Stir well until well combined and heated through.

Add the bean sprouts, cashew nuts, and chives. Stir briefly—just 1–2 minutes, otherwise the bean sprouts will wilt and loose their crispness—and serve hot.

Serves: 4 • Prep: 20 min • Cooking: 15 min

EGGPLANT NOODLE STIR-FRY

- 6 tablespoons peanut or other vegetable oil
- 1 red onion, finely chopped
- 1 garlic clove, crushed
- 1 fresh red chile, finely sliced (optional
- 8 baby eggplants, unpeeled, finely sliced on diagonal
- 2 tablespoons dark brown sugar
- 2 tablespoons light soy sauce
- 2 tablespoons oyster sauce
- 1 teaspoon Asian sesame oil
- 1 tablespoon Vietnamese or Thai fish sauce
- 4 (3-ounce) packages ramen noodles (350 g instant Chinese-style egg noodles), flavor packet discarded, cooked
- 2 scallions (spring onions), white and tender green parts only, trimmed and chopped

Heat 2 tablespoons of the oil in a large wok or frying pan over medium heat. Add the onion, garlic, and chile, and stir-fry until onion is softened, about 5 minutes. Remove from the pan and set aside.

Increase the heat to high and add 2 tablespoons of the oil. Stir-fry the eggplants in batches until golden brown, 3–4 minutes per batch. Remove from the pan and set aside.

Add the remaining 2 tablespoons of oil to the wok with the brown sugar and cook until caramelized, about 3 minutes. Add the soy sauce, oyster sauce, sesame oil, and fish sauce, and stir until heated through.

Add the noodles to the pan with the onion mixture and eggplants, and toss well. Add the scallions and serve hot.

Serves: 4 • Prep: 15 min • Cooking: 20 min

Quick Vegetarian Noodle Stir-Fry

SPICY BROCCOLI OMELET

- 10 ounces (300 g) broccoli, broken into small florets, stem diced
- 5 large eggs
- 1 tablespoon light soy sauce
- 2 medium fresh red chiles, seeded and finely chopped
- ½ cup (60 g) finely chopped roasted peanuts
- 4 tablespoons finely chopped fresh parsley
- 2 tablespoons extra-virgin olive oil
- 2 cloves garlic, finely chopped
- 6 scallions (spring onions), trimmed and finely chopped

Bring 1 cup (250 ml) of water to a boil in a medium frying pan over high heat. Add the broccoli and cook until tender but still crunchy, 5–7 minutes. Drain well and set aside.

Combine the eggs, soy sauce, chiles, peanuts, and parsley in a bowl with the broccoli.

Heat the oil in the frying pan over medium heat and sauté the garlic and scallions until soft, about 5 minutes.

Pour in the egg mixture and stir well. Cover and cook over medium-low heat until the bottom of the omelet is lightly browned. Brown the top of the omelet under the broiler (grill) and serve hot or at room temperature.

Serves 4 • Prep: 10 min • Cooking: 20 min

EGGS WITH SPICY SAUSAGE

Harissa is a spicy North African sauce. You can find it in North African food stores and specialty food stores.

- 6 large eggs
- 1 tablespoon harissa
- 1 teaspoon caraway seeds
  Salt and freshly ground black pepper
- 3 tablespoons extra-virgin olive oil
- 6 spicy lamb or pork sausages, cut into 1½-inch (4-cm) slices
- 3 fresh red chiles, thinly sliced
- 2 tablespoons tomato purée

Beat the eggs, harissa, caraway seeds, salt, and pepper in a large bowl until frothy.

Heat the oil in a large frying pan over medium heat. Brown the sausages in the oil, about 5 minutes.

Add the chiles and sauté until softened slightly, 5–7 minutes. Add the tomato purée. Pour in the beaten egg mixture. Cook over low heat, stirring often, until the eggs are cooked but still soft, 5–7 minutes. Serve hot.

Serves 4–6 • Prep: 10 min • Cooking: 20 min

SPICY SCRAMBLED EGGS WITH BLACK BEANS

- 4 tablespoons extra-virgin olive oil
- 1 large onion, finely chopped
- 2 cloves garlic, finely chopped
- 2 tablespoons finely chopped fresh parsley
- 2 fresh chiles, sliced
- 8 large eggs
  Salt and freshly ground black pepper
- 2 cups (500 g) cooked black beans, heated

Heat the oil in a large frying pan over medium-high heat. Add the onion, garlic, parsley, and chiles and sauté until softened, 5 minutes.

Beat the eggs in a small bowl with the salt and pepper until frothy. Pour into the pan and stir with a wooden spoon until the eggs are cooked, 5–7 minutes.

Spoon over the hot beans and serve.

Serves 4 • Prep: 10 min • Cooking: 15 min

CURRIED EGGS

If desired, serve the curried eggs on freshly made, lightly buttered toast.

- 4 tablespoons butter
- 1 large onion, finely chopped
- 1 cooking apple, peeled and diced
- 2 tablespoons all-purpose (plain) flour
- 1–2 tablespoons curry powder
- 1 teaspoon cumin seeds, crushed
- 2½ cups (625 ml) chicken broth or stock (see page 56), heated
- 6 eggs, hard-cooked, shelled and cut in half
- 1 tablespoon finely chopped fresh parsley

Melt the butter in a medium frying pan over medium-high heat. Add the onion and sauté until softened, 5 minutes.

Add the apple and cook until softened, 4 minutes. Add the flour, curry powder, and cumin and stir for 2 minutes.

Slowly add the broth, stirring constantly, to ensure a smooth texture. Simmer for a few minutes and then add the eggs. Sprinkle with the parsley and serve.

Serves 2–4 • Prep: 15 min • Cooking: 15 min

Bread and Bacon Fry with Bell Peppers

2 pounds (1 kg) day-old bread
6 tablespoons water
6 tablespoons extra-virgin olive oil
8 ounces (250 g) bacon, diced
4 ounces (125 g) salami, diced
6 cloves garlic, finely chopped

1 large green bell pepper (capsicum), seeded and diced
1 large red bell pepper (capsicum), seeded and diced
1 teaspoon cayenne pepper
Salt

Crumble the bread into a large bowl. Drizzle with the water and let stand for 12 hours.

Heat the oil in a large frying pan over medium heat. Sauté the bacon and salami for 5–7 minutes, until well browned. Transfer to a plate and set aside.

Sauté the garlic in the same pan until translucent, 2–3 minutes. Add the bell peppers and sauté until tender, about 10 minutes.

Season with the cayenne pepper and add the bread crumb mixture. Cook for 2–3 minutes, then add the bacon and salami and cook for 5 minutes more.

Serve hot.

Serves 6–8 • Prep: 15 min + 12 hr to stand • Cooking: 30 min

Chiles

Chiles, or chile peppers, are another gift from Central America, where they have been cultivated for more than 5,000 years. The Spanish and Portuguese settlers of the Americas brought them back to Europe and also took them to India and Indonesia. They were welcome wherever they were introduced and quickly became an essential ingredient in dishes around the world. There are many different types of chile, including habañero, jalapeño, cayenne, serrano, Fresno, and Anaheim. The range of heat generated by chiles goes from mild to dangerously hot. Chiles are hot because they contain an irritant called capsaicin, which creates the familiar burning sensation in the mouth and throat. Nutritionally, fresh chiles are high in vitamin C and also contain vitamins A and E. However, since we usually eat them in very small quantities (for obvious reasons!) or add them to cooked dishes, they don't make a significant contribution to our vitamin intake. Health benefits from eating chiles are said to include appetite stimulation, improved circulation, relief from pain (especially among people who suffer from rheumatoid arthritis), and the release of endorphins, which create a natural feeling of well being.

Egg-and-Vegetable Fry with Green Chile

This simple yet filling dish is so versatile it can be served at breakfast, lunch, or dinner. It also lends itself to variations, depending on what you have on hand. The basic method remains the same—sauté the vegetables in the oil until tender, then add the lightly beaten eggs. You can also add more or less chile, or leave it out entirely, according to your taste.

⅓ cup (80 ml) vegetable oil
1 large onion, thinly sliced
2 cloves garlic, thinly sliced
2 stalks celery, thinly sliced
4 medium potatoes, peeled and thinly sliced
2 carrots, thinly sliced

1–2 fresh green chiles, thinly sliced
Salt and freshly ground black pepper
1 large tomato, finely chopped
3 tablespoons finely chopped fresh cilantro (coriander)
4–6 large eggs, lightly beaten

Heat the oil in a large frying pan over medium heat. Add the onion and garlic and sauté until softened, about 5 minutes.

Add the celery, potatoes, carrots, and chiles. Mix well and season with salt and pepper. Sauté until the vegetables are tender, about 12 minutes. Add the tomato and stir until all the moisture has evaporated, about 5 minutes.

Stir 2 tablespoons of the cilantro into the beaten eggs. Lower the heat and add the eggs to the pan with the vegetables. Let the eggs cook through, about 5 minutes.

Transfer to a serving dish and garnish with the remaining 1 tablespoon cilantro.

Serves: 4–6 • Prep: 15 min • Cooking: 30 min

Potato and Zucchini Fry with Eggs

4 tablespoons extra-virgin olive oil
1 large onion, finely chopped
2 cloves garlic, finely chopped
4 ounces (125 g) bacon, cut into small cubes
Salt and freshly ground black pepper
½ teaspoon cumin

4 medium potatoes, peeled and cut into cubes
4 medium zucchini (courgettes), cut into cubes
4 large eggs
2 tablespoons finely chopped fresh parsley

Heat the oil in a large frying pan over medium heat. Add the onion and garlic and sauté until the onion is lightly browned, 7–8 minutes.

Add the bacon and sauté until browned, 5 minutes. Season with salt and pepper and add the cumin.

Add the potatoes and cook for 10 minutes, stirring often. Add the zucchini and cook for 10 minutes, stirring often.

When the vegetables are almost tender, break the eggs over the mixture, stirring to break the yolks. Cook for 5 minutes, or until the eggs are set. Sprinkle with parsley and serve hot.

Serves: 4 • Prep: 15 min • Cooking: 30 min

Beef, Egg, and Vegetable Fry

4 tablespoons extra-virgin olive oil
1 large onion, finely chopped
2 cloves garlic, finely chopped
1 pound (500 g) ground (minced) beef
Salt and freshly ground black pepper

1 teaspoon ground cinnamon
2 medium potatoes, cut into cubes
2 medium zucchini (courgettes), diced
6 large eggs
2 tablespoons finely chopped fresh flat-leaf parsley

Heat the oil in a large, deep frying pan over medium heat. Add the onion and garlic and sauté until softened, about 5 minutes.

Add the beef and brown for 10 minutes. Season with salt, pepper, and cinnamon.

Add the potatoes and cook for 10 minutes, stirring occasionally. Add the zucchini and cook for 10 minutes more, stirring occasionally.

When the potatoes and zucchini are almost tender, break the eggs over the mixture, stirring to break the yolks. Cook until the eggs are set, 5 minutes. Sprinkle with the parsley and serve hot.

Serves: 4 • Prep: 15 min • Cooking: 40 min

Beef, Egg, and Vegetable Fry

ASPARAGUS FRITTATA

Serve this nourishing frittata at breakfast or brunch. If desired, serve with a few baked cherry tomatoes. Drizzle the tomatoes with olive oil and season with salt and pepper. Bake in the oven at 400°F (200°C/gas 6) for 15 minutes.

1 tablespoon extra-virgin olive oil

1 pound (500 g) asparagus (wild asparagus is best, if available), trimmed and cut into 1-inch (2.5-cm) pieces

½ teaspoon salt

Pinch of crushed red pepper flakes

2 cloves garlic, finely chopped

1 tablespoon finely chopped flat-leaf parsley

1 tablespoon marjoram leaves

1 tablespoon chopped fennel leaves

6 large eggs

2 cups (250 g) finely grated aged pecorino cheese

Freshly ground black pepper

1 tablespoon butter

4 leaves fresh sage, coarsely chopped

Heat the oil in a large frying pan over medium heat. Add the asparagus, salt, and red pepper flakes and mix well. Sauté until the asparagus is tender, about 12 minutes.

Add the garlic, parsley, marjoram, and fennel. Cook for 1–2 minutes, just long enough to gently soften the garlic and herbs. Remove from the heat and let cool.

Beat the eggs and cheese in a large bowl. Season with pepper. Add the cooled asparagus mixture.

In the same pan used for the asparagus, melt the butter over medium heat. Add the sage and fry until crisp but still green, 3–4 minutes.

Add the egg mixture. Use a spatula to loosen the edges of the frittata. Shake the pan to make sure the frittata is not sticking to the bottom.

When the frittata holds together as one piece, flip it by inverting onto the pan lid and sliding back into the pan. Cook for 2 minutes then cut into triangular slices.

Serves 4–6 • Prep: 15 min • Cooking: 25 min

BULGUR WITH LAMB AND GARBANZO BEANS

¼ cup (60 ml) extra-virgin olive oil

2 medium onions, finely chopped

12 ounces (350 g) lamb, cut into small cubes

2 cups (300 g) coarse-grind bulgur

2 cups (500 ml) water + more as needed

Salt and freshly ground black pepper

½ teaspoon ground cinnamon

1 (14-ounce/400-g) can garbanzo beans (chick peas), drained

2 tablespoons finely chopped fresh cilantro (coriander)

Heat the oil in a large frying pan over medium heat. Add the onions and sauté until softened, about 5 minutes. Add the lamb and sauté until browned, 10 minutes.

Add the bulgur and enough water to cover. Season with salt, pepper, and cinnamon. Partially cover the pan and cook over medium-low heat for about 30 minutes, or until the lamb and bulgur are both tender. Stir often during cooking, adding more water if it has all been absorbed and the bulgur begins to stick to the pan.

Stir in the garbanzo beans and cook until heated through. Sprinkle with the cilantro and serve hot.

Serves: 4 • Prep: 15 min • Cooking: 50 min

FISH STOCK

 Fish stock keeps for 4–5 days in the refrigerator and 3 months in the freezer.

1 pound (500 g) heads and bones mixed fish

3 quarts (3 liters) cold water

1 carrot, chopped

1 stalk celery, chopped

1 onion, chopped

1 shallot, chopped

4 sprigs parsley

1 bay leaf

4 black peppercorns

½ cup (125 ml) dry white wine

1 clove garlic

1 sprig thyme

1 tablespoon coarse sea salt

Soak the fish heads and bones in a large bowl of cold water for 1 hour. This will remove any traces of blood.

Drain and place in a large saucepan with the 3 quarts water over low heat. Bring to a boil. Add all the other ingredients. Simmer for about 1½ hours. Drain the stock and filter through cheesecloth before using.

Makes: 8 cups (2 liters) • Prep: 15 min + 1 hr to soak • Cooking: 1½ hr

STEW POT

STEWS, TAGINES, CURRIES, AND CHILIS

Our word "stew" covers an enormous range of dishes, from slowly cooked, melt-in-your-mouth meat and vegetable combinations to the more exotic chilis, curries, tagines, and gumbos that are surprisingly easy to make at home, especially now that Asian and African spices and ingredients are so readily available in supermarkets and specialty stores. Here you will find a range of recipes, from classic beef and chicken stews with vegetables to spicy and sweet ethnic curries and tagines.

Beef Stew with Herbs and Beer

- 2 pounds (1 kg) beef chuck roast, cut into small chunks
- 2 tablespoons canola oil
- ½ teaspoon salt
- ½ teaspoon freshly ground black pepper
- ½ teaspoon dried basil
- ¼ teaspoon dried rosemary
- ¼ teaspoon dried sage
- ¼ teaspoon dried tarragon
- 1 bay leaf
- 1¼ cups (310 ml) beef broth or stock (see page 28)
- 1¼ cups (310 ml) beer or stout
- 4 medium carrots, diced
- 4 medium potatoes, peeled and diced
- 6 small onions, peeled and cut into quarters
- ¼ cup (30 g) all-purpose (plain) flour
- ¼ cup (60 ml) water

Heat the oil in a large saucepan over medium heat. Add the beef and cook until browned all over, about 10 minutes.

Add the salt, pepper, basil, rosemary, sage, tarragon, and bay leaf. Pour in the broth and beer. Cover and simmer for 1½ hours.

Add the carrots, potatoes, and onions and continue cooking until the vegetables are tender, about 30 minutes.

Mix the flour and water in a small bowl until smooth. Stir into the stew and continue cooking until it has thickened slightly. Discard the bay leaf and serve hot.

Serves: 4–6 • Prep: 15 min • Cooking: 2 hr

Stout Stew

If you don't want to make the dumplings to go with this stew, cook it for 2 hours and serve with boiled or mashed potatoes.

- 1 tablespoon all-purpose (plain) flour
- 1 teaspoon English mustard
- ½ teaspoon salt + more as needed Freshly ground black pepper
- 2 pounds (1 kg) stew beef, cut into small chunks
- 3 tablespoons butter or cooking juices from a roasted meat
- 2 medium onions, finely chopped
- 4 medium carrots, cut into large chunks
- 2 bay leaves
- 2 cups (500 ml) stout or dark beer
- 1 tablespoon dark brown sugar
- 1 tablespoon tomato paste (concentrate)
- 1⅔ cups (400 ml) beef broth or stock (see page 28) or water
- 1½ cups (200 g) dumpling dough (see page 114)
- 1 tablespoon finely chopped fresh parsley

Mix the flour and mustard. Season with ¼ teaspoon of the salt and pepper and coat the beef with this mixture.

Melt 1 teaspoon of the butter in a large saucepan over high heat. Add the meat in small batches and brown, adding more butter between batches and transferring the browned meat to a separate plate.

Add any remaining butter and the onions to the juices in the saucepan. Cook over low heat until the onions are soft and golden, about 10 minutes. Return the meat to the pan.

Stir in the carrots, the remaining ¼ teaspoon of salt, and bay leaves. Mix the stout, brown sugar, tomato paste, and broth. Pour the mixture over the meat. If the liquid does not cover the meat, add more water or broth. Stir well to make sure you have scraped up any bits from the bottom of the pan and bring to a boil.

Cover and simmer over low heat until the meat is tender, about 1¾ hours. Stir the stew after 1 hour, adding more water if the stew begins to dry out.

Season with salt and pepper. Discard the bay leaf. Prepare 12 small dumplings and place on top of the stew. If more liquid is needed to cook the dumplings, add some boiling water.

Cover and cook for 20 minutes more. Sprinkle with the parsley and serve hot.

Serves: 4–6 • Prep: 15 min • Cooking: 2 ¼ hr

BEEF AND BEER STEW

- 3 pounds (1.5 kg) beef chuck roast, cut into 1-inch (2.5-cm) chunks
- Salt and freshly ground black pepper
- 3 bay leaves
- 3 sprigs thyme
- 3 sprigs rosemary
- ¼ cup (60 ml) extra-virgin olive oil
- 2 tablespoons butter
- 2 large white onions, coarsely chopped
- ⅓ cup (50 g) all-purpose (plain) flour
- 1 (12-ounce/350 ml) bottle dark beer
- 4 cups (1 liter) hot beef broth or stock (see page 28)
- 1 (14-ounce/400-g) can crushed tomatoes
- 3 medium potatoes, peeled and diced
- 3 medium carrots, diced
- 3 stalks celery, finely sliced
- 1 small rutabaga (swede), peeled and diced
- 2 parsnips, peeled and diced

Season the beef generously with salt and pepper. Tie the stems of bay leaves and sprigs of rosemary and thyme tightly with cotton to make a bouquet garni.

Heat the oil and butter in a large saucepan over medium-high heat. Add the beef and sauté until browned all over, 8–10 minutes. Remove and set aside.

Add the onions to the saucepan and cook over medium heat until softened, about 5 minutes. Decrease the heat to low and cook until golden and caramelized, about 45 minutes. Sprinkle the onions with the flour and stir.

Return the beef to the saucepan and add the beer, broth, tomatoes, and bouquet garni. Season with salt and pepper. Bring the stew to a boil over medium-high heat, stirring often. Decrease the heat to low, cover the pot, and cook for 45 minutes more. Add the potatoes, carrots, celery, rutabaga, and parsnips and simmer for 1 hour more. Remove the bouquet garni. Serve hot.

Serves: 4–6 • Prep: 30 min • Cooking: 3 hr

SPICED GREEK STEW

- ¼ cup (60 ml) extra-virgin olive oil
- 4 pounds (2 kg) stew beef, cut into small chunks
- 2 onions, finely chopped
- 2 cloves garlic, finely chopped
- 1 teaspoon ground cumin
- 1 cup (250 ml) dry red wine
- 2 cups (500 ml) water
- 2 tablespoons tomato paste (concentrate)
- 1 2-inch (5-cm) stick cinnamon
- 8 cloves
- 1 bay leaf
- 2 teaspoons sugar
- Salt and freshly ground black pepper
- 2 pounds (1 kg) baby (pickling) onions

Heat the oil in a large Dutch oven (casserole) over medium heat. Add the beef in 2–3 batches and sauté until browned all over, 7–8 minutes per batch.

Add the onions, garlic, and cumin and sauté until softened and aromatic, about 5 minutes. Pour in the wine and cook until evaporated.

Return all the beef to the pan. Stir in the water and tomato paste. Bring to a boil and add the cinnamon, cloves, bay leaf, and sugar. Season with salt and pepper. Cover and simmer over low heat for 1 hour.

Stir in the baby onions. Cover and simmer until the meat and onions are tender, about 1½ hours more. Discard the cinnamon stick and bay leaf. Serve hot.

Serves: 6–8 • Prep: 20 min • Cooking: 2 ¾ hr

BOILED BEEF IN LEEK AND TOMATO SAUCE

Making beef broth or stock always leaves you with a large piece of beautifully cooked beef (see page 28). Here is an excellent way to use it up. Serve as is, or over a bed of cooked short-grain rice or sliced boiled potatoes.

- 4 tablespoons extra-virgin olive oil
- 4 leeks, trimmed and sliced
- 1 cup (250 ml) beef broth or stock (see page 28)
- 1 pound (500 g) boiled beef, cut into bite-sized pieces
- 1 (14-ounce/400-g) can tomatoes, chopped, with juice
- Salt and freshly ground black pepper

Heat the oil in a large saucepan over medium heat. Sauté the leeks until translucent, about 5 minutes.

Pour in the broth and partially cover the pan. Cook until the liquid has almost completely reduced, about 10 minutes. Add the meat and tomatoes, season with salt and pepper, and simmer until the meat is literally falling apart, about 20 minutes. Serve hot.

Serves: 4 • Prep: 15 min • Cooking: 35 min

FRENCH VEAL STEW

- 4 tablespoons butter
- 3 pounds (1.5 kg) boneless veal shoulder, cut into cubes
- 4 shallots, finely chopped
- 4 carrots, cut into thin strips
- 4 leeks, trimmed and finely sliced
- 3 cloves garlic, thinly sliced
- ½ cup (125 ml) dry white wine Water
- 1 bay leaf
- ⅛ teaspoon freshly grated nutmeg

- 8 ounces (250 g) mushrooms, thinly sliced
- Salt and freshly ground black pepper
- ¾ cup (200 ml) heavy (double) cream
- Juice of 1 lemon
- 2 tablespoons cornstarch (cornflour)
- 2 large egg yolks
- Freshly cooked long-grain rice, to serve

Melt the butter in a large saucepan over medium heat. Add the veal and sauté until pale, about 4 minutes.

Add the shallots, carrots, leeks, garlic, wine, and enough water to cover the veal. Add the bay leaf and nutmeg. Simmer over low heat for 45 minutes.

Cook the mushrooms in a large saucepan over medium heat for 5–7 minutes. Drain the juices they release and add them to the stew. Season with salt and pepper.

Beat the cream, lemon juice, cornstarch, egg yolks, and 2 tablespoons of the cooking juices from the stew in a medium bowl. Add this mixture to the stew together with the mushrooms and mix well. Cook for 2 minutes, or until the sauce is thickened. Serve hot with the rice.

Serves: 6–8 • Prep: 15 min • Cooking: 35 min

BOEUF BOURGUIGNON

This slowly cooked beef stew is a popular French dish from Burgundy. Recipes vary according to the cook's interpretation and taste, but the beef is usually cooked with wine, lardons or bacon, and button mushrooms and onions. You can make this dish in advance—its flavors improve with reheating.

- 1 tablespoon all-purpose (plain) flour
- Salt and freshly ground black pepper
- 1½ pounds (750 g) stew beef, trimmed and cut into small chunks
- ¼ cup (60 ml) extra-virgin olive oil
- 5 ounces (150 g) bacon, finely chopped
- 8 shallots, peeled
- 1 cup (250 ml) dry red wine
- ½ cup (125 ml) beef broth or stock + more as needed (see page 28)

- 1 clove garlic, unpeeled
- ½ teaspoon dried thyme or 2 sprigs fresh
- 2 sprigs fresh flat-leaf parsley
- 2 bay leaves
- 1 tablespoon tomato paste (concentrate)
- 8 ounces (250 g) baby button mushrooms, stems removed
- Boiled potatoes, to serve

Place the flour in a plastic bag and season generously with salt and pepper. Add the beef. Shake the bag until the meat is well coated.

Heat ½ tablespoon of the oil in a large saucepan over medium heat. Sauté the bacon until it releases its fat and becomes crisp, about 5 minutes. Remove the bacon from the pan and set aside.

Add the shallots to the pan and sauté over low heat until nicely colored, 7–8 minutes. Remove the shallots and set aside.

Pour the remaining 3½ tablespoons of oil into the pan. Sauté the beef in small batches until browned all over, about 5 minutes. Shake the pan so that the fat absorbs all the flour.

Pour in the wine and broth and boil for 30 seconds. Stir in all the browned beef, garlic, thyme, parsley, bay leaves, and tomato paste. Cover and simmer over very low heat for 1½ hours. Add a little more broth if the mixture begins to dry out—the liquid should only just cover the meat.

Add the bacon, shallots, and mushrooms. Cook until the meat is tender, 40–60 minutes, stirring occasionally to prevent it from sticking.

Season with salt and pepper. Discard the herbs and garlic. Serve hot.

Serves: 4–6 • Prep: 25 min • Cooking: 2 ¾ hr

RUSTIC ITALIAN STEW

- 2 pounds (1 kg) beef chuck, round, or shank (beef chuck or shin), cut into small chunks
- 1/2 cup (75 g) all-purpose (plain) flour
- 5 tablespoons extra-virgin olive oil
- 1 large onion, chopped
- 2 stalks celery, chopped
- 2 cloves garlic, finely chopped
- 1 tablespoon finely chopped fresh sage
- 1 tablespoon finely chopped fresh rosemary

- 1 (15-ounce/400 g) can Italian tomatoes, with juice
- 2–4 potatoes, peeled and cut into cubes
- Salt and freshly ground black pepper
- 1 cup (250 ml) dry red wine
- 1 cup (250 ml) beef broth or stock + more as needed (see page 28)

Toss the meat in the flour, shaking off the excess.

Heat the oil in a large saucepan over medium heat. Add the onion, celery, garlic, sage, and rosemary and sauté until the vegetables are softened, about 5 minutes.

Add the meat and sauté until brown, about 8 minutes. Add the tomatoes and potatoes and season with salt and pepper. Cook for 5 minutes more.

Pour in the wine and $1/2$ cup (125 ml) broth, partially cover, and simmer until the meat is tender, about $1^3/4$ hours. Add the remaining broth during cooking as the sauce dries out; it should resemble a thick gravy. Serve hot.

Serves: 4 • Prep: 20 min • Cooking: 2 hr

MUSHROOMS

A mushroom is an edible fungus with a round-shaped top and a stalk. Within that very broad definition, there are many different types, including the numerous varieties of wild mushrooms that are eagerly gathered in most parts of the world. In Southern Europe, the porcini mushroom is one of the most sought after. Other common wild varieties include the blewit, the cep, the chanterelle, and the common field mushroom. The champignon is the most popular type of cultivated mushroom, but oyster mushrooms, shiitakes, enokitake, and wood-ear mushrooms are also being grown. Nutritionally, mushrooms contain some B vitamins and small amounts of protein.

SCOTCH BEEF WITH DRIED FRUIT

8 ounces (200 g) pitted prunes
6 ounces (180 g) dried apricots
  Water
3 pound (1.5 kg) piece beef silverside or brisket
  Salt and freshly ground black pepper
2 tablespoons butter
2 medium onions, thinly sliced
1 large apple, thinly sliced

1 tablespoon dark brown sugar
1 teaspoon crushed cloves
  About ½ cup (125 ml) whisky
1 bay leaf
1 tablespoon all-purpose (plain) flour
2 tablespoons finely chopped fresh parsley

Soak the prunes and apricots in cold water overnight. Drain, reserving the soaking water, and set aside.

Season the beef well with the salt and pepper.

Melt the butter in a large saucepan over medium-high heat. Brown the beef all over, 8–10 minutes.

Lower the heat to medium and add the onions, apple, brown sugar, cloves, ⅓ cup (80 ml) of the whisky, ¾ cup (180 ml) water, and the bay leaf.

Bring to a boil. Cover and simmer over low heat for 1½ hours. Check occasionally and turn the meat over. Add a little hot water and more whisky if the liquid has evaporated.

Test the meat at the end of the cooking time, and if it is not quite tender, cook for 30 minutes more.

Arrange the prunes and apricots around the beef, adding about ½ cup (125 ml) of their soaking liquid to make sure that the meat and fruit are covered. Cook for 30 minutes more.

Season with salt and pepper. Slice the meat and transfer it to a serving dish. Place the fruit around the meat. Keep the meat and fruit in a warm oven while you prepare the sauce.

Blend the flour with a little water until smooth. Stir into the cooking juices to thicken into a sauce. Cook for 2 minutes, stirring constantly.

Spoon the sauce over the meat and fruit and sprinkle with the parsley. Serve hot.

Serves: 4–6 • Prep: 15 min + 12 hr to soak • Cooking: 2 ½ hr

BEEF STEW WITH POTATOES

⅓ cup (80 ml) extra-virgin olive oil
2 cloves garlic, finely chopped
1 large onion, finely chopped
1 large carrot, finely chopped
1 large stalk celery, finely chopped
1 tablespoon finely chopped fresh mixed herbs (sage, parsley, oregano, rosemary, and thyme)
2 pounds (1 kg) beef chuck, trimmed of fat and cut into bite-size pieces

  Salt and freshly ground black pepper
1 cup (250 ml) red wine
6 large tomatoes, peeled and chopped
2 pounds (1 kg) potatoes, peeled and cut into bite-sized chunks
2 cups (500 ml) beef broth or stock (see page 28)

Heat the oil in a large, heavy saucepan over medium heat. Add the garlic, onion, carrot, celery, and mixed herbs and sauté for 5 minutes.

Add the beef, season with salt and pepper, and sauté until brown, about 8 minutes.

Pour in the wine and cook until it evaporates, about 5 minutes.

Add the tomatoes and potatoes. Cover the pan and simmer until the meat and potatoes are very tender, about 1 hour. Gradually add the broth during cooking to keep the meat moist, stirring frequently to keep the meat from sticking to the bottom of the pan. Serve hot.

Serves: 4–6 • Prep: 25 min • Cooking: 80 min

Scotch Beef with Dried Fruit

SHREWSBURY STEW

- 2 tablespoons all-purpose (plain) flour
- 4¹⁄₂ teaspoons dry mustard powder
  Salt and freshly ground black pepper
- 2 pounds (1 kg) stew beef (preferably shin), cut into small cubes
- 4 tablespoons butter or cooking juices from roasted beef
- 1 rutabaga (swede), peeled and cubed
- 2 large onions, quartered
- 2 medium carrots, peeled and diced
- 2 parsnips, peeled, halved, and quartered lengthwise
- 2 cloves garlic, finely chopped (optional)

- 1 tablespoon tomato paste (concentrate)
- 2 tablespoons whole-grain mustard
- 4¹⁄₄ cups (310 ml) beef broth or stock (see page 28)
- 1¹⁄₄ cups (310 ml) hard (dry) cider
- 1 teaspoon dried thyme, or 1 tablespoon fresh
  Water (optional)
  Juice of ¹⁄₂ lemon
- 1 tablespoon finely chopped fresh parsley
  Freshly cooked boiled potatoes, to serve

Mix 1 tablespoon of the flour with the mustard powder, ¹⁄₄ teaspoon salt, and ¹⁄₄ teaspoon pepper in a medium bowl. Add the beef and toss to coat.

Melt 3 tablespoons of the butter in a large Dutch oven or saucepan over medium-low heat until very hot. Sauté the meat in small batches until browned, 7–8 minutes per batch. Transfer the meat to a plate.

Melt the remaining tablespoon of butter in the pot and add the rutabaga, onions, carrots, parsnips, and garlic, if using. Cook over low heat, turning often, until the vegetables begin to soften, about 10 minutes. Remove and set aside with the meat.

Remove the pan from the heat and stir in the remaining tablespoon of flour until all the juices have been absorbed. Return to the heat. Mix in the tomato paste and 1 tablespoon of the whole-grain mustard. Gradually pour in the broth and cider. Stir with a balloon whisk until the sauce begins to thicken. Season with salt and pepper and add the thyme.

Return the meat and vegetables to the pan, stir well, and return to a simmer.

Cover and cook over low heat until the meat is tender, about 2 hours. Check occasionally and add a little more water if the sauce dries out too much during cooking.

Stir in the remaining tablespoon of whole-grain mustard and the lemon juice. Sprinkle with parsley and serve with the boiled potatoes.

Serves: 6 • Prep: 20 min • Cooking: 2 ¹⁄₄ hr

GREEN BEAN AND MEAT STEW

- 4 tablespoons extra-virgin olive oil
- 2 large onions, coarsely chopped
- 2 cloves garlic, finely chopped
- 1 pound (500 g) beef or lamb, cut into small chunks
- 2 pounds (1 kg) fresh or frozen green beans, trimmed and cut into short lengths
- 2 cups (500 ml) water + more as needed

- 1 (14-ounce/400-g) can tomatoes, chopped, with juice
- ¹⁄₂ teaspoon ground cinnamon
  Salt and freshly ground black pepper
  Freshly cooked short-grain rice, to serve

Heat the oil in a large saucepan over medium heat. Add the onions and garlic and sauté until the onions are lightly browned, 7–8 minutes.

Add the beef and sauté until browned, 10 minutes.

Add the green beans and pour in the water. Bring to a boil, partially cover, and simmer over low heat until the meat is almost tender, 40–45 minutes. Add more water if the mixture becomes too dry.

Add the tomatoes and cinnamon and season with salt and pepper. Cook over low heat for 30 minutes more. Serve hot with the rice.

Serves 4 • Prep: 30 min • Cooking: 1 ¹⁄₂ hr

BEEF AND VEGETABLE STEW WITH COCONUT MILK AND BANANA

Naan is a delicious Indian flat bread made with wholewheat (wholemeal) or white flour, salt, a little fat (usually butter or ghee) and a leavening agent. It is widely available in Asian supermarkets and specialty stores.

- 2 tablespoons all-purpose (plain) flour
- 1 teaspoon salt
- 1 teaspoon black pepper
- 1 teaspoon ground red chile
- 1½ pounds (750 g) beef, thinly sliced
- 2 tablespoons extra-virgin olive oil
- 2 teaspoons sesame seeds
- 2 medium onions, peeled and finely sliced
- 8 baby corn (sweet corn)
- 12 tiny new season's potatoes, scrubbed
- 2 cloves garlic, finely chopped
- 1 teaspoon minced fresh ginger
- 1 pound (500 g) tomatoes, peeled and chopped
- 1 teaspoon Tabasco
- 2 (3½-ounce/100-g) cans coconut milk
- 2 bananas, cut into thin slices
- 2 cups (100 g) fresh or frozen green beans (thawed, if frozen)
  Handful of finely chopped fresh dill
  Freshly cooked rice or naan, to serve

Stir together the flour, salt, pepper, and chile in a shallow bowl. Add the beef and toss until well coated.

Heat the oil in a large saucepan or Dutch oven over medium-high heat. Add the sesame seeds. Stir for a few seconds then add the meat. Sauté until browned, 8–10 minutes.

Turn the heat down to low and add the onions, corn, potatoes, garlic, ginger, tomatoes, and Tabasco. Cook, stirring occasionally, until the potatoes are almost tender, about 20 minutes.

Pour in the coconut milk and add the bananas and green beans. Simmer until the beef is tender and the liquid has thickened, about 30 minutes.

Sprinkle with the fresh dill and stir. Serve over rice or accompanied by naan.

Serves: 4 • Prep: 10 min • Cooking: 1 hr

SOUTH AFRICAN BEEF AND VEGETABLE STEW

- 2 tablespoons vegetable oil
- 2 tablespoons melted ghee or clarified butter
- 1 large onion, peeled and finely sliced
- 1½ pounds (750 g) stewing beef, cubed
- 2 cups (500 ml) boiling water
- 2 medium potatoes, peeled and cut into quarters
- 1 pound (500 g) frozen mixed vegetables
- 1 (14-ounce/400-g) can tomatoes, chopped, with juice
- 2 teaspoons ground coriander
- 1 teaspoon ground red chile
- 1 teaspoon tandoori or curry powder
- ½ teaspoon ground turmeric
  Salt and freshly ground black pepper
- 1 tablespoon cornstarch (cornflour)
- 2 tablespoons water
- ½ teaspoon garam masala
  Freshly cooked long-grain rice or crusty fresh bread, to serve

Heat the oil and ghee over medium heat in a large saucepan or Dutch oven. Add the onion and sauté until golden brown, about 7 minutes. Add the beef and stir until the meat is well browned, about 8 minutes.

Add the water, potatoes, mixed vegetables, tomatoes, coriander, chile, tandoori powder, and turmeric. Season with salt and pepper. Cover and simmer over low heat until the meat and vegetables are tender, about 1½ hours.

Make a paste with the cornstarch and 2 tablespoons water and stir into the stew to thicken. Boil for a few minutes, stirring continuously, until thickened. Stir in the garam masala. Serve with rice or crusty fresh bread.

Serves: 4–6 • Prep: 10 min • Cooking: 2 hr

VEGETABLE STOCK

 Vegetable stock is light and tasty, as well as being easy to make. It will keep for 4 to 5 days in the refrigerator and freezes well.

- 2 tablespoons extra-virgin olive oil
- 2 medium onions, studded with 2 cloves
- 2 medium carrots, cut in half
- 2 stalks celery, with leaves
- 2 small tomatoes
  Small bunch fresh parsley
- 6 whole black peppercorns
- 2 bay leaves
- 1 teaspoon salt
  About 10 cups (2.5 liters) cold water

Heat the oil in a large saucepan over medium heat. Add the onions, carrots, celery, tomatoes, parsley, peppercorns, bay leaves, and salt.

Sauté for 5 minutes, then pour in the water. Partially cover and bring to a boil. Simmer for 1 hour.

Pour through a strainer, discarding the vegetables.

Makes: about 8 cups (2 liters) • Prep: 15 min • Cooking: 1 hr

Beef and Vegetable Stew with Coconut Milk and Banana

DUMPLING-TOPPED SCOTTISH HIGHLAND STEW

- 1½ pounds (750 g) stew beef, cut into small chunks
- 2 tablespoons all-purpose (plain) flour
  Salt and freshly ground black pepper
- 4 tablespoons extra-virgin olive oil
- 1 large onion, coarsely chopped
- 2 large carrots, coarsely chopped
- ¼ rutabaga turnip, peeled and coarsely chopped (about 2 cups)
- 1½ cups (375 ml) beef broth or stock (see page 28)
- 1½ cups (250 g) dumpling dough (see below)

Roll the beef in the flour, shaking off the excess. Season the beef generously with salt and pepper.

Heat the oil in a large Dutch oven or saucepan over medium heat. Add the beef in small batches and sauté until browned all over, 8–10 minutes.

Add the onion, carrots, and rutabaga and sauté over medium heat until lightly browned, 8–10 minutes.

Pour in the broth. Season with salt and pepper. Simmer over low heat for 1¼ hours.

Prepare 6 dumplings and place on the top of the stew.

Cover and simmer until the dumplings have doubled in size and the beef is tender, 30–45 minutes. Serve hot.

Serves: 4 • Prep: 30 min • Cooking: 2 ½ hr

PAN-ROASTED GARLIC PORK WITH VEGETABLES

- 3 pounds (1.5-kg) bone-in pork loin rib roast
- 5 cloves garlic
- 3 sprigs fresh rosemary, chopped
- 6 fresh sage leaves, chopped
- 4 ounces (125 g) smoked bacon, diced
  Salt and freshly ground black pepper
- ½ cup (125 ml) extra-virgin olive oil
- 2 cups (500 ml) beef broth or stock (see page 28)
- 3 pounds (1.5 kg) potatoes, peeled and cut into bite-size pieces
- 2 large carrots, quartered
- 2 large parsnips, peeled and quartered

Detach the loin from the ribs. Use a sharp knife to make 6 incisions in the loin. Peel 3 of the garlic cloves and cut in half. Fill the slits with the garlic. Sprinkle the pork with the rosemary, sage, and bacon and season with salt and pepper. Tie the ribs to the loin with kitchen string.

Heat the oil in a heavy-bottomed pan over medium heat. Add the meat and brown all over, about 10 minutes.

Add a ladleful of the broth to the pan. Partially cover and simmer, adding more broth to keep the pan moist.

When the pork has been cooking for 30 minutes, add the potatoes, carrots, parsnips, and the remaining 2 unpeeled cloves of garlic. Continue cooking until the meat is tender and the vegetables are cooked, 50 minutes.

Untie the ribs and cut into 8–12 pieces. Arrange the meat and vegetables in a heated serving dish. Spoon the cooking juices over the top and serve hot.

Serves: 4–6 • Prep: 20 min • Cooking: 1 ½ hr

DUMPLINGS

Dumplings probably arose independently in the various peasant cuisines of Europe where vegetable stews were flavored with just a little meat (an expensive commodity for most) and considerably extended by these simple and economical mixes of flour and water.

- 1 cup (150 g) all-purpose (plain) flour
- ¼ cup (60 g) vegetable shortening
- or beef suet
- 4 tablespoons water + more as needed

Mix the flour and suet together with enough water to make a dough. Form the mixture into balls and place on top of the stew.

Makes: about 1 ½ cups (200 g) • Prep: 15 min • Cooking: 25 min

TOULOUSE CASSOULET

There are many versions of this dish, which originally comes from the Languedoc region of southern France. The main ingredients of a traditional cassoulet are haricot beans, garlic-flavored pork sausage, mutton, salt pork, pork, and duck or goose. The dish can be adapted with more or less meat, but canned beans should never be used. The name cassoulet comes from the glazed earthenware pot in which the dish is cooked.

2½ cups (250 g) dried haricot beans, soaked overnight and drained

2–3 tablespoons duck fat or extra-virgin olive oil

4 duck legs (optional)

10 ounces (300 g) unsmoked bacon or pancetta, diced

1 large onion, finely chopped

2 stalks celery, finely chopped

3 cloves garlic, finely chopped

1 pound (500 g) boneless lamb, from shoulder or neck, cut into small cubes

12 ounces (350 g) pork loin, cut into small cubes

Salt and freshly ground black pepper

6 tomatoes, chopped, or 1 (14-ounce /400-g) can tomatoes, chopped, with juice

1 tablespoon tomato paste (concentrate)

4 cups (1 liter) chicken broth or stock (see page 56)

1 carrot, halved

1 bouquet garni (see page 168)

1 pound (500 g) Toulouse sausage or other garlic-flavored pork sausage, skinned and thickly sliced on the diagonal

2 tablespoons finely chopped fresh flat-leaf parsley

2 tablespoons finely chopped fresh thyme

8 tablespoons fresh bread crumbs + extra, as required

Place the beans in a cassoulet, Dutch oven, or flameproof casserole dish. Fill with cold water and bring to a gentle boil. Simmer until tender, about 1 hour. Drain and set aside.

In the same pan, heat 1 tablespoon of duck fat over medium-high heat. Brown the duck legs, if using, 8–10 minutes. Remove the legs, retaining the fat.

Sauté the bacon in the fat over high heat until crispy, about 3 minutes.

Add 1 tablespoon of duck fat (or 2 tablespoons if the bacon did not produce much fat) and heat until hot and sizzling. Add the onion, celery, and garlic and sauté over low heat for 10 minutes until softened. Scrape up the bits from the bottom of the pan as you stir the mixture. Remove with a slotted spoon and set aside.

Add the lamb and pork in batches and brown, 8–10 minutes, adding more fat if needed. Season the meat with salt and pepper and set aside.

Return the reserved ingredients to the cassoulet except for the duck legs. Stir in the tomatoes and tomato paste. Season with salt and pepper. Add three-quarters of the beans and pour in the broth. Bring to a boil and simmer over low heat for 3 minutes, stirring constantly.

Add the duck legs, if using, carrot, and the bouquet garni. Top with the sausage and cover with the remaining beans. Make sure the liquid comes about halfway up and add water if needed. Cover and simmer for 1 hour. Stir twice during that time and add a little more water if the pan dries out too much. Uncover and stir in half the parsley and thyme.

Simmer for 1 hour more, or until the meat is tender and the sauce has thickened.

Preheat the oven to 425°F (220°C/gas 7).

Stir in the remaining parsley and thyme. Sprinkle the bread crumbs over the top, pressing them down into the liquid with the back of the spoon to form a crust. Bake, uncovered, for about 20 minutes, or until the crust is golden brown.

Remove from the oven, partly break up the crust and give the cassoulet a good stir. It should be quite thick. If it is too liquid, stir in the crust and sprinkle with another layer of bread crumbs. Bake at 450°F (235°C/gas 8) for about 15 minutes, until another crust has formed. The bread crumbs should absorb the liquid.

Serves: 8–10 • Prep: 30 min + 12 hr to soak and cook the beans • Cooking: 4 hr

Ecuadorian One-Pot Stew

2 tablespoons extra-virgin olive oil

2 tablespoons minced fresh ginger

3 garlic cloves, finely chopped

¼ jalapeño, minced

1 green bell pepper (capsicum), diced

1 small onion, finely chopped

1 pound (500 g) pork loin, cut into small chunks

1 teaspoon ground cumin

½ teaspoon salt + more as needed

¼ teaspoon freshly ground black pepper + more as needed

1 (14-ounce/400-g) can red kidney beans, rinsed and drained

1⅔ cups (400 g) canned tomatoes

1⅔ cups (400 ml) chicken broth or stock (see page 56)

2 medium yellow sweet potatoes, peeled and diced

Heat the oil in a large saucepan over medium heat. Add the ginger, garlic, and jalapeño and sauté until the garlic is pale gold, about 2 minutes.

Add the bell pepper and onion and sauté for 5 minutes.

Season the pork with the cumin, salt, and pepper. Add the pork to the pan and cook until browned all over, 7–8 minutes.

Add the beans, tomatoes, broth, and sweet potatoes and bring to a boil. Simmer over low heat until the pork is tender, about 45 minutes.

Season with salt and pepper and serve hot.

Serves: 4–6 • Prep: 15 min • Cooking: 1 hr

Bell Peppers

Bell peppers, or capsicums, belong to the same family as chiles (see page 95) and also come from South America. Usually available in red, yellow, and green, these large, fleshy vegetables are sweet and mild and can add color and flavor to many stews. Their crisp texture makes them a wonderful addition to salads, while grilling or roasting them until the skins blacken and can be peeled off seems to heighten their flavor, making them an ideal appetizer or flavoring for pasta sauces or salads. Bell peppers are rich in vitamins A and C and in carotenoids.

SZEGED GOULASH

A hearty central European pork stew with sauerkraut. This stew is named after Szeged, a town in southern Hungary famous for the quality—and quantity—of the paprika grown there.

- ¼ cup (60 ml) sunflower oil
- 1 pound (500 g) lean pork, cut into small cubes
- 8 ounces (250 g) bacon or pancetta, chopped
- 3 large onions, thinly sliced
- 2 green bell peppers (capsicums), seeded and cut into thin strips
- 2 cloves garlic, finely chopped
- 1 tablespoon fresh thyme leaves, or 1 teaspoon dried
- 1 teaspoon crushed caraway seeds
- 1 teaspoon salt
- 1–1⅔ cups (250–400 ml) vegetable broth or stock (see page 112), heated
- 1 tablespoon tomato paste (concentrate)
- 1 tablespoon sweet paprika

- 1 pound (500 g) sauerkraut, drained, rinsed under cold water, and drained again
- 1 apple, peeled, cored, and diced
- 2 medium potatoes, peeled and thickly sliced
- ¼ cup (60 ml) dry red wine
- ⅔ cup (150 ml) sour cream
- Salt and freshly ground black pepper
- ½ teaspoon hot paprika
- 1 tablespoon all-purpose (plain) flour
- 3 tablespoons cold water
- Handful of fresh dill, coarsely chopped
- Pickled chile, to serve

Heat the oil in a large saucepan over high heat. Add the pork and bacon and sauté until browned, 4–5 minutes.

Lower the heat to medium and add the onions, bell peppers, garlic, thyme, caraway, and salt. Sauté for 5–8 minutes, until the vegetables begin to soften.

Add a few tablespoons of hot vegetable broth and stir in the tomato paste and sweet paprika. Cook for 5 minutes. Chop the sauerkraut and add to the pan with the apple and potatoes. Cook for 5 minutes, until nicely coated.

Pour 1 cup (250 ml) of the hot broth into the mixture. Cover and simmer over low heat for 1¼ hours. Stir after 30 minutes, adding more broth if the stew is dry or sticks to the pan. Stir in the wine and 1 tablespoon of the sour cream. Cook for 15 minutes more. Season with salt and pepper to taste. Add the hot paprika.

Blend the flour with the water and stir it in. Cook until the sauce has thickened. Stir in the remaining sour cream and sprinkle with dill and pickled chile. Serve hot.

Serves: 4–6 • Prep: 15 min • Cooking: 2 hr

CZECH LAMB GOULASH

This Czech goulash is based on the Hungarian dish, but with added tomatoes and bell peppers (capsicums). For an extra flourish, serve the goulash in a hollowed-out loaf of bread. Just slice off the top of a round loaf, hollow it out, fill with goulash, and put the top back on.

- 2 tablespoons vegetable oil or lard
- 2 onions, thinly sliced
- 2 pounds (1 kg) lean lamb (leg or shoulder), cut into small cubes
- Salt and freshly ground black pepper
- 2 cloves garlic, finely sliced
- 2 tablespoons sweet paprika
- About 1 cup (250 ml) vegetable broth or stock (see page 112), heated
- 6 plum tomatoes, peeled and chopped, or 1 (14-ounce/400-g) can plum tomatoes, drained
- 2 green bell peppers (capsicum), seeded and cut into thin strips

- 1 red bell pepper (capsicum), seeded and cut into thin strips
- 1 tablespoon finely chopped fresh marjoram
- ½ teaspoon crushed caraway seeds
- 1 fresh green or red chile, seeded and finely chopped
- 1 tablespoon all-purpose (plain) flour
- 2 tablespoons cold water
- ¼ cup (60 ml) dry red wine
- 1 teaspoon hot paprika (optional)
- 1 clove garlic, peeled and lightly crushed

Heat the oil in a large saucepan over medium heat. Add the onions and sauté until softened, about 5 minutes.

Add the lamb and sauté until browned all over, about 8 minutes Season with salt and pepper.

Stir in the sliced garlic and sprinkle the lamb with the sweet paprika. Pour in a few spoonfuls of hot broth and stir for 2 minutes until the meat is coated with paprika.

Add the tomatoes, bell peppers, half the marjoram, caraway seeds, and chile. Pour in about ½ cup (125 ml) of the hot broth, just enough to prevent the meat from sticking to the pan. Cover and simmer over low heat until the lamb is tender, about 1½ hours. Add more broth if the stew looks very dry.

Shortly before the end of the cooking time, blend the flour with the cold water and stir into the goulash to thicken the sauce.

Add the wine, the remaining marjoram, hot paprika, if using, and the crushed garlic. Simmer for 10 minutes. Season with salt and pepper to taste. Serve hot.

Serves: 4–6 • Prep: 20 min • Cooking: 2 hr

Lamb Stew with Spring Vegetables

- 2 pounds (1 kg) lamb, shoulder or leg, cut into bite-size pieces
  Salt and freshly ground black pepper
- 4 tablespoons butter
- 2 cloves garlic, finely chopped
- 2 tablespoons all-purpose (plain) flour
- 4 cups (1 liter) beef broth or stock (see page 28)
- 1 bay leaf
- 1 pound (500 g) small new potatoes, scrubbed
- 10 baby carrots, scrubbed
- 8 small white onions
- 1 cup (150 g) frozen peas
- 1 tablespoon finely chopped fresh parsley
- 1 tablespoon finely chopped fresh thyme

Season the lamb generously with salt and pepper.

Melt the butter in a large saucepan over medium-high heat. Add the lamb and garlic and sauté until browned, 8–10 minutes.

Add the flour and cook for 3–4 minutes, stirring constantly. Add the broth, bay leaf, potatoes, carrots, onions, peas, parsley, and thyme. Cover and cook over low heat until the meat and vegetables are tender, about 1 hour.

Remove the bay leaf and serve hot.

Serves: 4–6 • Prep: 20 min • Cooking: 1 ¼ hr

Lamb with Sun-Dried Tomatoes and Zucchini

- 4 tablespoons (60 ml) extra-virgin olive oil
- 2 pounds (1 kg) lamb shoulder, boned and cut into 1-inch (2.5-cm) cubes
  Salt and freshly ground black pepper
- 2 cloves garlic, finely chopped
- 2 pounds (1 kg) tomatoes, peeled and chopped
- 4 ounces (125 g) sun-dried tomatoes, finely chopped
- 1 teaspoon dried oregano
- 4 medium zucchini (courgettes), sliced

Heat the oil in a large, heavy-bottomed pan over medium heat. Add the lamb and sauté until browned all over, 8–10 minutes. Season with salt and pepper.

Add the garlic and sauté for 2–3 minutes more.

Stir in the fresh and sun-dried tomatoes and oregano and cook until the lamb is almost tender, 25–30 minutes.

Add the zucchini and cook until tender, 10–15 minutes. Serve hot.

Serves: 4 • Prep: 20 min • Cooking: 1 hr

Lamb and Bell Pepper Stew

- 4 tablespoons (60 ml) extra-virgin olive oil
- 2 pounds (1 kg) lamb shoulder, boned and cut into 1-inch (2.5-cm) cubes
  Salt
- 1 cup (150 g) diced pancetta
- 2 cloves garlic, finely chopped
- 1 large onion, coarsely chopped
- 3 large bell peppers (preferably mixed red, yellow, and green), seeded and chopped
- ½ cup (125 ml) dry white wine
- 1 (14-ounce/400-g) can tomatoes, chopped, with juice
- 2 tablespoons finely chopped fresh parsley
  Freshly ground black pepper
  Freshly cooked short-grain rice, to serve

Heat 2 tablespoons of the oil in a large saucepan over medium heat. Add the lamb and sauté until browned all over, 8–10 minutes. Season with salt. Remove the meat from the pot and set aside on a warm plate

Heat the remaining 2 tablespoons of oil in the same pan. Add the pancetta, garlic, and onion. Sauté until the onion is softened, about 5 minutes. Add the bell peppers and cook for 5 minutes more.

Pour in the wine. When it has evaporated, add the tomatoes, partially cover the pan, and cook for 15 minutes.

Add the lamb and parsley, season with pepper, and cook until the lamb is tender, about 40 minutes. Serve hot with the rice.

Serves: 4 • Prep: 20 min • Cooking: 1 ¼ hr

Lamb and Bell Pepper Stew

BRAISED LAMB WITH CHEESE

This recipe comes from Sicily, where a little of the local pecorino cheese is often added to the cooking juices for extra flavor.

- 3 tablespoons extra-virgin olive oil
- 2 tablespoons finely chopped fresh pork fat or lard
- 2 large scallions (green onions) or 1 small onion, thinly sliced
- 2 pounds (1 kg) lamb, from the shoulder or leg, diced
- 1 cup (250 ml) dry red wine
- 1 tablespoon finely chopped fresh parsley
- 2 cloves garlic, lightly crushed
- Salt and freshly ground black pepper
- About 2 cups (500 ml) beef broth or stock (see page 28)
- 2 pounds (1 kg) small new potatoes or large potatoes, diced
- ¾ cup (125 g) freshly grated pecorino cheese

Heat the oil and pork fat in a large saucepan over medium heat. Add the scallions and sauté until softened, 5 minutes. Add the lamb and brown all over, 6–8 minutes.

Pour in the wine and cook, uncovered, until it has evaporated.

Stir in the parsley and garlic. Season with salt and pepper. Pour in 1 cup (250 ml) of the broth. Cover and cook over low heat for 45 minutes.

Add the potatoes and the remaining 1 cup (250 ml) of broth. Cover and cook until the potatoes and meat are tender, about 30 minutes.

Sprinkle with the cheese, stir briefly, and turn off the heat. Let stand for 4–5 minutes before serving.

Serves: 4 • Prep: 20 min • Cooking: 1½ hr

EASY LAMB STEW

- 1½ pounds (750 g) boneless lamb, cut into small cubes
- 1½ pounds (750 g) savoy cabbage, finely shredded
- 10 ounces (300 g) potatoes, peeled and cut into cubes
- 3 firm-ripe tomatoes, thinly sliced
- 2 medium carrots, thinly sliced
- 2 red onions, finely chopped
- 1 stalk celery, finely chopped
- Salt and freshly ground black pepper
- 1 tablespoon finely chopped fresh parsley
- 4 cups (1 liter) beef broth or stock (see page 28)

Arrange the lamb, cabbage, potatoes, tomatoes, carrots, onions, and celery in layers in a large saucepan. Season with salt and pepper. Add the parsley.

Pour in the broth, cover, and cook over medium heat for about 3 hours, or until the lamb is very tender. Serve hot.

Serves 4 • Prep: 15 min • Cooking: 3 hr

LAMB STEW WITH ROSEMARY, GARLIC, AND PEAS

- ⅓ cup (90 ml) extra-virgin olive oil
- 4 cloves garlic, finely chopped
- 1 tablespoon finely chopped fresh rosemary
- ½ cup (60 g) diced pancetta
- 3 pounds (1.5 kg) lamb shoulder, cut into 1-inch (2.5-cm) pieces
- Salt and freshly ground black pepper
- 1 cup (250 ml) dry white wine
- 6 large tomatoes, peeled and chopped
- 2 large potatoes, peeled and diced
- 2 cups (300 g) frozen peas

Heat the oil in a large saucepan over medium heat. Add the garlic, rosemary, and pancetta and sauté until the pancetta is lightly browned, 4–5 minutes.

Add the lamb, season with salt and pepper, and sauté until lightly browned, 7–8 minutes.

Pour in the wine and cook until it has evaporated. Stir in the tomatoes, decrease the heat, and partially cover the pan. Simmer for about 50 minutes, stirring from time to time.

Add the potatoes and peas and cook until the potatoes are tender, about 30 minutes. Serve hot.

Serves: 6 • Prep: 20 min • Cooking: 1½ hr

MAYDAY STEW

- 3 pounds (1.5 kg) boneless lamb shoulder, cut into small chunks
- Salt and freshly ground black pepper
- ¼ cup (60 ml) extra-virgin olive oil
- 1 onion, finely chopped
- 2 cloves garlic, finely chopped
- 1 stalk celery, finely chopped
- 1 tablespoon all-purpose (plain) flour
- 3 cups (750 ml) chicken broth or stock (see page 56)
- 1 sprig fresh thyme
- 1 cup (100 g) green beans, trimmed
- 5 ounces (150 g) baby carrots
- 8 ounces (250 g) snow peas (mangetout)
- 2 cups (250 g) frozen petits pois (baby peas), thawed
- Oven baked potatoes, to serve

Season the lamb generously with salt and pepper.

Heat 2 tablespoons of the oil in a large Dutch oven or saucepan over high heat. Add the lamb and sauté until browned all over, about 8 minutes. Remove the lamb from the pan and discard any fat.

Sauté the onion, garlic, and celery in the remaining 2 tablespoons of oil until the garlic is pale gold, about 5 minutes.

Stir in the flour and cook for 1 minute. Pour in the broth and add the lamb and thyme. Season with salt and pepper. Bring to a boil. Cover and simmer over low heat for 1 hour.

Add the green beans, carrots, snow peas, and petits pois. Cook until the vegetables and lamb are tender, about 15 minutes. Serve hot with the baked potatoes.

Serves: 6–8 • Prep: 20 min • Cooking: 1 ½ hr

PEAS

Green or garden peas are a type of legume that originally comes from West Asia, where it has been cultivated for thousands of years. The ancient Greeks and Romans certainly grew peas, although they mainly consumed them in dried form. Dried and split peas were a staple food for poor people all over Europe until modern times because they were a cheap form of protein. Nowadays frozen peas are the most convenient and nutritious way to eat them when they are not available fresh from the garden or farmers' market. From a nutritional point of view, peas are a rich source of low-fat protein: a cup of peas has the same amount of protein as an egg. Snow peas and sugar snaps are part of the same group.

INDIAN ALMOND AND CARDAMOM LAMB CURRY

This dish comes from northern India.

Curry Paste

- 2 large cloves garlic, finely chopped
- 2 large green chile peppers, seeded and finely chopped
- 1 small onion, finely chopped
- ¼ teaspoon salt
- 2 tablespoons ground almonds
- 1 teaspoon water

Lamb Curry

- 1½ tablespoons butter
- 1 tablespoon sunflower oil
- 4 whole green cardamom pods, crushed
- ½ teaspoon ground cardamom
- 1 1¼-inch (3 cm) cinnamon stick
- 1½ pounds (750 g) boneless leg of lamb, cut into small cubes
  Salt
- 3 tablespoons plain yogurt
- ½ cup (125 ml) water + more as needed
- ⅔ cup (150 ml) light (single) cream
  Freshly ground white pepper
- 1 tablespoon fresh cilantro (coriander) leaves, to garnish
- 1 tablespoon flaked almonds, toasted, to garnish
  Freshly cooked basmati rice, to serve

Curry Paste: Pound the garlic with the chiles, onion, and salt with a mortar and pestle. Mix in the almonds and water to make a smooth paste. Set aside.

Lamb Curry: Heat the butter and oil in a large saucepan over medium heat. Add the cardamom pods and cinnamon stick and stir for 10 seconds to release their flavor.

Add the curry paste and cook for 5 minutes, stirring constantly and scraping up the paste from the bottom of the pan.

Add the lamb and cook over medium heat until browned all over, 8–10 minutes. Season with salt.

Stir in the yogurt and enough water to just cover the meat. Stir well and cover the pan. Simmer over low heat for 45 minutes, stirring occasionally so the meat does not stick to the bottom.

Uncover and cook for 15 minutes more until the meat is cooked (it will look slightly oily) and the sauce is well reduced.

Increase the heat and pour in the cream. Bring to a boil, stirring constantly. Stir in the ground cardamom and season with salt and white pepper.

Garnish with the cilantro and flaked almonds. Serve hot with the rice.

Serves: 4 • Prep: 20 min • Cooking: 1 ¼ hr

EXOTIC LAMB STEW

Serve this unusual stew over a bed of freshly cooked basmati rice.

- ¼ cup (60 ml) peanut oil
- 1 large onion, finely chopped
- 1 clove garlic, finely chopped
- 1½ pounds (650 g) boneless lamb shoulder, cut into small chunks
- ¼ teaspoon ground turmeric
  Salt and freshly ground black pepper
- ¼ teaspoon saffron threads, crumbled
- ½ teaspoon ground cinnamon
- 1 cup (100 g) walnuts, very finely chopped
- 1½ cups (375 ml) chicken broth or stock (see page 56)
- 2 tablespoons tomato paste (concentrate)
- 1 cup (250 ml) pomegranate juice
- 3 tablespoons fresh lemon juice
- 1 pound (500 g) canned chestnuts
  Freshly cooked basmati rice, to serve

Heat the oil in a large saucepan over medium heat. Add the onion and garlic and sauté until softened, 5 minutes.

Add the lamb and turmeric and sauté over high heat until the lamb is browned all over, 7–8 minutes. Season with salt and pepper.

Stir in the saffron, cinnamon, and walnuts. Pour in the broth and add the tomato paste. Mix well and bring to a boil. Cover and simmer over low heat for 1½ hours.

Add the pomegranate juice, lemon juice, and chestnuts. Cover and simmer for 10 minutes more. Serve hot over the basmati rice.

Serves: 4–6 • Prep: 15 min • Cooking: 2 hr

SWEET AND SPICY LAMB STEW

In spring, use tiny potatoes, cooked whole, in this dish. Later in the year you can replace them with 2 large potatoes, well-scrubbed and diced. The lemon zest, added right at the end of the cooking time, adds a fresh flavor to the dish. Be sure to use an unwaxed, preferably organic lemon.

½ cup (75 g) all-purpose (plain) flour
Salt and freshly ground white pepper
2 pounds (1 kg) boneless lamb shoulder, cut into small cubes
4 tablespoons extra-virgin olive oil
4 cloves garlic, finely chopped
1 teaspoon cumin seeds, crushed
1 teaspoon coriander, crushed
1 teaspoon ground cinnamon

1 bay leaf
¼ cup (60 ml) sweet sherry
2 cups (500 ml) boiling water
3 leeks, chopped
3 carrots, chopped
16 tiny new potatoes, scrubbed
½ cup (90 g) golden raisins (sultanas)
2 tablespoons very finely grated lemon zest

Place the flour on a large plate and season generously with salt and white pepper. Toss the lamb in the seasoned flour to coat well. Shake off any excess.

Heat the oil in a large saucepan over medium-high heat. Add the lamb and sauté until browned, 8–10 minutes. Remove and set aside. Leave the cooking juices in the pan.

Add the garlic to the pan and cook over medium heat for 30 seconds. Add the cumin, coriander, cinnamon, and bay leaf. Cook for 1–2 minutes, then pour in the sherry. Stir until the sherry has evaporated. Pour in the water and stir well to mix. Return the lamb to the pan. Cover and simmer over low heat, stirring often, for 1 hour.

Add the leeks, carrots, potatoes, and golden raisins. Season with salt and white pepper. Cover and simmer over low heat until the meat and vegetables are tender, about 1 hour. Remove the bay leaf. Sprinkle with the lemon zest and serve hot.

Serves: 4–6 • Prep: 30 min • Cooking: 2 ¼ hr

HOT AND SPICY LAMB AND TOMATO STEW

4 tablespoons extra-virgin olive oil
1 onion, coarsely chopped
1 carrot, coarsely chopped
1 stalk celery, coarsely chopped
2 cloves garlic, finely chopped
2 tablespoons finely chopped fresh parsley
1 teaspoon crushed red pepper flakes
1 cup (150 g) diced pancetta

3 pounds (1.5 kg) lamb, from shoulder or leg, cut into bite-size pieces
Salt and freshly ground black pepper
1 cup (250 ml) dry white wine
1 pound (500 g) tomatoes, peeled and chopped
Hot water, as needed

Heat the oil in a large saucepan over medium heat. Add the onion, carrot, celery, garlic, parsley, red pepper flakes, and pancetta and sauté until softened, about 5 minutes.

Add the lamb and sauté until browned, about 8 minutes. Season with salt and pepper and add the wine. Cook until the wine has evaporated.

Add the tomatoes, decrease the heat to medium, and partially cover. Cook until the meat is tender, about 1 hour, adding a little hot water if the sauce reduces too much.

Serves: 4–6 • Prep: 15 min • Cooking: 1 ¼ hr

CORN BREAD

 Corn bread is the perfect accompaniment to soups and stews. Try this recipe with the lamb stews on this page or with any of the others in this chapter.

1 tablespoon butter
1 cup (150 g) stone-ground cornmeal
2 teaspoons sugar
½ teaspoon salt
1 teaspoon baking powder

¼ teaspoon baking soda (bicarbonate of soda)
½ cup (125 ml) boiling water
¾ cup (180 ml) milk
1 large egg, lightly beaten

Preheat the oven to 450°F (225°C/gas 8). Place the butter in a cast-iron skillet and place in the oven.

Combine the cornmeal, sugar, salt, baking powder, and baking soda in a medium bowl. Pour in the water all at once and beat with a wooden spoon. Add the milk and egg and beat until smooth.

Stir the melted butter into the batter. Pour the batter into the skillet and bake until golden brown, 20 minutes.

Serves: 4–6 • Prep: 10 min • Cooking: 20 min

SPICY MEATBALL STEW

Meatballs

- 1 pound (500 g) finely ground chicken
- 2 tablespoons ground coriander
- 1 teaspoon finely chopped green chile
- 1 teaspoon red chile paste
- 1 teaspoon minced peeled fresh ginger
- 2 cloves garlic, minced
- ½ teaspoon salt
- ½ teaspoon ground turmeric
- ½ teaspoon garam masala
- Handful of finely chopped fresh coriander (coriander)
- Handful of finely chopped fresh flat-leaf parsley
- Juice from ½ lemon

Stew

- 4 tablespoons extra-virgin olive oil
- 1 red onion, peeled and grated
- 1 medium yellow onion, peeled and grated
- 1 (14-ounce/400-g) can chopped diced tomatoes, with juice
- 1 tablespoon ground red chile
- 1 teaspoon salt
- 2 cloves garlic, minced
- ½ teaspoon ground turmeric
- 1 red bell pepper (capsicum), seeded and sliced thickly
- 1 green bell pepper (capsicum), seeded and sliced thickly
- 1 yellow bell pepper (capsicum), seeded and sliced thickly
- 6 large potatoes, peeled and quartered
- 2 cups (500 ml) chicken broth or stock (see page 56)
- 2 tablespoons fresh lemon juice
- 2 tablespoons finely chopped fresh cilantro (coriander)
- Freshly cooked long-grain rice, to serve

Meatballs: Mix together all the meatball ingredients in a large bowl. Knead for about 5 minutes to ensure the mixture is well blended. Form into walnut-size meatballs. Set aside in a plate.

Stew: In a Dutch oven or saucepan, heat the oil over medium heat. Add the onions and sauté until lightly golden, about 7 minutes.

Add the tomatoes, ground red chile, salt, garlic, and turmeric. Cook over low heat until the oil has risen to the top, about 20 minutes.

Add the peppers, potatoes, and prepared meatballs. Pour in the chicken broth and cover. Simmer gently for about 25 minutes, stirring occasionally.

Add the lemon juice and garnish with the cilantro. Serve over the rice.

Serves: 4–6 • Prep: 15 min • Cooking: 1 hr

AFGHAN-STYLE CHICKEN

- 5 cups (1.25 liters) water
- 4 chicken drumsticks
- 4 chicken thighs
- 2 (14-ounce/400-g) cans garbanzo beans (chickpeas)
- 1 medium onion, finely chopped
- 1 stalk celery with leaves attached, thinly sliced
- 1 large carrot, thinly sliced
- 8 ounces (250 g) zucchini
- (courgettes), thinly sliced
- ¼ teaspoon ground cumin
- 1 teaspoon salt
- ¼ teaspoon freshly ground white pepper
- ¼ cup (30 g) finely chopped fresh cilantro (coriander)
- ¼ cup (30 g) finely chopped fresh dill
- ¼ cup (60 ml) fresh lemon juice

Bring the water to a boil in a large saucepan. Add the chicken pieces, garbanzo beans, onion, celery, carrot, zucchini, cumin, salt, and white pepper.

Cover and simmer over medium heat for 45 minutes.

Add the cilantro, dill, and lemon juice. Simmer over low heat for 15 minutes more, or until the chicken is tender. Serve warm.

Serves: 4 • Prep: 20 min • Cooking: 1 hr

CHICKEN WITH MUSHROOMS, TOMATOES, AND OLIVES

- 1 cup (250 ml) canned tomatoes, with juice
- 1 tablespoon Tabasco
- 2 cups (200 g) sliced mushrooms
- 2 cloves garlic, finely chopped
- 1 tablespoon fresh lime juice
- 1 teaspoon garam masala
- 1 red onion, finely chopped
- Salt
- 2 tablespoons Asian chili oil
- 3 chicken breasts, sliced into ½-inch- (1-cm-) thick pieces
- Handful of finely chopped fresh cilantro (coriander) leaves
- 6 cherry tomatoes
- 10 whole black olives
- Freshly cooked long-grain rice, to serve

Mix the tomato sauce, Tabasco, mushrooms, garlic paste, lime juice, garam masala, and onion in a large saucepan. Season with salt. Stir in the chili oil.

Make deep cuts in the chicken pieces and add them to the sauce, turning to coat both sides. Cover and cook over medium heat for 30 minutes. Turn the chicken over and cook until tender, about 30 minutes more.

Garnish with the cilantro, cherry tomatoes, and olives. Serve with freshly cooked rice.

Serves: 4–6 • Prep: 15 min • Cooking: 1 hr

HOT AND SPICY CHICKEN STEW

- 6 tablespoons golden raisins (sultanas)
- 2 tablespoons extra-virgin olive oil
- 1 large onion, finely chopped
- 1 green bell pepper (capsicum), seeded and thinly sliced
- 1 teaspoon ground turmeric
- 1–2 teaspoons chili paste or harissa

- 3 pounds (1.5 kg) chicken pieces
- 3 tablespoons white wine vinegar
- 4 large potatoes, peeled and diced
- 4 large tomatoes, finely chopped
- 8 ounces (250 g) green beans, cut into short lengths
- Salt
- 1 cup (250 ml) cold water

Soak the raisins in warm water for 10 minutes. Drain.

Heat the oil in a large saucepan over medium heat. Add the onion and bell pepper and sauté until softened, about 5 minutes.

Add the turmeric and chili paste and sauté over medium heat for 2 minutes. Add the chicken and sauté until well browned, 7–9 minutes. Drizzle with the vinegar and cook until it evaporates.

Add the potatoes, tomatoes, green beans, and golden raisins, and season with salt. Mix well and pour in the water. Partially cover and cook over low heat until the chicken is tender, about 1¼ hours. Serve hot.

Serves: 4 • Prep: 25 min • Cooking: 1 ½ hr

COCONUT AND BELL PEPPER CHICKEN STEW

- 4 tablespoons extra-virgin olive oil
- 1 large white onion, coarsely chopped
- 2 cloves garlic, finely chopped
- 3 pounds (1.5 kg) chicken pieces
- 2 red bell peppers (capsicums), seeded and cut into strips
- 2 large tomatoes, peeled and chopped

- Salt and freshly ground black pepper
- ½ cup (125 ml) coconut milk
- 1 tablespoon finely chopped fresh flat-leaf parsley
- Freshly cooked Thai or jasmine rice, to serve

Heat the oil in a large saucepan over medium heat. Add the onion and garlic and sauté until softened, about 5 minutes.

Add the chicken pieces and sauté until well browned, 7–9 minutes.

Add the bell peppers and tomatoes and season with salt and pepper. Cover and cook over low heat for 15 minutes.

Stir in the coconut milk and parsley and simmer until the chicken is tender and the juices run clear, about 1 hour.

Place the rice in a large serving dish and spoon the chicken stew over the top. Serve hot.

Serves: 4–6 • Prep: 15 min • Cooking: 1 ½ hr

TURKEY AND TURNIP STEW

- 1 tablespoon extra-virgin olive oil
- ½ cup (60 g) diced bacon or pancetta
- 1 shallot, finely chopped
- 1 tablespoon extra-virgin olive oil
- 6 turkey breast fillets (about 1½ pounds/750 g), cut into small chunks
- 1 pound (500 g) turnip, peeled and

- cut into cubes
- 1 bay leaf
- 1 cup (250 ml) chicken broth or stock (see page 56)
- ⅔ cup (150 ml) heavy (double) cream
- Salt and freshly ground black pepper

Heat the oil in a large saucepan over medium heat. Add the bacon and shallot and sauté until softened, about 5 minutes.

Add the turkey and turnip. Sauté over medium heat until browned all over, 7–9 minutes.

Add the bay leaf. Pour in the broth and bring to a boil. Simmer over low heat until the turkey and turnip are tender, about 30 minutes.

Discard the bay leaf. Stir in the cream and season with salt and pepper. Cook for 2 minutes more. Serve hot.

Serves: 4–6 • Prep: 15 min • Cooking: 45 min

Hot and Spicy Chicken Stew

BRAISED CHICKEN AND VEGETABLES

- 1 chicken, about 3 pounds (1.5 kg)
- 4 tablespoons (60 ml) extra-virgin olive oil
- 2 medium onions, finely chopped
- 2 cloves garlic, finely chopped
- ½ cup (125 ml) dry white wine
- 1 pound (500 g) potatoes, peeled and coarsely chopped
- 4 large carrots, coarsely chopped
- 4 stalks celery, cut into 1-inch (2.5-cm) lengths
- 2 tablespoons finely chopped fresh parsley
  Salt and freshly ground black pepper
- 1 cup (250 ml) chicken broth or stock (see page 56)

Rinse the chicken under cold running water and dry with paper towels. Cut into 8 pieces.

Heat the oil in a large saucepan over medium heat. Add the onions and garlic and sauté until softened, about 5 minutes.

Add the chicken, in two batches, and sauté until well browned, 7–9 minutes.

Pour in the wine and cook until it evaporates. Add the potatoes, carrots, celery, and parsley and season with salt and pepper.

Pour in enough broth to moisten the dish. Cover and cook over medium heat, stirring frequently. Add more broth as needed to keep the chicken and vegetables moist.

Cook until the chicken and vegetables are tender, about 30 minutes. Serve hot.

Serves: 4 • Prep: 20 min • Cooking: 45 min

COQ AU VIN

- 3 tablespoons extra-virgin olive oil
- 1 chicken, weighing about 4 pounds (2 kg), cut into 8 pieces
- 2 tablespoons all-purpose (plain) flour
- 2 cups (250 g) diced bacon
- 8 ounces (250 g) button mushrooms
- 2 onions, finely chopped
- 2 shallots, finely chopped
- 3 cloves garlic, finely chopped
- 1 teaspoon tomato paste (concentrate)
- 1 bouquet garni (see page 168)
  Salt and freshly ground black pepper
- 2 cups (500 ml) full-bodied dry red wine
- 1½ cups (375 ml) beef broth or stock (see page 28)
  Freshly cooked short-grain rice or boiled potatoes, to serve

Heat the oil in a large saucepan over medium heat. Add the chicken in a single layer and sauté until well browned, 7–9 minutes. Sprinkle the chicken with the flour, letting it soak up the oil. Remove and set aside.

Add the bacon, mushrooms, onions, and shallots to the same pan and sauté over medium heat until lightly browned, about 10 minutes.

Add the garlic, tomato paste, and bouquet garni. Season with salt and pepper. Pour in the wine and broth. Return the chicken to the pan. Cover and simmer over low heat until the chicken is cooked through, about 30 minutes. The sauce should be thick. Remove the bouquet garni. Serve hot with the rice or potatoes.

Serves: 4–6 • Prep: 20 min • Cooking: 50 min

Scottish Chicken Stew

- 4 tablespoons (60 g) butter
- 4 boneless, skinless chicken breasts, thinly sliced
- 2 pounds (1 kg) potatoes, peeled and sliced ¼-inch (5-mm) thick
- ½ teaspoon dried thyme
  Salt and freshly ground black pepper
- 2 large leeks, trimmed and thinly sliced
- 2 large carrots, sliced
- 2 cups (500 ml) chicken broth or stock (see page 56)
  Water (optional)

Melt 2 tablespoons of the butter in a large saucepan over medium heat. Add the chicken in batches and sauté until well browned, 7–9 minutes per batch. Remove from the heat and set aside.

Line the bottom of the pan with the potato slices. Sprinkle with the thyme. Season generously with salt and pepper. Add a layer of chicken, followed by a layer of leeks, carrots, and more potatoes. Repeat until all the ingredients are used, finishing with a layer of potatoes.

Pour in the broth and add the remaining 2 tablespoons of butter. Bring to a boil. Cover and simmer over low heat until the chicken is very tender, about 2 hours. If the dish appears to be drying out, add a little water.

Serve hot.

Serves: 4–6 • Prep: 20 min • Cooking: 2 hr

Potatoes

Potatoes are another food with their origins in the New World; they were first grown by the pre-Inca people, high in the Andes Mountains. The Spanish brought them back to Europe, where, at least initially, many people thought they were poisonous and refused to eat them. Slowly they began to catch on, and in Ireland potatoes became the main food of many poor people. When potato blight struck in Ireland in the 1830s and 1840s, more than a million people died and another million were forced to emigrate. As a food, potatoes are extremely versatile and can be boiled, baked, fried, scalloped, puréed, stewed, and braised in an endless variety of ways. Eaten in moderation, potatoes are a healthy food, rich in potassium and with useful amounts of vitamin C, vitamin B6, and dietary fiber.

CHICKEN TAGINE WITH GARBANZO BEANS AND ONIONS

A tagine is a round earthenware pot with a tall cone-shaped cover. Generally used to cook slowly simmered stews, the tagine can be placed over hot coals, on the stove burner, or in the oven. To prevent cracking, a tagine must be glazed and seasoned before being used the first time.

- 2 tablespoons extra-virgin olive oil
- 1 red onion, finely chopped
- 1 yellow onion, finely chopped
- 1 red bell pepper (capsicum), seeded and sliced
- 1 green bell pepper (capsicum), seeded and sliced
- 2 medium carrots, coarsely chopped
- 1 large chicken, about 2 pounds (1 kg), skinned and cut into 8 pieces
- 1 teaspoon ground red chile
- 1 teaspoon sweet paprika
- 1 teaspoon salt
- ½ teaspoon black pepper
- 2 ears corn (sweet corn), cut into thirds
- 1 (14-ounce/400-g) can tomatoes, chopped, with juice
- 1 tablespoon tomato purée
- 1 tablespoon harissa
- 2 cups chicken broth or stock (see page 56)
- 1 (14-ounce/400-g) can garbanzo beans (chickpeas), drained and rinsed
- 1 tablespoon finely chopped fresh cilantro (coriander)
  Freshly cooked couscous, to serve

Heat the oil in a tagine or saucepan over medium heat. Add the onions and sauté until softened, about 5 minutes.

Add the bell peppers, carrots, and the chicken. Sprinkle the ground chile, paprika, salt, and pepper and stir well. Reduce the heat to a simmer and add the corn, tomatoes, tomato purée, harissa, and broth. Stir well. Cover and cook over low heat until the chicken is cooked, about 30 minutes.

Stir in the beans. Cover and cook for 10 minutes more, until heated through. Uncover and sprinkle with the chopped cilantro. Serve hot with couscous.

Serves: 4–6 • Prep: 15 min • Cooking: 45 min

CHICKEN TAGINE WITH PEARS AND CINNAMON

- 4 tablespoons (60 g) butter
- 4 firm-ripe pears, peeled, cored, and quartered
- ¼ teaspoon ground cardamom
- ¼ cup (60 ml) honey
- ¼ cup (60 ml) extra-virgin olive oil
- 2 Spanish onions, finely chopped
- 4 chicken breast halves
- ⅛ teaspoon saffron threads, crumbled
- 2 teaspoons minced fresh ginger, or 1 teaspoon ground
  Salt and freshly ground black pepper
- 2 (2-inch/5-cm) cinnamon sticks, broken in half
- ⅓ cup (50 g) golden raisins (sultanas), soaked in warm water for 15 minutes and drained
- 1 bunch fresh cilantro (coriander), tied with string
  Juice of 1 lemon
- 1 cup (250 ml) water
- 4 strips orange zest
- 3 orange slices, halved
- 2 tablespoons orange-flower water or fresh orange juice
- 2 tablespoons blanched almonds, lightly toasted
  Freshly cooked brown rice, to serve

Melt the butter in a large tagine or saucepan over medium heat. Add the pears and sauté for 2 minutes. Sprinkle with the cardamom.

Add the honey and gently turn the pears until lightly caramelized all over. Remove the pears with a slotted spoon and set aside.

Add the oil to the tagine and sauté the onions over low heat until golden, 7–8 minutes.

Add the chicken, saffron, and ginger. Season with salt and pepper. Sauté over medium-high heat until the chicken is seared all over, 2–3 minutes.

Add the cinnamon sticks, raisins, and cilantro. Pour in the lemon juice and water. Bring to a boil and cover. Simmer until the chicken is cooked through, 20–25 minutes, basting regularly.

Return the pears to the tagine and add the orange zest, orange slices, and orange-flower water. Simmer, uncovered, for 10 minutes.

Discard the cilantro and cinnamon sticks. Sprinkle with almonds and serve hot with the brown rice.

Serves: 4–6 • Prep: 15 min • Cooking: 50 min

Chicken Tagine with Pears and Cinnamon

ZUCCHINI AND CHICKEN TAGINE

- 4 large tomatoes, peeled and chopped
- ½ cup (125 ml) extra-virgin olive oil
- 2 pounds (1 kg) boneless, skinless chicken breasts, cut into small chunks
- 4 medium zucchini (courgettes), cut into cubes
- 3 onions, finely chopped
- 3 firm-ripe tomatoes, peeled, seeded, and coarsely chopped
- 1¼ cups (125 g) black olives, such as Kalamata, pitted
- 2 preserved lemons (see page 138)
- 1 small bunch fresh flat-leaf parsley, finely chopped
- 1 small bunch fresh cilantro (coriander), finely chopped
- 1 cup (250 ml) chicken broth or stock (see page 56)
- 2 cloves
- ¼ teaspoon ground cinnamon
  Salt and freshly ground black pepper
  Freshly cooked couscous, to serve

Heat 3 tablespoons of the oil in a tagine, earthenware pot, or Dutch oven over high heat. Add the chicken and sauté until well browned, 7–9 minutes. Remove the chicken and set aside.

Add the remaining 5 tablespoons of oil and the zucchini and sauté until browned, about 5 minutes. Remove the zucchini and set aside.

In the same oil, sauté the onions over medium heat until softened, about 5 minutes. Stir in the tomatoes and cook for 5 minutes more.

Add the chicken, zucchini, olives, preserved lemons, half the parsley, half the cilantro, the broth, cloves, and cinnamon. Season with salt and pepper. Partially cover and simmer over very low heat for 1 hour.

Garnish with the remaining parsley and cilantro. Serve hot over a steaming platter of couscous.

Serves: 4–6 • Prep: 40 min • Cooking: 1 ½ hr

BIGOS (POLISH HUNTERS' STEW)

Bigos, or Polish hunters' stew, is made with pork and venison. You can cook it with boned shoulder, saddle, or leg of venison, or leg of wild boar. Alternatively, use top round steak. The sauerkraut sharpens the flavor.

- 3 tablespoons all-purpose (plain) flour
  Salt and freshly ground black pepper
- 1 pound (500 g) lean boneless venison, cut into small cubes
- 1 pound (500 g) pork loin or belly, cut into cubes
- 8 ounces (250 g) boneless smoked pork chop, cut into thin strips
- ⅓ cup (80 ml) vegetable oil
- 8 ounces (250 g) bacon, cut into thin strips
- 2 onions, thinly sliced
- 2 pounds (1 kg) sauerkraut, drained, rinsed under cold water, and drained again
- 4 tomatoes, peeled and finely chopped
- 2 bay leaves
- 8 ounces (250 g) mushrooms, quartered
- 5 cloves
- 8 allspice berries
- ½ teaspoon dill seeds
- ¼ cup (60 ml) dry white wine
- 1 cup (250 ml) apple juice
- 1⅔ cups (400 ml) vegetable broth or stock (see page 112)
- 1 pound (500 g) cabbage, finely shredded
- 8 ounces (200 g) kielbasa or wild boar sausages, thickly sliced
- 2 tablespoons finely chopped fresh parsley

Season the flour generously with salt and pepper. Toss the venison, pork loin, and smoked pork chop in the flour, shaking off the excess.

Heat 3 tablespoons of the oil in a large saucepan over medium heat. Add the bacon and sauté for 3 minutes. Add the onions and sauté until soft and golden, about 10 minutes. Transfer to a bowl and set aside.

Add 2 tablespoons of the oil to the pan and increase the heat. Fry a single layer of meat over high heat until well browned, 5–7 minutes. Transfer to the bowl with the onions and bacon. Repeat the process, adding the remaining oil, if needed, until all the meat is browned.

Return everything to the pan and add the sauerkraut, tomatoes, bay leaves, mushrooms, cloves, allspice, dill, and ½ teaspoon of salt. Pour in the wine and apple juice. Simmer for 2 minutes, stirring well. Pour in half the broth. Stir well and bring to a boil. Cover and simmer over low heat for 1½ hours.

Add the cabbage, kielbasa, and remaining broth if there is not enough moisture in the saucepan. Simmer for 30 minutes more, or until the cabbage is cooked. Uncover for the last 15 minutes, so the liquid reduces by half.

Season with salt and pepper to taste. Remove the bay leaves. Sprinkle with parsley and serve hot.

Serves: 6–8 • Prep: 30 min • Cooking: 2 ½ hr

BEEF AND POTATO TAGINE WITH MOROCCAN PRESERVED LEMONS

Preserved lemons are lemons preserved in salt. They are common ingredients in vegetable and meat tagines. They provide a distinctive sweet-and-sour flavor to Moroccan food. You can buy them wherever Middle Eastern foods are sold.

1½ pounds (750 g) tender beef steak, cut into bite-size chunks
2 cloves garlic, finely chopped
1 teaspoon minced fresh ginger
2 tablespoons all-purpose (plain) flour
1 teaspoon ground cumin
½ teaspoon ground red chile
1 teaspoon salt
½ teaspoon ground fennel seeds
½ teaspoon freshly ground black pepper
½ teaspoon ground turmeric
4 tablespoons extra-virgin olive oil
2 large onions, peeled and finely chopped
1 preserved lemon, sliced thinly
2 cups (500 ml) beef broth or stock (see page 28)
2 large potatoes, peeled and cut into 8 pieces
Freshly cooked couscous, to serve

Combine the beef with the garlic, ginger, flour, cumin, red chile, salt, fennel, pepper, and turmeric in a large bowl. Mix well to ensure the steak is well coated. Set aside for 2 hours.

Heat the oil in a tagine or large saucepan over medium heat. Add the onions and sauté until softened, about 5 minutes.

Add the beef and lemon slices. Stir for a few minutes oven a high heat to brown the meat.

Pour in the broth and cover. Simmer for 15 minutes, then add the potatoes. Continue to simmer until the beef and potatoes are tender, about 45 minutes. Serve hot over couscous.

Serves: 4 • Prep: 10 min + 2 hr to marinate • Cooking: 65 min

LAMB TAGINE WITH RAISINS, ALMONDS, AND HONEY

Tagine, which means stew, originated in North Africa and comes from the Berbers. The same word also describes the special earthenware cooking pot with a pointed lid in which the stew is cooked. Spiced Moroccan dishes were traditionally prepared by simmering them over an open fire or a bed of charcoal. Many, such as this lamb tagine, combine savory and sweet with a fusion of spices, including saffron, the most expensive spice in the world.

¼ teaspoon saffron threads
3 tablespoons boiling water + more as needed
¼ cup (60 ml) sunflower oil
3 tablespoons butter
1 (1⅓-inch/3-cm) piece fresh ginger, peeled and finely grated, or 2 teaspoons ground
Salt and freshly ground black pepper
½ teaspoon freshly ground white pepper
½ teaspoon ground turmeric
3 small red onions, 1 finely grated and 2 coarsely chopped
3 cloves garlic, finely chopped
2½ pounds (1.2 kg) boneless lamb, trimmed of fat and cut into small chunks
1 tablespoon honey
¾ cup (150 g) raisins
½ cup (100 g) dried apricots, halved
2 dried figs, quartered
Juice of 1 lemon
3 (2-inch/5-cm) cinnamon sticks
1⅓ cups (120 g) flaked almonds, toasted, to garnish
1 tablespoon finely chopped fresh cilantro (coriander) leaves
Freshly cooked couscous, to serve

Toast the saffron in a large tagine or saucepan over very low heat until just brittle, 2–3 minutes. Crumble into a cup. Add the boiling water and infuse for 10 minutes.

Heat the oil and butter in the same tagine or saucepan over medium-high heat. Add the ginger, 1 teaspoon of salt, white pepper, turmeric, grated onion, and garlic. Sauté for 30 seconds.

Add the lamb, stirring until the meat is well coated with the spice mixture, about 3 minutes. Stir in the chopped onions, the saffron water, and honey. Pour in enough water to cover the meat. Cover and simmer over medium-low heat until the meat is almost tender, 1½ hours. Stir during cooking and add more water if needed to prevent the stew from drying out.

After the stew has been cooking for 45 minutes, soak the raisins, apricots, and figs in a ladleful of the cooking liquid, the lemon juice, and a little hot water, if not fully covered (you might have to add a little more water to the stew at the same time). Let soften for 30 minutes.

About 30 minutes before the end of cooking, when the meat is almost tender, add the fruit mixture and cinnamon sticks to the tagine. Cover and simmer for 30 minutes more, until the lamb is completely tender. Season with salt and pepper. Discard the cinnamon sticks and sprinkle with almonds and cilantro. Serve hot with couscous.

Serves: 6 • Prep: 20 min • Cooking: 2 hr

Lamb Tagine with Raisins, Almonds, and Honey

MONKFISH TAGINE

In many North African dishes, fish is first marinated in chermoula, *a hot marinade of garlic, cumin, ground hot red pepper, cilantro, and lemon. This tagine is made with monkfish, but you can use hake or any other white fish.*

Chermoula
- 2 cloves garlic
- 1 teaspoon salt
- 3 tablespoons extra-virgin olive oil
- 4 tablespoons finely chopped fresh cilantro (coriander)
- 2 tablespoons sweet smoked Spanish paprika (pimentòn)
- 1 teaspoon ground cumin seeds
- ¼ teaspoon cayenne pepper
  Juice of 1 large lemon

- 2 pounds (1 kg) monkfish fillet, cut into 6 portions

Sauce
- 2 cloves garlic, thinly sliced
- 5 tablespoons extra-virgin olive oil
- 1 teaspoon finely grated fresh ginger
- ½ teaspoon salt

- ½ teaspoon freshly ground white pepper
- ½ teaspoon saffron threads infused in ½ cup (125 ml) boiling water (or 2 teaspoons ground turmeric in ½ cup (125 ml) cold water)
- 3 large green bell peppers (capsicums), roasted, peeled, and cut into thin strips
- 15 black olives, cured in oil
- 6 cherry tomatoes, cut in half
- 3 large ripe tomatoes, peeled and cut into quarters
  Salt and freshly ground black pepper
- 1 preserved lemon, cut into 6 strips
- 1 tablespoon coarsely chopped fresh cilantro (coriander)
  Freshly cooked couscous or Moroccan bread, to serve

Chermoula: Pound the garlic with the salt to a smooth paste with a mortar and pestle. Add the oil, cilantro, paprika, cumin, cayenne, and lemon juice and mix.

Spread two-thirds of the mixture over the fish and let marinate in the refrigerator for 3 hours. Keep the remaining *chermoula* in a separate bowl.

Sauce: Mix the garlic, oil, ginger, salt, and white pepper with the reserved chermoula and add the saffron mixture. Set aside.

Arrange the bell pepper strips in crosses at the bottom of a tagine or Dutch oven. Place the fish on top of the bell peppers. Sprinkle with the olives and cherry tomatoes.

Pour three-quarters of the sauce over the fish and top with the tomatoes. Spoon the remaining sauce over the top. Cover and simmer over medium-low heat for 30 minutes. Season with salt and pepper to taste.

If the sauce is too runny, transfer the fish to a warmed plate. Boil the sauce hard for a few minutes over high heat until thickened.

Return the fish to the pan and add the lemon strips. Simmer over low heat for 5 minutes. Sprinkle with the cilantro. Serve with couscous or Moroccan bread.

Serves: 6 • Prep: 40 min + 3 hr to marinate • Cooking: 35 min

SICILIAN-STYLE SALT COD

Try to buy salt cod that is presoaked and ready to cook. In many areas of North America it may be difficult to find presoaked salt cod, so you may end up buying large slabs of dried fish. The desalting process is fairly straightforward and well worth the effort.

- 1½ pounds (750 g) salt cod
- ½ cup (125 ml) extra-virgin olive oil
- 1 medium onion, finely chopped
- 1 whole clove garlic, lightly crushed
- ⅓ cup (50 g) all-purpose (plain) flour
  Salt and freshly ground black pepper
- 1 pound (500 g) fresh or canned tomatoes, peeled and chopped
  About 1 cup (250 ml) boiling water
- 1¼ pounds (600 g) potatoes, peeled and sliced

- 2 slightly underripe pears, peeled, cored, and sliced
- 5 ounces (150 g) green olives, pitted
- 2 small, tender stalks celery, sliced
- 2 tablespoons capers
- 3 tablespoons pine nuts
- 3 tablespoons seedless golden raisins (sultanas), soaked and drained

Desalting: Cut the salt cod into large pieces, removing the center bone (sometimes this has already been removed). Soak in a large bowl of cold water for 24 hours, changing the water at least 4 times.

Rinse the salt cod and dry with paper towels. Cut into pieces roughly 3 inches (8 cm) square.

Heat the oil in a large saucepan over medium heat. Add the onion and garlic and sauté until softened, 5 minutes.

Coat the pieces of salt cod lightly with flour and cook for a few minutes over a slightly higher heat, turning them once. Season with a little salt and pepper.

Add the tomatoes and enough boiling water to just cover the fish. Cover the pot and simmer over low heat for 45 minutes.

Add the potatoes, pears, olives, celery, capers, pine nuts, and raisins. Stir carefully, cover, and simmer for another 40 minutes. There should be plenty of liquid; if not, moisten with hot water. Serve hot.

Serves: 4 • Prep: 15 min + 24 hr to soak • Cooking: 1 ½ hr

BELL PEPPER AND POTATO COUSCOUS

- 4 tablespoons extra-virgin olive oil
- 1 large white onion, finely chopped
- ½ teaspoon cumin seeds
- 2 cloves garlic, finely chopped
- 1 teaspoon sweet paprika
- 1 (14-ounce/400-g) can tomatoes, chopped, with juice
- 1 teaspoon sugar
- 1 teaspoon salt
- 1 teaspoon chili powder
- 2 tablespoons ground coriander
- 1 teaspoon garam masala
- 2 cups (500 ml) vegetable broth or stock (see page 112)
- 1 green bell pepper (capsicum), seeded and thinly sliced
- 1 red bell pepper (capsicum), seeded and thinly sliced

- 1 orange or yellow bell pepper (capsicum), seeded and thinly sliced
- 2 baby eggplant (aubergines), with peel, chopped
- 2 zucchini (courgettes), sliced lengthwise
- 2 medium potatoes, not peeled, cut in small dice
- 2 tablespoons finely chopped fresh parsley
- 2 tablespoons finely chopped fresh dill
- 10 black olives
- 5 dried apricots, coarsely chopped
  Freshly cooked couscous, to serve

Heat the oil in a large frying pan over medium heat. Add the onion, cumin seeds, and garlic and sauté until the onions are softened, about 5 minutes.

Add the paprika, tomatoes, sugar, salt, chili powder, coriander, garam masala, vegetable broth, bell peppers, eggplant, zucchini, and potatoes.

Stir everything together over medium heat for a few minutes. Cover and simmer until all the vegetables are tender, about 25 minutes.

Stir in the parsley, dill, olives, and apricots.

Pile the couscous high on a large serving platter. Spoon the vegetables and sauce over the top and serve hot.

Serves: 4–6 • Prep: 15 min • Cooking: 30 min

COUSCOUS

Couscous, from North African, is a type of tiny pasta made from semolina, although we usually think of it as a grain. It is thought that the word originated from the French *sutsoo*, which describes the sound the vapor makes when it passes through the grains as they steam. Couscous is served on large round, shallow platters. The grains are heaped up with a small depression made in the top where the meat or vegetables stews and tagines are placed. Nowadays most couscous is sold precooked and is simple and easy to prepare. As a food, couscous is a good source of complex carbohydrates.

VEGETARIAN COUSCOUS

- 3 tablespoons extra-virgin olive oil
- 1 red onion, finely chopped
- 1 white onion, finely chopped
- 2 cloves garlic, finely chopped
- 1 red bell pepper (capsicum), seeded and sliced
- 1 yellow bell pepper (capsicum), seeded and sliced
- 1 orange bell pepper (capsicum), seeded and sliced
- 2 medium eggplants (aubergines), unpeeled and chopped
- 4 medium-large potatoes, diced
- 1 small marrow or 2 medium zucchini (courgettes), diced
- 8 baby corns (sweet corns)
- ½ cup (60 g) canned bamboo shoots, drained
- 2 cups (400 g) cooked (or canned) garbanzo beans (chickpeas)
- 1 teaspoon salt
- ½ teaspoon freshly ground black pepper
- 1 fresh red chile, finely chopped
- 1 (14-ounce/400-g) can tomatoes, chopped, with juice
- 1 tablespoon tomato purée
- 1 tablespoon harissa
- ½ teaspoon cumin seeds
- 2 cups (500 ml) chicken broth or stock (see page 56)
- 2 tablespoons finely chopped fresh cilantro (coriander)
  Freshly cooked couscous, to serve

Heat the oil in a tagine or Dutch oven over medium heat. Add the onions and garlic and sauté until softened, about 5 minutes.

Add the bell peppers, eggplant, potatoes, marrow, corn, bamboo shoots, and the garbanzo beans. Stir well and sauté until the vegetables begin to soften, about 5 minutes.

Add the salt, pepper, chile, tomatoes, purée, harissa, cumin, and broth. Stir well and cover tightly, allowing no steam to escape.

Reduce the heat and simmer on the lowest setting until the vegetables are tender, about 40 minutes

Sprinkle with the cilantro and serve hot with couscous.

Serves: 4–6 • Prep: 15 min • Cooking: 50 min

VEGETARIAN CHILI SUPREME

- 2 tablespoons extra-virgin olive oil
- 1 teaspoon cumin seeds
- 1 large onion, finely sliced
- 2 stalks celery, chopped
- 2 cloves garlic, finely chopped
- 1 teaspoon green curry paste
- ½ red bell pepper (capsicum), seeded , cored, and sliced
- ½ green bell pepper (capsicum), seeded and sliced
- 2 zucchini (courgettes), thickly sliced
- 1 medium eggplant (aubergine), unpeeled and chopped
- 8 ounces (250 g) mushrooms, quartered
- 2 (14-ounce /400-g) cans Italian
- tomatoes, chopped, with juice
- 1 tablespoon tomato purée
- 1 tablespoon sweet chili sauce
- 1 teaspoon chili powder
- 1 teaspoon ground cumin powder
- 2 teaspoons ground coriander
- 1 teaspoon salt
- 1 (14-ounce/400 g) can red kidney beans, rinsed and drained
- 1 tablespoon plain yogurt
  Juice of 1 lemon
  Handful of finely chopped fresh cilantro (coriander)
  Freshly cooked long-grain rice, to serve

Heat the oil in a large saucepan over medium heat. Add the cumin seeds and heat until they are fragrant, about 2 minutes. Add the onion, celery, garlic, and green curry and cook until the onions are softened, about 5 minutes.

Add the bell peppers, zucchini, eggplant, mushrooms, and tomatoes. Cover and cook over medium heat until the vegetables are softened, about 5 minutes.

Add the tomato purée, chili sauce, chili powder, cumin, coriander, and salt. Mix well, then add the kidney beans. Cover and cook until the vegetables are tender, about 25 minutes. Stir occasionally during cooking.

Stir in the yogurt, lemon juice, and fresh cilantro. Stir well and serve over rice.

Serves: 4–6 • Prep: 10 min • Cooking: 40 min

EASY BROCCOLI STEW

- 2 tablespoons extra-virgin olive oil
- 1 large onion, finely chopped
- 1 clove garlic, finely chopped
- 1 (¾-inch/2-cm) piece fresh ginger, peeled and finely grated
- 1 red bell pepper (capsicum), seeded and finely chopped
- 1 teaspoon finely chopped fresh thyme
- 1 teaspoon finely chopped fresh mint
- 1 teaspoon dried mixed Italian herbs
- 1 pound (500 g) broccoli florets
- halved and stalks diced
- 1 cup (250 ml) carrot juice
- 2 cups (400 g) canned garbanzo beans (chickpeas), rinsed and drained
- 1 tablespoon balsamic vinegar
  Salt and freshly ground black pepper
- ½ cup (60 g) toasted cashews or walnuts, to garnish
- 1 small bunch mint leaves, torn
  Freshly cooked brown rice, to serve

Heat the oil in a saucepan over medium heat. Add the onion, garlic, and ginger and sauté until softened, about 5 minutes.

Add the bell pepper, thyme, mint, and mixed herbs. Sauté over low heat for 5 minutes. Add the broccoli and carrot juice. Cover and simmer for 10 minutes. Add the garbanzo beans and balsamic vinegar and simmer for 5 minutes more. Season with salt and pepper. Garnish with the nuts and mint. Serve hot with brown rice.

Serves: 4 • Prep: 10 min • Cooking: 20 min

CREAMY VEGETABLE CURRY

- 2 tablespoons extra-virgin olive oil
- ½ teaspoon mustard seeds
- ½ teaspoon cumin seeds
- 2 fresh green chiles, cut into slivers
- 2 cloves garlic, finely chopped
- ½ teaspoon minced fresh ginger
- 2 onions, finely chopped
- 1 marrow or 4 large zucchini (courgettes), cut into bite-size chunks
- 2 large potatoes, peeled and cut in bite-size chunks
- 4 ounces (125 g) okra, trimmed and sliced in half
- 4 ounces (125 g) winter squash or pumpkin, peeled, seeded, and cubed

- 4 ounces (125 g) button mushrooms, chopped
- ½ teaspoon white pepper
- 1 teaspoon salt
- 1 tablespoon Worcestershire sauce
- 2 tablespoons dark soy sauce
- 2 cups (500 ml) chicken broth or stock (see page 56), boiling
- 1 cup (250 ml) light (single) cream
  Handful of finely chopped fresh cilantro (coriander), to garnish
  Freshly cooked brown rice, to serve

Heat the oil over medium heat in a large saucepan. Add the mustard and cumin seeds and stir until fragrant, about 3 minutes.

Add the chiles, garlic, ginger, and onions and sauté until the onion is softened, about 5 minutes.

Stir in the marrow, potatoes, okra, winter squash, and mushrooms. Add the white pepper, salt, Worcestershire sauce, and soy sauce.

Add the broth, cover, and simmer until all the vegetables are tender, about 30 minutes. The liquid should reduce a little in volume and the vegetables should be tender.

Stir in the cream and simmer for 5 minutes. Garnish with the cilantro and serve hot with brown rice.

Serves: 4 • Prep: 15 min • Cooking: 45 min

GREEN CURRY WITH COCONUT AND SHRIMP

- 1 tablespoon Thai green curry paste
- 1 2/3 cups (400 ml) coconut milk
- 1 long eggplant (aubergine), weighing about 8 ounces (250 g), cut into 1-inch (2.5-cm) cubes
- 8 ounces (250 g) green beans, trimmed and chopped
- 1 red bell pepper (capsicum), sliced into thin 2-inch (5-cm) long strips
- 1 zucchini (courgette), cut in half lengthwise and sliced
- 1 yellow crookneck squash, cut in half lengthwise and sliced
- ½ cup (100 g) thinly sliced bamboo shoots

- 1 teaspoon Thai fish sauce
- 1 pound (500 g) medium-large shrimp (prawns), peeled and deveined
- 12 fresh basil leaves, torn
- ½ cup (125 ml) vegetable broth or stock (see page 112) or water
  Salt
  Freshly cooked Thai or jasmine rice, to serve
  Few sprigs of Vietnamese or regular mint, to garnish
  Lime wedges, to garnish

Heat the green curry paste and half the coconut milk in a large saucepan over medium heat until very fragrant and bubbly.

Add the eggplant, toss in the sauce, and cook for 3 minutes. Add the green beans and bell pepper. Stir, then cover, and cook for 5–7 minutes, until the vegetables begin to soften.

Add the zucchini, yellow squash, bamboo shoots, the remaining coconut milk, and fish sauce.

Simmer until the vegetables are tender but still al dente, about 5 minutes. Add the shrimp and basil. Add some vegetable broth if the curry gets too dry. Cook until the shrimp are pink, about 5 minutes. Taste for salt and seasoning. Remove from the heat.

Serve hot with the rice. Garnish with the mint and wedges of lime.

Serves: 4 • Prep: 15 min • Cooking: 20 min

Green Curry with Coconut and Shrimp

COCONUT SEAFOOD CURRY

- 2 tablespoons peanut or other vegetable oil
- 1 medium onion, thinly sliced
- 2 cloves garlic, thinly sliced
- 1 teaspoon minced fresh ginger
- 2 tablespoons mild curry paste
- 1 tablespoon tomato purée
- 1 pound (500 g) skinless, boneless white fish (such as pollock or perch), cut into small chunks
- 12 ounces (350 g) shrimp (prawns), peeled and deveined, tails intact
- 2 cups (500 ml) canned coconut milk
- 1/4 cup (60 ml) chicken or fish broth or stock (see pages 56 or 98)
- 1 teaspoon sugar
- Salt and freshly ground black pepper
- 2 tablespoons fresh lime juice
- 2 tablespoons finely chopped fresh cilantro (coriander), plus whole leaves, to garnish
- Freshly cooked Thai rice, to serve
- Lime wedges, to serve

Heat the oil in a medium saucepan over medium heat. Add the onion and sauté until softened, about 5 minutes.

Stir in the garlic and ginger and cook for a few seconds. Add curry paste and tomato puree, and cook, stirring, until fragrant, about 1 minute.

Add the fish and shrimp and stir until coated in the sauce.

Pour in the coconut milk, broth, and sugar and season with salt and pepper. Bring to a boil, then reduce the heat to low and continue cooking until the seafood is cooked through, about 5 minutes.

Stir in lime juice and cilantro.

Spoon some of the rice into individual serving bowls and top with the curry. Garnish each dish with cilantro leaves and a lime wedge.

Serves: 4 • Prep: 15 min • Cooking: 15 min

SHRIMP AND MANGO CURRY

- 1/4 cup (60 ml) peanut oil
- 4 fresh red chiles, seeded and finely chopped
- 5 cardamom pods
- 2 curry leaves (optional)
- 2 onions, very finely chopped
- 4 cloves garlic, very finely chopped
- 1 small slice fresh ginger, minced
- 2 tablespoons garam masala
- 2 cups (500 g) canned chopped tomatoes, with juice
- 1/2 cup (125 ml) water
- 2 mangoes, peeled and cut into small chunks
- 1 2/3 cups (400 ml) coconut milk
- 12 ounces (350 g) shrimp (prawn), peeled and deveined, tails intact
- Freshly cooked basmati rice, to serve

Heat the oil in a large saucepan over medium heat. Add the chiles and cardamom and sauté for 2 minutes.

Add the curry leaves, if using, and sauté for 30 seconds. Stir in the onions, garlic, ginger, and garam masala. Sauté for 1 minute more.

Stir in the tomatoes and water. Simmer until the sauce begins to thicken, about 15 minutes.

Stir in the mangoes and coconut milk. Simmer over low heat for 10 minutes more.

Add the shrimp and simmer until pink, about 3 minutes. Serve hot over the rice.

Serves: 4 • Prep: 15 min • Cooking: 35 min

CURRIED CHICKEN AND PEANUT STEW

- 4 tablespoons peanut oil
- 1 medium sized chicken (about 3 pounds/1.5 kg), cut into 8 pieces
- 1 large onion, chopped
- 2 cloves garlic, finely chopped
- 1 teaspoon minced fresh ginger
- 1 teaspoon salt
- 1 teaspoon sweet paprika
- 1 teaspoon ground red chile
- ½ teaspoon ground turmeric
- 2 red bell peppers (capsicums), seeded and sliced thickly
- 3 tablespoons tomato purée

- 1 cup (100 g) dried black-eyed peas, soaked overnight and drained
- 1 cup (100 g) dried lima beans, soaked overnight and drained
- 1 chicken bouillon (stock) cube
- 6 cups (1.5 liters) boiling water
- ½ cup (125 g) peanut butter
  Handful of finely chopped fresh cilantro (coriander)
- 2 fresh green jalapeño chiles, seeded and chopped
  Freshly cooked long-grain rice or naan, to serve

Heat the oil over medium heat in a saucepan. Add the chicken and sauté until well browned, 7–9 minutes. Remove the chicken and set aside.

Add the onion, garlic, and ginger and sauté until the onion is softened, about 5 minutes. Stir in the salt, paprika, ground chile, and turmeric.

Add the peppers and tomato purée and sauté until the peppers are beginning to wilt, about 5 minutes.

Return the chicken to the pan and add the black-eyed peas, beans, stock cube, and boiling water. Cover and simmer over low heat until the chicken is tender, about 45 minutes.

Just before the chicken is ready, place the peanut butter in a small bowl and stir in about ¹/₂ cup (125 ml) of the cooking juices, stirring until smooth. Stir the peanut mixture into the sauce.

Garnish the dish with cilantro and jalapeños and serve hot with the rice or naan.

Serves: 4–6 • Prep: 15 min • Cooking: 1 hr

GREEN CURRY WITH CHICKEN AND GREEN BEANS

- 1 cup (250 ml) coconut cream (spooned from the top of canned coconut milk)
- 4 tablespoons store-bought or homemade green curry paste (see page 78)
- 1 (14-ounce/400-g) can coconut milk
- 2 tablespoons fish sauce
- 2 tablespoons dark brown sugar
- 2 pounds (1 kg) boneless, skinless chicken breasts, cut into small chunks
  Salt and freshly ground black pepper
- 1 medium white onion, coarsely chopped

- 12 ounces (350 g) green beans, trimmed and cut into short lengths
- 6 ounces (180 g) white mushrooms, sliced
- 1 red bell pepper (capsicum), seeded and cut into thin strips
- 1 fresh green chile, thinly sliced
- 2 tablespoons fresh lime juice
- 4 tablespoons coarsely chopped fresh basil
- 4 tablespoons coarsely chopped fresh cilantro (coriander)
  Freshly cooked basmati or Thai rice, to serve

Combine the coconut cream and curry paste in a large saucepan over medium-high heat. Stirring constantly, bring to a boil. Lower the heat and simmer, stirring frequently, until almost all the liquid evaporates and the oil and solids in the coconut cream have separated, about 10 minutes.

Stir in the coconut milk, fish sauce, and brown sugar and return to a boil. Simmer until the sauce begins to thicken, about 5 minutes.

Season the chicken with salt and pepper and add it in batches to the pot. Stir until all the pieces are separated and coated with the sauce.

Add the onion, green beans, mushrooms, and bell pepper and simmer until the vegetables are almost tender, about 15 minutes.

Remove from the heat and stir in the green chile, lime juice, basil, and cilantro. Serve hot with the rice.

Serves: 6 • Prep: 20 min • Cooking: 35 min

Green Curry with Chicken and Green Beans

BULGUR PILAF WITH LAMB

- 4 tablespoons butter
- 1 medium onion, finely chopped
- 1 pound (500 g) boneless lamb, cut into small cubes
- 1 cup (250 ml) peeled and chopped tomatoes
- 1 teaspoon ground cumin
  Salt and freshly ground black pepper
- 1 pound (500 g) bulgur
- 3 cups (750 ml) hot water + more as needed

Melt the butter in a large saucepan over medium heat. Add the onion and sauté until lightly browned, 7–8 minutes.

Add the lamb and sauté until browned, 8–10 minutes.

Stir in the tomatoes and cumin. Season with salt and pepper. Lower the heat, cover the pan, and simmer until the lamb is almost tender, 35–40 minutes, adding a little water if the mixture begins to dry.

Stir in the bulgur and cook for 5 minutes. Pour in the water. Cover and cook over high heat for 5 minutes. Lower the heat and cook until the bulgur is tender, 10–15 minutes. Serve hot.

Serves 4 • Prep: 15 min • Cooking: 1 ¼ hr

CHICKEN WITH PASTA

- 4 tablespoons extra-virgin olive oil
- 2 medium onions, finely chopped
- 2 cloves garlic, finely chopped
- 1 stick cinnamon
- 2 cloves
- 1 chicken, weighing about 1½ pounds (750 g), cut into 8 pieces
- 3 large tomatoes, coarsely chopped
  Salt and freshly ground black pepper
- 4 cups (1 liter) boiling water
- 1 pound (500 g) tagliatelle, broken up

Heat the oil in a large saucepan over medium heat. Add the onions and sauté until lightly browned, 7–8 minutes.

Stir in the garlic, cinnamon, and cloves. Add the chicken and sauté until well browned, 7–9 minutes.

Add the tomatoes and season with salt and pepper. Lower the heat and cook until the chicken is tender, 25–30 minutes.

Add the boiling water, followed by the tagliatelle, and cook until the pasta is al dente, 10–15 minutes. Serve hot.

Serves 4 • Prep: 30 min • Cooking: 1 hr

HALUSKA

This rich cabbage-and-noodle dish is a traditional Hungarian farmhouse recipe.

- 12 ounces (350 g) wide, flat egg noodles
- 8 tablespoons butter
- 1 large onion, thinly sliced
- 1 small savoy cabbage, finely shredded
- 1 teaspoon salt
- ¼ teaspoon freshly ground black pepper
- 1 teaspoon caraway seeds
- 1 tablespoon water
  Scant 2½ cups (600 ml) sour cream
- 2 tablespoons finely chopped fresh flat-leaf parsley

Bring a large pot of salted water to a boil. Add the egg noodles and cook until al dente. Drain well.

Melt the butter in a large saucepan over medium heat. Add the onion and sauté until softened, about 5 minutes.

Stir in the cabbage and sauté over low heat until almost tender, about 5 minutes.

Add the salt, pepper, caraway seeds, and water. Cover and simmer over low heat for 10–15 minutes, stirring occasionally.

Stir in the noodles and sour cream. Heat gently, garnish with the parsley, and serve hot.

Serves: 4 • Prep: 15 min • Cooking: 30 min

CHICKEN AND SAUSAGE GUMBO

Gumbo is a spicy dish, somewhere between a soup and a stew. It is a famous Cajun dish from the state of Louisiana. There are many different versions; this one is based on chicken and sausage. Andouille sausage is a spicy specialty of Louisiana; if you can't find it, substitute with another type of cooked, smoked sausage.

- 3 pounds (1.5 kg) chicken thighs
  Salt and freshly ground white pepper
- ½ cup (125 ml) vegetable oil
- ½ cup (75 g) all-purpose (plain) flour)
- 2 onions, finely chopped
- 1 stalk celery, finely chopped
- 6 cloves garlic, finely chopped
- 1 teaspoon dried marjoram

- 8 cups (2 liters) chicken broth or stock (see page 56)
- 2 bay leaves
- 1 pound (500 g) andouille sausage, cut in short chunks
- 2 tablespoons finely chopped fresh parsley
- 2 scallions (spring onions), tender white and green parts only, sliced

Season the chicken thighs generously with salt and white pepper. Heat 2 tablespoons of the oil in a large Dutch oven or saucepan over medium-high heat. Add the chicken in 2 batches and sauté until well browned and crisp, about 10 minutes each batch. Set aside.

Wipe the pot clean and add the remaining 6 tablespoons of oil. Place over medium heat for 2 minutes. Gradually stir in the flour, mixing with a wooden spoon, until the mixture is a deep, red-brown color, about 10 minutes.

Add the onions, celery, garlic, marjoram, salt, and pepper. Simmer, stirring often, until the vegetables begin to soften, about 10 minutes.

Add the broth a little at a time, stirring constantly with the wooden spoon so that no lumps form.

Add the bay leaves and chicken and simmer for 30 minutes. Add the sausage and simmer for 30 minutes more. Remove from the heat. Remove the bay leaves. Stir in the parsley and scallions and serve hot.

Serves 4–6 • Prep: 30 min • Cooking: about 2 hr

TOMATOES

From soup and tomato salad, to tomato sauce for pasta, to salsa: there are literally thousands of dishes from around the world in which tomato is an important—if not the main— ingredient. There are now hundreds of different varieties, from marble-size cherry tomatoes to large fleshy greenish red tomatoes favored for salads in Italy and everything in between. Nutritionally, tomatoes are a good source of vitamin C. Many people also believe that they contain trace elements that protect against cancer and heart disease.

SAUSAGES AND BEANS IN TOMATO SAUCE

- 2 tablespoons extra-virgin olive oil
- 8 large Italian pork sausages, halved
- 4 cloves garlic, finely chopped
- 8 leaves fresh sage
- 2 (14-ounce/400-g) cans Italian tomatoes, with juice
- Salt and freshly ground black pepper
- 2 (14-ounce/400-g) cans cannellini or white kidney beans, rinsed and drained

Heat the oil in a large saucepan over medium heat. Prick the sausages with a fork and add to the pot. Add the garlic and sage and sauté until the sausages are browned, 8–10 minutes. Remove the sausages and set aside.

Add the tomatoes to the same pot and season with salt and pepper. Simmer over low heat until the tomatoes have reduced and the oil is visible around the edges of the pot, about 25 minutes.

Add the sausages and beans and cook for a few minutes so that they absorb the seasoning. Serve hot.

Serves: 6 • Prep: 10 min • Cooking: 40 min

VEGETABLE CHILI WITH RED AND WHITE KIDNEY BEANS

- 4 tablespoons extra-virgin olive oil
- 1 large white or yellow onion, finely chopped
- 1 large green bell pepper (capsicum), seeded and finely chopped
- 6 cloves garlic, finely chopped
- 2 teaspoons cumin seeds
- 2 tablespoons chili powder
- ½ teaspoon cayenne pepper
- Salt
- 2 cups (500 ml) water
- 2 (14-ounce/400-g) cans tomatoes, chopped, with juice
- 1 teaspoon dried oregano
- 1 tablespoon dark brown sugar
- 1 (14-ounce/400-g) can cannellini or white kidney beans, rinsed and drained
- 1 (14-ounce/400-g) can red kidney beans, rinsed and drained
- 1 cup (150 g) frozen peas
- 2 tablespoons fresh lime juice
- 4 tablespoons coarsely chopped fresh cilantro (coriander)
- 2 tablespoons finely chopped fresh parsley

Heat the oil in a large saucepan over medium-high heat. Add the onion and garlic and sauté until softened, about 5 minutes.

Add the bell pepper and sauté until softened, about 5 minutes.

Push the vegetables to the edges of the pot and add the cumin seeds in the cleared space. Stir to toast the seeds a little, about 30 seconds, then stir them into the vegetables. Simmer for 2 minutes, then add the chili powder and cayenne. Season with salt.

Pour in the water and stir well to combine with the vegetables. Bring to a boil, then simmer over medium heat until slightly thickened, about 5 minutes.

Stir in the tomatoes, oregano, and brown sugar and simmer until reduced, about 25 minutes.

Add the beans and peas and simmer until the peas are cooked, about 5 minutes.

Remove from the heat and stir in the lime juice, cilantro, and parsley. Serve hot.

Serves: 4 • Prep: 15 min • Cooking: 45 min

CHICKEN CHILI

- 1 tablespoon extra-virgin olive oil
- 1 onion, finely chopped
- 2 teaspoons ground cumin
- 1 teaspoon crushed red pepper flakes
- 2 cups (500 g) canned chopped tomatoes, with juice
- 1½ cups (375 ml) chicken broth or stock (see page 56)
- 8 ounces (250 g) Spanish chorizo sausage, diced
- 6 skinless chicken thighs
- 2 red bell peppers (capsicums), seeded and diced
- 1 (14-ounce/400 g) can cannellini or white kidney beans, rinsed and drained
- Sour cream, to serve

Heat the oil in a large saucepan over medium heat. Add the onion and sauté until softened, about 5 minutes.

Add the cumin and red pepper flakes and sauté for 1 minute.

Stir in the tomatoes and chicken broth. Bring to a boil and add the chorizo and chicken. Cover and simmer over low heat for 20 minutes.

Stir in the bell peppers and beans. Cook until the chicken is tender, about 20 minutes more.

Serve hot with the sour cream served on the side.

Serves: 4–6 • Prep: 15 min • Cooking: 50 min

BEEF CHILI

- 3 tablespoons peanut oil
- 2 onions, finely chopped
- 2 cloves garlic, finely chopped
- 2 green chiles, seeded and finely chopped
- 1½ pounds (750 g) stew beef, cut into small chunks
- 1 (14-ounce/400-g) can red kidney beans, rinsed and drained
- 1 (14-ounce/400-g) can tomatoes, chopped, with juice
- 2 teaspoons ground cumin
- 2 teaspoons sugar
- ¾ cup (180 ml) beef broth or stock (see page 28)
- 1 red bell pepper (capsicum), seeded and finely chopped
- 1 small bunch fresh cilantro (coriander), finely chopped
- 1 ounce (30 g) bittersweet (dark chocolate), coarsely chopped
- Salt
- ¼ cup (60 ml) sour cream

Heat the oil in a large saucepan over medium heat. Add the onions and sauté until softened, about 5 minutes.

Add the garlic and chiles and sauté for 5 minutes more.

Add the beef and cook until browned all over, 8–10 minutes.

Stir in the beans, tomatoes, cumin, and sugar. Pour in the broth and bring to a boil. Cover and simmer over low heat for 1 hour.

Add the bell pepper and simmer for 30 minutes more.

Mix in the cilantro and chocolate. Season with salt. Serve hot with the sour cream served on the side.

Serves: 6–8 • Prep: 20 min • Cooking: 2 hr

CHILI CON CARNE WITH BEANS

- 1 onion, finely chopped
- ½ cup (60 g) diced bacon
- 1 tablespoon extra-virgin olive oil
- 2 cloves garlic, finely chopped
- 1 teaspoon cumin seeds
- 2 pounds (1 kg) stew beef, cut into small chunks
- 1 (14-ounce/400-g) can tomatoes, chopped, with juice
- 2½ cups (625 ml) beef broth or stock (see page 28)
- 1 teaspoon chili powder
- 1 teaspoon sugar
- Salt and freshly ground black pepper
- 1 (14-ounce/400-g) can pinto or red kidney beans, rinsed and drained
- ⅔ cup (150 ml) sour cream

Heat the oil in a large saucepan over medium heat. Add the onion and bacon and sauté until lightly browned, 7–8 minutes.

Add the garlic and cumin and sauté for 1 minute.

Add the beef and pour in the tomatoes and broth. Stir in the chili powder and sugar. Season with salt and pepper.

Simmer over medium heat for 10 minutes. Cover and simmer over low heat for 1 hour.

Uncover and stir in the beans. Cook until the beef is very tender, about 1 hour.

Serve hot with the sour cream served on the side.

Serves: 6 • Prep: 15 min • Cooking: 2 ½ hr

MEDITERRANEAN VEGETABLE STEW

You can adjust the ingredients in the stew pot depending on the vegetables in season and your preferences. Zucchini flowers have only a very brief summer season and are difficult to find. You can replace them with asparagus tips or small artichoke hearts. It is best to cut the vegetables into large, uniform pieces and cook until tender. If you are including root vegetables, such as carrots or beets, remember that they need longer cooking times and should be added to the pot first.

- 12 zucchini (courgette) flowers, or asparagus tips (optional)
- ⅓ cup (90 ml) extra-virgin olive oil
- 1 large onion, finely chopped
- 2 red onions, finely chopped
- 3 cloves garlic
- 1 red or green bell pepper (capsicum), seeded and thinly sliced
- 1 yellow bell pepper (capsicum), seeded and thinly sliced
- 1 small eggplant (aubergine), peeled and cut into chunks
- 1 small green chile, seeded and finely chopped
- 6 firm-ripe tomatoes, peeled and coarsely chopped
- 2 bay leaves

- ⅔ cup (150 ml) dry white or red wine
- 2 pounds (1 kg) potatoes, peeled and cut into small cubes
- 1 tablespoon chopped fresh oregano, or 1 teaspoon dried Water, as needed
- 8 ounces (250 g) green beans, trimmed
- 2 medium zucchini (courgettes), thinly sliced Salt and freshly ground black pepper
- 2 tablespoons fresh lemon juice
- 1 tablespoon finely chopped fresh marjoram
- 2 tablespoons finely chopped fresh flat-leaf parsley

Wipe and clean the zucchini flowers carefully, making sure there are no tiny insects in them. Trim the stems just below the flower.

Heat the oil in a large saucepan over low heat. Add the onions and sauté until softened, about 5 minutes.

Add the garlic, bell peppers, eggplant, and chile. Sauté over low heat until softened, 8–10 minutes.

Stir in the tomatoes and bay leaves. Simmer until the eggplant is tender, 15–20 minutes.

Pour in the wine and bring to a boil.

Add the potatoes and oregano. Cover and simmer over low heat for 15 minutes. Check halfway through to make sure the potatoes are not sticking to the pan. Add a little water if there is not enough sauce for the vegetables.

Test the potatoes, and when they are almost soft, add the green beans and zucchini. Season with salt and pepper to taste. (If you are using asparagus instead of zucchini flowers, add the tips now.)

Cover and cook for 5–8 minutes more. The green beans should retain some bite.

Stir in the zucchini flowers, if using, and cook for 3 minutes. Stir in the lemon juice, marjoram, and half the parsley. Season with salt and pepper. Sprinkle with the remaining parsley and serve hot.

Serves: 4–6 • Prep: 40 min • Cooking: 65 min

UKRAINIAN VEGETABLE STEW

- 3 tablespoons butter
- 3 red onions, finely sliced
- 2 cloves garlic, crushed (optional)
- 4 stalks celery, finely chopped
- 3 cups (750 ml) water
- 1 small savoy cabbage, weighing about 1½ pounds (750 g), finely shredded
- 2 carrots, finely chopped
- 1 pound (500 g) potatoes, peeled and thickly sliced
- 6 medium uncooked beets (beetroot), peeled and cut into small cubes
- 1 (14-ounce/400 g) can tomatoes, chopped, with juice
- 2 tablespoons cider vinegar or white wine vinegar

- 1 teaspoon salt
- 1 (14-ounce/400-g) can red kidney beans, rinsed and drained
- 1 (14-ounce/400-g) can cannellini or white kidney beans, rinsed and drained
- 2 tablespoons finely chopped fresh dill Freshly ground black pepper
- 1 tablespoon fresh lemon juice
- 6 scallions (spring onions), tender green and white parts only, thinly sliced
- ⅔ cup (150 ml) sour cream Black bread, to serve

Melt the butter in a large saucepan over low heat. Add the onions, garlic, if using, and celery and sauté until softened, about 5 minutes.

Pour in 1 cup (250 ml) water. Cover and simmer over low heat for 5 minutes.

Stir in the cabbage and carrots. Cover and simmer for 5 minutes.

Pour in the remaining 2 cups (500 ml) water and add the potatoes, beets, tomatoes, vinegar, and salt. Bring to a boil. Simmer over low heat for 30 minutes.

Stir in the beans and dill. Season with pepper and add the lemon juice. Stir in the scallions and the sour cream. Serve hot, accompanied by black bread.

Serves: 6 • Prep: 15 min • Cooking: 50 min

Mediterranean Vegetable Stew

MIXED VEGETABLE CASSEROLE WITH BEANS

2 cloves garlic, finely chopped
3 tablespoons extra-virgin olive oil
1 large red onion, coarsely chopped
1 fresh red chile pepper, seeded and coarsely chopped
1 pound (500 g) carrots, diagonally sliced
3 sun-dried tomatoes, cut into small strips
2 cups (300 g) cherry tomatoes, halved
1 pound (500 g) zucchini (courgettes), diagonally sliced
2 stalks celery, diagonally sliced

2 tablespoons finely chopped fresh flat-leaf parsley
1 tablespoon finely chopped fresh rosemary
   Salt and freshly ground black pepper
2 (14-ounce/400-g) cans cannellini or white kidney beans, drained
⅔ cup (150 ml) water or vegetable broth or stock (see page 112)
1 cup (60 g) fresh bread crumbs
½ cup (60 g) freshly grated Parmesan cheese
1 twig rosemary, to garnish

Heat the oil in a large flameproof Dutch oven or casserole over medium heat. Add the onion, chile, and garlic and sauté for 2 minutes.

Add the carrots and cook over low heat for 5 minutes.

Stir in the sun-dried and cherry tomatoes, zucchini, and celery. Add the parsley and rosemary, stir well, and season with salt and pepper. Cover and simmer over low heat for 10 minutes.

Add the beans and the water or broth. Cover and cook for 5 minutes. Season with salt and pepper to taste. The vegetables should be in a thick sauce.

Preheat the oven to 350°F (180°C/gas 4).

Mix together the bread crumbs and Parmesan. Sprinkle over the casserole and bake for 10 minutes, or until golden. Garnish with more rosemary and serve hot.

Serves: 4–6 • Prep: 30 min + 1 hr to soak beans • Cooking: 35 minutes

FAVA BEAN, LEEK, AND POTATO STEW

3 tablespoons extra-virgin olive oil
1 tablespoon butter
6 leeks, trimmed and thinly sliced
2 cloves garlic, finely chopped
1½ pounds (750 g) waxy potatoes, peeled and cut into small cubes
   Salt and freshly ground black pepper
1 pound (500 g) fresh or frozen shelled (hulled) fava (broad) beans

1 tablespoon finely chopped fresh mint
   Grated zest and juice of ½ lemon
1¼ cups (310 ml) chicken broth or stock (see page 56)
4 tablespoons sour cream
20 basil leaves, torn

Heat the oil and butter in a large saucepan over low heat. Add the leeks and garlic, cover, and cook until softened but not colored, about 5 minutes.

Add the potatoes and season with salt and pepper. Stir in the fava beans, mint, lemon zest, and 1 cup (250 ml) of the broth. Simmer until the potatoes and beans have softened, 15–20 minutes.

Drizzle with the lemon juice and add the remaining ¼ cup (60 ml) of broth if the mixture is very dry. If desired, break the stew up a little with a potato masher; otherwise leave it chunky.

Stir in the sour cream and basil. Heat gently, about 3 minutes. Check the seasoning and serve hot.

Serves: 4 • Prep: 25 min • Cooking: 35 min

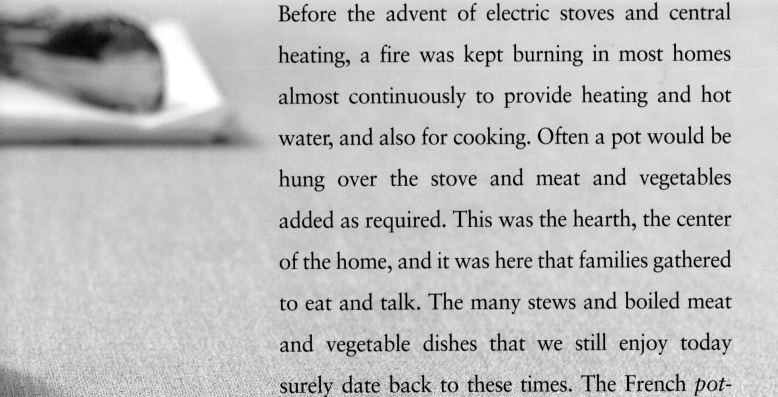

BOILING POT

VEGETABLE AND MEAT DISHES, POLENTA, AND PASTAS

Before the advent of electric stoves and central heating, a fire was kept burning in most homes almost continuously to provide heating and hot water, and also for cooking. Often a pot would be hung over the stove and meat and vegetables added as required. This was the hearth, the center of the home, and it was here that families gathered to eat and talk. The many stews and boiled meat and vegetable dishes that we still enjoy today surely date back to these times. The French *pot-au-feu* and Italian *bollito misto* are just two of the classics we have included in this chapter.

SPANISH-STYLE BOILED MEATS

1¾ pounds (750 g) boneless beef brisket or chuck

1 beef bone

4 ounces (125 g) jamón serrano ham or prosciutto (Parma ham)

12 cups (3 liters) water + more as needed

½ chicken, about 1 pound (500 g)

1 pound (500 g) dried garbanzo beans (chickpeas), soaked overnight and drained

1 carrot

1 turnip, peeled

½ stalk celery

1 small onion, studded with 1 clove

8 waxy potatoes
 Salt and freshly ground black pepper

1 large savoy cabbage, cut into wedges

1 Spanish chorizo sausage

Place the beef brisket, beef bone, and ham in a large saucepan and cover with cold water. Bring to a boil. Add the chicken, beans, carrot, turnip, celery, and onion. Simmer over low heat for 2 hours.

Add the potatoes and cook for 30 minutes more.

Taste the cooking liquid and season with salt and pepper. Add the cabbage and chorizo and cook for 30 minutes, or until tender and well cooked.

Drain the stock from the meats and vegetables. If desired, serve as a soup as a first course.

Discard the beef bone. Cut the meats into pieces and serve hot with the vegetables on a large serving dish.

Serves: 6–8 • Prep: 40 min + 12 hr to soak the beans • Cooking: 3 hr

SPANISH OXTAILS WITH POTATOES

Oxtails are the tails of beef cattle and they make especially tasty soups, stews, and boiled dishes. They require slow and lengthy cooking to become tender but their superb taste is worth the wait. Oxtails are not always easy to find, in which case you may want to substitute with meaty veal or beef neck, short rib, or shank.

3 large oxtails
 Salt and freshly ground black pepper

4 tablespoons extra-virgin olive oil

2 pounds (1 kg) onions, finely chopped

4 cups (1 liter) water

2 bay leaves

2 cups (500 ml) dry red wine

2 pounds (1 kg) potatoes, peeled and cut into small cubes

Season the oxtails with salt and pepper.

Heat the oil in a large, heavy saucepan over medium heat. Sauté the oxtails until well browned, 10–15 minutes. Remove from the pan and set aside.

Sauté the onions in the same pan until lightly browned, 7–8 minutes.

Add the water and bay leaves and return to a boil. Add the wine, cover, and simmer until the meat is very tender, 2½–3 hours. Add more water during cooking if necessary; the oxtails should always be covered.

About 30 minutes before the oxtails are cooked, place the potatoes in a steamer over the pan and steam until tender.

Place the potatoes on a serving dish with the oxtails and spoon the cooking juices over the top.

Serves: 6–8 • Prep: 15 min • Cooking: 3 hr

BOLLITO MISTO (MIXED MEATS AND VEGETABLES, ITALIAN-STYLE)

In Italy, the meats and vegetables in this dish vary according to the region and the season. You may also vary them according to personal taste and what you have on hand. Cotechino sausage is now available both in Italy and abroad in a pre-cooked version sealed in a bag that usually only requires about 45 minutes boiling to finish cooking.

- 2 medium onions, studded with 4–6 cloves
- 3 stalks celery, trimmed
- 9 large carrots, cut into chunks
- 20 black peppercorns
- 2 tablespoons coarse salt
- 4 pounds (2 kg) boneless beef, cut from brisket, bottom round, or rump roast
- 2 pounds (1 kg) boneless veal, cut from breast or shoulder
- 1 chicken, about 3 pounds (1.5 kg)
- 1 pound (500 g) calf's tongue
- 1 pre-cooked cotechino sausage, about 1½ pounds (750 g)
- 8 large potatoes, unpeeled, cut in half

Fill a large pot with about 6 quarts (6 liters) of cold water. Add the onions, celery, 1 of the carrots, peppercorns, and salt.

Bring to a boil over medium-high heat. Add the beef, and when the water has returned to a boil, decrease the heat a little and cover. Simmer for 1 hour.

Add the veal, chicken, and tongue. Simmer for 1 hour, adding boiling water to cover the meats if necessary.

Add the potatoes and remaining 8 carrots. Simmer until the meat and potatoes are very tender, about 1 hour.

Cook the pre-cooked cotechino sausage separately following the instructions on the package.

Drain and serve the meats and vegetables on a large heated serving platter.

Serves: 8–10 • Prep: 30 min • Cooking: 3 hr

CORNED BEEF AND VEGETABLES

- 6 pounds (3 kg) corned beef brisket
- 1 onion studded with 3 cloves
- 8 cloves garlic, peeled and left whole
- 1 tablespoon freshly ground black pepper
- 6 onions
- 6 potatoes
- 6 carrots
- ½ teaspoon dried marjoram
- 6 turnips, peeled

Place the corned beef in an 8-quart (8-liter) pot. Pour in enough water to cover the beef completely. Bring to a boil over high heat and boil for 5 minutes.

Skim off the froth from the surface. Add the onion with cloves, garlic, and pepper and boil for 10 minutes more.

Skim off any froth. Cover and simmer over very low heat for 1 hour. Add the onions and simmer for 30 minutes.

Add the potatoes, carrots, and marjoram and simmer for 10 minutes.

Add the turnips and simmer until all the vegetables are tender and the beef is cooked through, about 20 minutes.

Remove the beef and discard the stock and the onion studded with cloves.

Slice the beef and serve hot on a large platter with the vegetables.

Serves: 8–10 • Prep: 20 min • Cooking: 2 ¼ hr

GERMAN BOILED BEEF

4 cups (1 liter) beef broth or stock (see page 28)

2 carrots, diced

½ celery root (celeriac), peeled and diced

2 leeks, trimmed and finely sliced

½ cup (50 g) freshly grated horseradish

1½ pounds (750 g) beef tenderloin

½ cup (125 ml) half-and-half (or low fat milk)

¼ cup (60 g) butter

Salt and freshly ground black pepper

Bring the broth to a boil in a large saucepan. Add the carrots, celery root, and leeks. Cook for 3 minutes. Add the horseradish. Simmer for 15 minutes.

Add the beef. Cover, bring to a boil, and simmer for 15 minutes. Remove the beef and let rest for 10 minutes.

Strain the broth and continue cooking over high heat until reduced by half. Stir in the half-and-half and butter. Season with salt and pepper.

Slice the beef and arrange on a heated serving dish with the vegetables. Serve hot.

Serves: 4 • Prep: 20 min • Cooking: 45 min

RUSSIAN BOILED BEEF

This recipe produces a wonderful beef stock. Be sure to reserve it when you take out the meat and vegetables. It can be stored in the refrigerator for up to five days or frozen.

1 tablespoon black peppercorns

2 bay leaves

1 small bunch fresh parsley, finely chopped

1 small bunch fresh dill, finely chopped

12 cups (3 liters) water

1 pound (500 g) beef bones

2 onions, coarsely chopped

3 stalks celery with leaves attached, thinly sliced

2 teaspoons salt

4 pounds (2 kg) boneless beef rump roast

2 pounds (1 kg) carrots, thickly sliced

2 pounds (1 kg) potatoes, well scrubbed

Place the peppercorns, bay leaves, parsley, and dill in a small cloth bag and tie it tightly.

Put the water, beef bones, onions, celery, salt, and the bag containing the herbs in a very large saucepan. Bring to a boil over high heat. Skim off any froth from the surface. Boil for 10 minutes.

Add the beef roast and boil for 3 minutes. Cover and simmer over low heat until the meat is tender, about 3½ hours. Add the carrots and potatoes about 45 minutes before the beef is tender.

Remove the cloth bag. Discard the beef bones, onions, and celery. Slice the beef and arrange on a heated serving platter with the potatoes and carrots. Serve hot.

Serves: 8–10 • Prep: 20 min • Cooking: 4 hr

WELSH CAWL

Cawl is the Welsh word for broth, and this dish contains two very Welsh ingredients—lamb and leeks. It was traditionally made with leftover roasted meat.

3 tablespoons butter or meat drippings

2 onions, thinly sliced

3 leeks, trimmed and thinly sliced

2 large carrots, diced

1 large parsnip, peeled and diced

1 stalk celery, finely chopped

1½ pounds (750 g) lamb or mutton fillet, cut into small chunks

Salt

6–8 cups (1.5–2 liters) hot lamb broth or stock (use beef stock or broth if lamb not available)

1 pound (500 g) new potatoes, thinly sliced

1 medium rutabaga (swede), peeled and diced

1 small turnip, peeled and diced

2 bay leaves

1 sprig fresh thyme

Freshly ground black pepper

1 tablespoon finely chopped fresh mint, to garnish

Melt the butter in a large saucepan over medium heat. Add the onions, leeks, carrots, parsnip, and celery and sauté until softened, about 5 minutes.

Add the lamb and season with ½ teaspoon salt. Cover and cook over low heat for 10 minutes.

Pour in 6 cups (1.5 liters) of the broth. Add the potatoes, rutabaga, turnip, bay leaves, and thyme. Season with salt and pepper. Simmer over low heat until the lamb is tender, about 2 hours. Add more broth if the sauce dries out too much during cooking.

Garnish with the mint and serve hot.

Serves: 4–6 • Prep: 35 min • Cooking: 2 ¼ hr

Pot-au-Feu

- 2 pounds (1 kg) beef tenderloin
- 2 pounds (1 kg) chicken
- 1 pound (500 g) lamb shoulder roast
- 4 ounces (125 g) salt pork
- 4–5 quarts (4–5 liters) water
- 1 cup (250 ml) dry white wine
- 2 cloves
- 2 medium onions
- 4 cloves garlic, finely chopped
- 3 turnips, peeled and halved
- 4 tomatoes, halved
- 1 pound (500 g) whole carrots
- 2 leeks, trimmed
- 1 bouquet garni (see below)
  Salt and freshly ground black pepper
- 6–8 slices firm-textured bread, toasted

Cover the beef, chicken, lamb, and salt pork in a large pot with water. Bring to a boil over medium heat.

Pour in the wine. Press a clove into each onion and add to the pot with the garlic, turnips, tomatoes, carrots, leeks, and the bouquet garni. Season with salt and pepper.

Bring to a boil and skim off any foam. Simmer over low heat until the meat is very tender, 2–3 hours.

Place the toast in individual soup bowls and ladle the stock over the top. Serve the meat and chicken, sliced, and vegetables on a large platter.

Serves: 6–8 • Prep: 25 min • Cooking: 2–3 hr

Poule au Pot

- 1 chicken, weighing about 6 pounds (3 kg)
- 6 quarts (6 liters) water
- 6 onions, peeled
- 1 whole head garlic
- 1 bouquet garni (see below)
  Salt and freshly ground black pepper
- 6 carrots
- 6 leeks, white parts only, trimmed
- 6 turnips, peeled
- 1 cabbage, finely shredded
- 4 pounds (2 kg) potatoes, peeled

Preheat the oven to 350°F (180°C/gas 4). Wrap the garlic and onion in aluminum foil and bake for 45 minutes.

Meanwhile, combine the chicken and water in a large pot over medium heat. Bring to a boil and simmer gently.

Add the baked onion and garlic to the chicken. Simmer for 45–50 minutes over low heat. Add the bouquet garni. Season with salt and pepper.

Simmer for 2 hours. Add the carrots, leeks, turnips, and remaining 3 onions. Simmer for 30 minutes more.

Add the cabbage and potatoes and simmer until tender, about 1 hour.

Remove the chicken from the pot and carve. Serve with the vegetables and stock.

Serves: 6–8 • Prep: 1 hr • Cooking: 5 hr

Bouquet Garni

A bouquet garni is a bunch of fresh herbs tied together with kitchen string or wrapped in cheesecloth (muslin). It is added to a dish during cooking and then removed before serving. There are many possible combinations; for the two dishes on this page; we suggest the following classic combination.

- 4 bay leaves
- 1 small stalk celery
- Small bunch fresh thyme
- Small bunch fresh parsley

Tie the bay leaves, celery, thyme, and parsley together with kitchen string. Alternatively, lay a 12-inch (30-cm) square of cheesecloth (muslin) out on a clean work surface. Place the herbs in the center. Gather the edges of the cheesecloth together and tie securely with kitchen string.

Makes: 1 bouquet garni • Prep: 5 min

BOILED CHICKEN WITH VEGETABLES AND TRUFFLES

Be sure to use black truffles in this innovative Italian recipe. White truffles are not suitable for boiling, but the aroma of black truffles will be exulted by this method of cooking. If it is not truffle season (or they are prohibitively expensive), make this dish without the truffles.

- 8 cups (2 liters) water
- 1 tablespoon coarse sea salt
- 1 ounce (30 g) fresh black truffles
- 1 chicken, weighing about 3 pounds (1.5 kg)

- 3 large carrots, sliced
- 2 medium turnips, peeled and cut into ½-inch (1-cm) cubes
- 2 fennel bulbs, trimmed and cut into ½-inch (1-cm) cubes

Combine the water and sea salt in a large pot over medium heat and bring to a boil.

Clean the truffles by wiping them with a damp cloth. Make sure all the dirt has been removed. Use a sharp knife to slice as thinly as possible.

Use the knife to make incisions in the chicken between the skin and the flesh. Fill these incisions with slices of truffle.

Place the chicken in the boiling water. Partially cover the pan and adjust the heat so that the chicken is gently simmering. Cook for 40 minutes.

Add the carrots, turnips, and fennel and cook until the chicken and vegetables are tender, about 20 minutes more.

Drain the chicken and vegetables, reserving the stock. Cut the chicken into 6–8 pieces and place on a heated serving platter. Spoon the vegetables around it.

Pour about 1 cup (250 ml) of the reserved stock over the chicken and vegetables and serve at once.

Serves 4–6 • Prep: 25 min • Cooking: 1 hr

KIELBASA AND CABBAGE

- 2 heads cabbage
- 2 rings kielbasa or Polish sausage, cut into 3-inch (8-cm) lengths, about 2 pounds (1 kg)
- 6 medium potatoes, peeled and cut into quarters

- 2 teaspoons caraway seeds
- 4 cups (1 liter) water
  Salt and freshly ground black pepper

Cut the cabbage into wedges, discarding the outer leaves and core.

Put the kielbasa and potatoes in a large saucepan. Sprinkle with the caraway seeds. Top with the cabbage and pour in the water.

Bring to a boil and cook over medium heat until the cabbage and potatoes are tender, about 20 minutes.

Season with salt and pepper. Drain and serve straight from the pot.

Serves: 6–8 • Prep: 15 min • Cooking: 30 min

MUSHROOM AND APPLE SAUCE

If you have the time, do try the Boiled Chicken with Vegetables and Truffles recipe (above) with this delicious sauce; it makes for a superb taste combination. The sauce is also good with boiled meats and roast pork.

- 2 tablespoons extra-virgin olive oil
- 8 ounces (250 g) white button mushrooms, sliced
- 1 cooking apple, cored and sliced

- 1 tablespoon finely chopped fresh marjoram or thyme
  Salt

Heat the oil in a medium frying pan over medium heat. Add the mushrooms, apple, and marjoram and sauté until the mushrooms are tender, about 10 minutes. Season with salt.

Makes: about 1 cup (250 ml) • Prep: 5 min • Cooking: 10 min

SHRIMP BOIL WITH SPICY BUTTER

Re-create the taste of New Orleans and the Gulf Coast, where shrimp boils are served in late summer when shrimp are large and plentiful.

5 quarts (5 liters) water

2 lemons, cut in half

2 tablespoons coarse sea salt

4 garlic cloves, smashed with the flat side of a large knife blade

2 medium onions, halved
  Spice bundle (see below)

3½ pounds (1.75 kg) medium new potatoes, scrubbed

6–8 large carrots, cut into 2–3 pieces

6–8 ears fresh corn (sweet corn), shucked and broken in half

3½ pounds (1.75 kg) large shrimp (king prawns), with shell and tail on

Spicy Butter

1 cup (250 g) butter

1–2 teaspoons crushed red pepper flakes

2–4 cloves garlic, minced

Bring the water to a boil in a large kettle or pot.

Squeeze the lemon juice into water, then add the squeezed halves. Add the salt, garlic, onions, and spice bundle. Reduce the heat to a simmer, cover the pot, and cook for 10 minutes.

Add the potatoes and carrots to the pot. Cover the pot and return to a boil. Decrease the heat and simmer until the potatoes and carrots are almost tender, 15–20 minutes.

Add the corn and simmer for 5 minutes more.

Add the shrimp and boil until they are pink and tender, 3–5 minutes, depending on their size. Be careful not to overcook the shrimp because they will become tough and difficult to peel. They are ready when the shell begins to separate from the flesh along the back.

Drain the shrimp and vegetables, reserving 2 cups (500 ml) of the broth. Ladle this into 6 small bowls for dipping.

Arrange the shrimp and vegetables on a heated platter.

Spicy Butter: Soften the butter over very low heat. Transfer to a small bowl and stir in the red pepper flakes and garlic.

Whip with a fork until smooth and well blended. Place the butter in 6 small dishes, for smearing over the corn.

Serves: 6–8 • Prep: 40 min • Cooking: 40 min

SPICE BUNDLE

There are many crab or shrimp boil spice packs available commercially, but for added authenticity and flavor we suggest you prepare your own spice bundle following the instructions given here.

1 tablespoon crumbled dried bay leaves

8 whole allspice berries

3 tablespoons coriander seeds

1 tablespoon mustard seeds

1 tablespoon dill seeds

4–6 small dried hot chiles

Lay a 12-inch (30-cm) square of cheesecloth (muslin) out on a clean work surface. Spoon the spices into the center. Use a rolling pin to crush the seeds, releasing their aromas. Gather the edges of the cheesecloth together and tie securely with kitchen string.

Makes: about ½ cup • Prep: 5 min

Vegetables with Rice and Cumin

- 3 cups (600 g) short-grain rice
- 2 cups (300 g) fresh or frozen peas
- 4 firm-ripe tomatoes, coarsely chopped
- 2 carrots, coarsely chopped
- 3 zucchini (courgettes), coarsely chopped
- 2 large onions, finely chopped
- 2 cloves garlic, finely chopped
- 6 cups (1.5 liters) water
  Salt and freshly ground black pepper
- 4–6 threads saffron, crumbled
- 2 tablespoons finely chopped fresh parsley
- 1 teaspoon cumin
- 1 cup (250 ml) plain yogurt

Combine the rice, peas, tomatoes, carrots, zucchini, onions, and garlic in a large saucepan. Add the water, salt, pepper, and saffron. Bring to a boil, then lower the heat, cover, and cook until the water has been completely absorbed, 15–20 minutes.

Spoon the rice and vegetables onto a serving dish. Garnish with the parsley and cumin seeds. Spoon about half of the yogurt over the top. Serve hot, with the remaining yogurt passed on the side.

Serves: 6–8 • Prep: 15 min • Cooking: 20 min

Spinach and Cheese Gnocchi

- 1 tablespoon coarse sea salt
- 1½ pounds (750 g) frozen spinach, thawed
- 1 cup (200 g) ricotta cheese, well drained
- 1 large egg and 1 large yolk
- 1 cup (125 g) freshly grated Parmesan cheese + extra, to serve
- Pinch of nutmeg
  Salt and freshly ground black pepper
- ½ cup (125 g) salted butter
- 10 sage leaves, torn

Bring a large pot of water to a boil with the coarse salt. Cook the spinach until tender, 5–7 minutes. Drain, reserving the cooking water.

Let the spinach cool and chop finely. Return the cooking water to the pot and bring to a boil.

Place the spinach in a large bowl with the ricotta, egg, egg yolk, Parmesan, nutmeg, salt, and pepper. Mold the mixture into gnocchi about the size of golf balls.

Cook the gnocchi in the boiling water in batches of 6–8 until they bob up to the surface, 2–3 minutes.

Scoop out with a slotted spoon and place in a heated serving dish. Repeat until all the gnocchi are cooked.

Place the butter and sage in a small saucepan and place over the boiling water until melted. Drizzle the butter and sage over the gnocchi. Sprinkle with the extra Parmesan and serve hot.

Serves: 4 • Prep: 25 min • Cooking: 20 min

Finger-Licking Pepperpot

Cassareep is a favorite ingredient in Caribbean cuisine. It is a mixture of juices from the cassava plant, brown sugar, and spices. Track it down at Caribbean markets and ethnic food stores. If you can't find pig's feet, replace with the same weight of ham hock.

- 2 chickens, each weighing 2 pounds (1 kg), cut into 8 pieces
- 1 pig's foot (trotter)
- 8 cups (2 liters) water, + extra, as needed
- 2 teaspoons salt
- 3 pounds (1.5 kg) pork loin, cut into bite-size chunks
- ½ cup (125 ml) cassareep
- 1 large onion, finely chopped
- 2 tablespoons dark brown sugar
- 2 red fresh chiles, seeded and finely chopped
- 1 (2-inch/5-cm) stick cinnamon
- 4 cloves
- 1 tablespoon red wine vinegar

Place the chicken pieces, pig's foot, water, and salt in a large saucepan. Bring to a boil and skim off the foam. Partially cover and simmer over low heat for 1 hour. Skim off the foam and fat that gathers on the surface.

Add the pork loin, cassareep, onion, brown sugar, chiles, cinnamon stick, and cloves. Return to a boil and simmer until the pork is tender, about 1 hour.

Discard the cloves and cinnamon. Stir in the vinegar and serve hot.

Serves: 6–8 • Prep: 20 min • Cooking: 2 hr

Vegetables with Rice and Cumin

CREAMY GORGONZOLA CHEESE POLENTA

10 cups (2.5 liters) cold water
2 tablespoons coarse sea salt
3½ cups (500 g) polenta (stone-ground cornmeal)
¼ cup (60 g) butter, chopped

12 ounces (350 g) Gorgonzola cheese, chopped
¼ cup (60 ml) heavy (double) cream

Bring the water and salt to a boil in a large saucepan over medium heat. Gradually stir in the cornmeal. Cook, stirring constantly with a long-handled wooden spoon, until the polenta is cooked, about 45 minutes.

Stir in the butter, half the Gorgonzola, and the cream. The polenta should be soft and creamy. Pour it into individual soup plates, and sprinkle with the remaining Gorgonzola. Serve hot.

Serves: 4–6 • Prep: 10 min • Cooking: 50 min

BUCKWHEAT POLENTA WITH CHEESE

7 cups (1.75 liters) water
1 tablespoon coarse sea salt
3 cups (450 g) buckwheat flour
1 cup (250 g) butter

8 ounces (250 g) Fontina, Asiago, or Fontal cheese (or a mixture of the three), cut in slivers

Bring the water and salt to a boil in a large pan. Gradually sift in the buckwheat flour, stirring constantly with a wooden spoon. Add half the butter.

Cook, stirring frequently, until the polenta is cooked, about 40 minutes. The polenta will be rather soft.

Add the cheese and continue stirring over low heat. Add the remaining butter. Stir until the polenta is smooth and creamy, 5–8 minutes. Serve hot.

Serves: 4–6 • Prep: 15 min • Cooking: 50 min

POLENTA AND BEANS

2 tablespoons extra-virgin olive oil
½ cup (60 g) diced pancetta
½ onion, finely chopped
1⅓ cups (250 g) dried cranberry, borlotti, or pinto beans, soaked overnight and drained
1 tablespoon finely chopped fresh sage or rosemary

About 8 cups (2 liters) cold water
2½ cups (375 g) polenta (stone-ground cornmeal)
Salt
Warm water, as needed

Heat the oil in a large saucepan over medium heat. Add the pancetta and onion and sauté until softened, about 5 minutes. Add the beans, sage, and sufficient cold water to cover the beans. Bring to a boil, cover, and simmer until the beans are almost tender, 1 hour.

Gradually stir in the polenta. Season with salt. Cook for 45 minutes, stirring continuously with a long-handled wooden spoon, and adding warm water if necessary. Turn out onto a platter and serve.

Serves: 4 • Prep: 20 min + 12 hr to soak beans • Cooking: 2 hr

EASY BASIC POLENTA

Here is a simple method of preparing polenta. Normally the cornmeal and water should be stirred constantly over low heat until cooked, which usually takes about 50 minutes. You will need a 6-quart (6-liter) pot and a large metal bowl that fits into the top of the pot.

1½ cups (250 g) polenta (stone-ground cornmeal)
1½ quarts (1.5 liters) boiling water
1 teaspoon salt

2 tablespoons butter
½ cup (60 g) finely grated Parmesan cheese
Freshly ground black pepper

Fill the bottom of a 6-quart (6 liter) pot with water; cover with a metal bowl, making sure it does not touch the water. Bring to a boil. Place the boiling water and salt in the metal bowl. Gradually add the polenta, stirring for 1–2 minutes. Cover the bowl with foil. Simmer over low heat for 1½ hours. Stir every 30 minutes to make sure the polenta is not sticking. Stir in the butter, Parmesan, and black pepper.

Serves: 4–6 • Prep: 20 min • Cooking: 1½ hr

Pork and Polenta Casserole

*This hearty winter dish comes from Piedmont, in northwestern Italy.
We suggest you use a precooked polenta that only requires about 10 minutes
of constant stirring.*

- 1 pound (500 g) pork loin, cut into 1-inch (2.5-cm) cubes
- 1 pound (500 g) savoy cabbage, cut into thin strips
- 1 small onion, thickly sliced
- 1 large carrot, sliced
- 1 stalk celery, sliced
- 1 teaspoon salt

- 6 cups (1.5 liters) boiling water + more, as needed
- 1½ cups (250 g) precooked polenta (stone-ground cornmeal)
- ¼ cup (60 g) butter, cut into small pieces
- 4 tablespoons freshly grated Parmesan cheese

Place the pork in a large saucepan with the cabbage, onion, carrot, and celery. Add the salt and ½ cup (125 ml) of boiling water. Cover and bring quickly to a boil. Decrease the heat to medium and simmer for 30 minutes.

Uncover the pan and pour in the remaining 5½ cups (1.37 liters) of boiling water. Add the cornmeal, stirring continuously with a large wooden spoon to prevent lumps forming. Continue cooking over medium heat, stirring until the polenta is ready, 8–10 minutes (or according to the instructions on the package).

Add extra boiling water as needed to keep the polenta soft. Stir in the butter and Parmesan. Serve hot.

Serves: 4 • Prep: 15 min • Cooking: 1 hr

Barbadian Okra and Cornmeal Mix

- 12 okra pods, trimmed and sliced
- 6 cups (1.5 liters) water
- 1 teaspoon salt
- 1 tablespoon hot pepper sauce

- 2 cups (300 g) polenta (stone-ground cornmeal)
- 2 tablespoons butter

Place the okra in a large saucepan with 3 cups (750 ml) of the water. Season with salt and stir in the pepper sauce. Bring to a boil and simmer for 10 minutes.

Remove the pan from the heat. Pour in the remaining 3 cups (750 ml) water and add the polenta, stirring constantly to prevent any lumps from forming. Return the pan to the heat and cook over medium heat, stirring constantly, until the mixture becomes stiff and smooth and comes away from the sides of the pan, 45 minutes.

Dot with the butter and serve hot.

Serves: 6 • Prep: 10 min • Cooking: 55 min

Polenta with Fontina and Parmesan Cheeses

- 5 cups (1.25 liters) boiling water
- 5 cups (1.25 liters) hot milk
- 1 tablespoon coarse sea salt
- 2 cups (300 g) polenta (stone-ground cornmeal)
- 14 ounces (400 g) Fontina cheese, cut in slivers

- Freshly ground black pepper
- ½ cup (75 g) freshly grated Parmesan cheese
- ⅓ cup (90 g) butter, cut in small pieces

Bring the water, milk, and salt to a boil in a large saucepan. Gradually add the polenta, stirring constantly with a long-handled wooden spoon to prevent lumps from forming.

After the polenta has been cooking for about 30 minutes, add the Fontina and cook for 15 minutes more, stirring energetically.

Pour the polenta into a large serving dish, dust with pepper, and sprinkle with the Parmesan. Dot with the butter and serve hot.

Serves: 4–6 • Prep: 15 min • Cooking: 50 min

Pork and Polenta Casserole

OVEN POT

CASEROLES, DUTCH OVENS, GRATINS,
AND ROASTS

A host of nourishing one-pot meals can be baked in the oven. We have included a broad range of dishes, from traditional meat-and-vegetable casseroles such as Lancashire Hotpot, Shepherd's Pie, and Cassoulet, to meatloafs, pilafs, baked frittatas, and sausage, vegetable, and pasta bakes. These dishes make great family meals and delicious food for informal dinner parties. For special occasions, try the Baked Sea Bass and Vegetables.

WINTER CASSEROLE

- 2 tablespoons all-purpose (plain) flour
  Salt and freshly ground black pepper
- 2 pound (1kg) chuck steak, cut into 1-inch (2.5 cm) pieces
- 2 onions, coarsely chopped
- 6 cloves garlic, crushed
- 2 carrots, chopped
- 2 stalks celery, chopped
- 10 ounces (300 g) mushrooms, halved if large
- 4 large potatoes, peeled and chopped
- 1 head broccoli, broken into florets
- 2 tablespoons finely chopped fresh thyme
- 2 tablespoons extra-virgin olive oil
- 2 tablespoons tomato paste
- 12 ounces (350 ml) dark beer
- ½ cup (125 ml) beef broth or stock (see page 28)

Preheat the oven to 350 °F (180°C/gas 4).

Put the flour in a shallow bowl and season with the salt and pepper. Roll the meat in the flour until well coated.

Place the meat in a large casserole dish. Place all the chopped vegetables over the meat. Sprinkle with the thyme.

Mix together the oil, tomato paste, beer, and broth in a medium bowl. Season with salt and pepper and pour over the meat and vegetables.

Cover and bake until the meat is very tender, 1½–2 hours. Serve hot.

Serves: 4–6 • Prep: 25 min • Cooking: 1½–2 hr

SWEET AND NUTTY VEAL CASSEROLE

This unusual casserole is fairly hearty served on its own. If desired (or to stretch the number of servings to eight), serve over cooked brown rice.

- 2 tablespoons butter
- 2 pounds (1 kg) veal, cut into small cubes
- 2 large potatoes, peeled and cut into small cubes
- 2 large carrots, finely diced
- 1 large Granny Smith apple, peeled and diced
- 1 large onion, chopped
- 4 cloves garlic, finely chopped
- 1 tablespoon curry powder
- ½ teaspoon cumin seeds
- ¾ cup (100 g) slivered almonds
- ½ cup (75 g) unsweetened shredded (desiccated) coconut
- 6 tablespoons light corn syrup
- 1 (14-ounce/400-g) can onion soup
  Freshly cooked brown rice, to serve (optional)

Preheat the oven to 325°F (160°C/gas 3).

Put the butter in a Dutch oven or casserole dish. Add the veal and cover with the potatoes, carrots, apple, onion, garlic, curry powder, cumin, almonds, and coconut. Drizzle with the corn syrup. Pour the onion soup over the top.

Cover the casserole and bake for 2 hours. Stir carefully and bake until the meat and vegetables are very tender, about 1 hour more. Serve hot.

Serves: 4–6 • Prep: 25 min • Cooking: 3 hr

MEATLOAF WITH MIXED VEGETABLES

This is a great one-pot dish that can be served hot or at room temperature. It makes a terrific lunch dish on busy days that the whole family can enjoy even if they are eating on the go or at different times.

- ¾ cup (180 ml) canned sweetened condensed milk
- 4 threads saffron, dissolved in 3 tablespoons boiling milk
- 6 slices thickly sliced white sandwich (toast) bread, cut into small dice
- ½ onion, finely chopped
- 2 pounds (1 kg) lean ground (minced) lamb
- 2 tablespoons ketchup
- 1 teaspoon salt
- ½ teaspoon freshly ground black pepper
- ½ teaspoon ground chile
- 2 large eggs, lightly beaten
- 1 teaspoon mixed Italian herbs
- 1 teaspoon dry mustard powder
- 2 cups (300 g) frozen mixed vegetables

Preheat the oven to 350°F (180°C/gas 4). Butter a 9 x 5-inch (23 x 12-cm) loaf pan.

Pour the condensed milk and saffron milk over the bread. Let soak until the bread has absorbed all the milk. Stir in the onion, lamb, ketchup, salt, pepper, chile, eggs, mixed herbs, and mustard powder. Add the vegetables.

Spoon the mixture into the prepared loaf pan. Cover with aluminum foil. Bake for 1¼ hours. Remove the foil and bake until browned on top, about 15 minutes.

Let cool in the pan for 10 minutes until firm and slightly cooled. Slice and serve.

Serves: 4 • Prep: 10 min • Cooking: 1½ hr

LANCASHIRE HOTPOT

This dish comes from the county of Lancashire, in northwest England. The main ingredients are lamb or mutton (sometimes also kidney, black pudding, or oysters) and potatoes, with a top layer of overlapping potato slices. The traditional tall, round cooking dish is made of earthenware with a lid. It needed to be tall to fit the long bones, but modern cooks prefer the meat as cutlets or off the bone.

1½ tablespoons all-purpose (plain) flour
2 teaspoons salt
Freshly ground white pepper
2 pounds (1 kg) lamb shoulder or neck, cut into small chunks
4 tablespoons butter

4 medium onions, thinly sliced
3 large baking (floury) potatoes, peeled and very thinly sliced
1 sprig thyme
⅔ cup (150 ml) hot chicken broth or stock (see page 56) or water
Pickled red cabbage, to serve

Use a flameproof casserole dish or Dutch oven. If you want to cook the dish in a traditional earthenware pot, do not sauté the onions—just add them raw.

Preheat the oven to 300°F (150°C/gas 2).

Mix the flour with the salt and pepper in a medium bowl, add the meat, and toss to coat.

Melt 1 tablespoon of the butter in the casserole dish over medium heat. Add the onions and 1 teaspoon of the salt. Sauté for 4 minutes without letting them color. Remove from the pan and set aside.

Arrange the lamb in the casserole dish and add the thyme. Spread the onions over the meat. Layer the potatoes on top of the onions, overlapping each slice with the next one. Dot with the remaining 3 tablespoons of butter. Pour in the broth. Cover and bake for 2 hours.

Remove the lid, increase the temperature to 350°F (180°C/gas 4), and bake for 30–45 minutes more, or until the potatoes are golden brown.

Serve hot with pickled red cabbage.

Serves: 4–6 • Prep: 40 min • Cooking: 3 hr

DUBLIN STEW

3 pounds (1.5 kg) boneless lamb shoulder, cut into small chunks
Salt and freshly ground black pepper
¼ cup (60 g) butter

3 onions, finely thinly sliced
1 pound (500 g) baby new potatoes
2 bay leaves
1½ cups (375 ml) chicken broth or stock (see page 56)

Preheat the oven to 350°F (180°C/gas 4).

Season the lamb generously with salt and pepper. Melt the butter in a large Dutch oven or flameproof casserole over medium heat. Add the lamb and sauté until browned all over, 7–8 minutes. Remove the lamb from the pan and set aside.

Sauté the onions in the same pan over medium heat until softened, about 5 minutes.

Add the lamb, potatoes, and bay leaves. Season with more salt and pepper. Pour in the broth and bring to a boil. Cover and bake until the lamb and potatoes are tender, 45–50 minutes. Discard the bay leaves. Serve hot.

Serves: 4–6 • Prep: 20 min • Cooking: 1 hr

LAMB AND POTATO CASSEROLE

- 2 pounds (1 kg) lamb (from the shoulder), cut into bite-size pieces
- 2 pounds (1 kg) yellow, waxy potatoes, thickly sliced or cut into wedges
- 4 large tomatoes, quartered or cut into 6 pieces
- 1 medium onion, sliced
- ¼ cup (60 ml) extra-virgin olive oil
  Salt and freshly ground black pepper
  Leaves from a small sprig of rosemary
- 1 teaspoon dried oregano
- 1 cup (250 ml) boiling water

Preheat the oven to 400°F (200°C/gas 6).

Combine the lamb, potatoes, tomatoes, and onion in an ovenproof casserole. Drizzle with the oil and season with a little salt and plenty of pepper. Sprinkle with the rosemary and oregano.

Cover and bake until the meat is tender, about 1 hour. Baste at frequent intervals with a little boiling water. Serve hot.

Serves: 4 • Prep: 15 min • Cooking: 1 hr

SHEPHERD'S PIE

Traditionally, shepherd's pie is made with leftovers from a joint of lamb while cottage pie is made with leftovers from beef. Both became popular in the 1870s with the introduction of grinding machines. Because most people do not cook large roasts anymore, the filling today is made by slowly cooking ground meat. There is no need to worry about exact quantities or ingredients, just use what you have on hand—canned tomatoes, vegetable soup, and wine can be included.

- 2 tablespoons extra-virgin olive oil
- 1 onion, finely chopped
- 1 leek, trimmed and finely chopped
- 1–2 tablespoons butter
- 1 clove garlic, finely chopped
- 1 medium carrot, finely chopped
- 1 stalk celery, finely chopped
- 4 brown button mushrooms, thinly sliced
- 1 pound (500 g) ground (minced) lamb
- 1 tablespoon all-purpose (plain) flour
- 1 tablespoon tomato paste (concentrate)
- 1 tablespoon Worcestershire sauce
- 1 cup (250 ml) vegetable broth or stock (see page 112)
- 1 bay leaf
- 1 teaspoon finely chopped fresh thyme
  Salt and freshly ground black pepper
- 2 pounds (1 kg) potatoes, boiled and mashed with milk and butter

Heat the oil in a large frying pan over medium heat. Add the onion and leek and sauté until soft and golden, 7–8 minutes.

Add 1 tablespoon of the butter if the oil does not cover the bottom of the pan. Stir in the garlic, carrot, and celery and sauté for 5 minutes.

Add the remaining tablespoon of butter and the mushrooms. Cook for 4 minutes.

Add the meat, stirring it into the mixture. Cook over high heat until the meat browns, about 5 minutes. Stir with a wooden spatula to break up any clumps. Sprinkle with flour and mix in the tomato paste and Worcestershire sauce. Cook for 3 minutes, stirring constantly.

Pour in the broth. Add the bay leaf and thyme and bring to a boil. Cover and simmer over low heat for 15 minutes.

Cook, uncovered, until the sauce thickens, 10–15 minutes. Season with salt and plenty of pepper.

Preheat the oven to 375°F (190°C/gas 5).

Transfer the filling to a casserole or large deep baking dish and top with the mashed potatoes. Bake for 20 minutes, or until golden. Serve hot.

Serves: 4 • Prep: 20 min • Cooking: 1 ¼ hr

FRENCH BEEF DAUBE

¼ cup (60 ml) extra-virgin olive oil

8 ounces (200 g) bacon or lardons, coarsely chopped

2 pounds (1 kg) stew beef, cut into bite-size pieces

Salt and freshly ground black pepper

2 onions, thinly sliced

7 cloves garlic, finely chopped

2½ cups (625 ml) dry red wine

¾ cup/180 ml beef broth or stock (see page 28)

4 carrots, thinly sliced

1 (14-ounce/400-g) can tomatoes, chopped, with juice

3 salt-cured anchovies, rinsed and finely chopped

1 bouquet garni (celery, bay leaves, thyme, and parsley; see page 168)

1 tablespoon butter, melted

1 tablespoon all-purpose (plain) flour

1 cup (100 g) black olives, pitted

Preheat the oven to 300°F (150°C/gas 2).

Heat 2 tablespoons of oil in a large Dutch oven or flameproof casserole dish over medium heat. Add the beef and lardons and brown, about 10 minutes. Season generously with salt and pepper. Remove from the pan and set aside.

Heat the remaining 2 tablespoons of oil over medium heat. Add the onions and garlic and sauté until pale gold, about 7 minutes.

Pour in the wine and simmer over high heat until the liquid has reduced by half.

Add the broth, beef, bacon, carrots, tomatoes, anchovies, and bouquet garni. Mix well. Cover and bake until the beef and vegetables are very tender, about 2 hours.

Remove from the oven and discard the bouquet garni. Combine the butter and flour in a small bowl and mix until smooth. Stir into the casserole. Stir in the olives. Serve hot.

Serves: 4–6 • Prep: 20 min • Cooking: 2 ½ hr

BEEF AND VEGETABLE CASSEROLE WITH ORANGE

4 tablespoons extra-virgin olive oil

5 ounces (150 g) salt pork or bacon, diced

3 pounds (1.5 kg) chuck steak, cut into chunks

5 medium onions, finely chopped

2 cups (500 ml) dry white wine

4 cups (1 liter) water

2 stalks celery, diced

2 bay leaves

2 large carrots, thinly sliced

2 large potatoes, peeled and diced

Salt and freshly ground black pepper

1 tablespoon finely chopped fresh thyme

20 pitted black olives

20 green pitted olives

4 firm-ripe tomatoes, peeled, seeded, and finely chopped

6 garlic cloves, finely chopped

Grated zest of 1 small orange

Preheat the oven to 325°F (170°C/gas 3).

Heat the oil in a Dutch oven over medium heat. Sauté the salt pork until lightly browned, about 5 minutes.

Add the chuck steak and sauté until browned, 7–9 minutes.

Stir in the onions and cook for 10 minutes more.

Pour in one-third of the wine and cook until it has evaporated. Repeat twice until all the wine has been added.

Pour in the water, celery, bay leaves, carrots, and potatoes. Season with salt and pepper. Bring to a boil and simmer, covered, for 5 minutes. Add the thyme, olives, tomatoes, garlic, and orange zest. Cover and bake until the meat is very tender, about 3 hours.

Remove the bay leaves and serve hot.

Serves: 6–8 • Prep: 30 min • Cooking: 3½ hr

COUNTRY CASSOULET

A modern adaptation of the famous French dish from the southern Languedoc region.

2 tablespoons sunflower oil

2 large onions, finely chopped

¾ cup (90 g) diced bacon or lardons

2 pounds (1 kg) pork shoulder, boned, skinned, and cut into ¾-inch (2-cm) pieces

Salt and freshly ground black pepper

8 ounces (250 g) garlic sausage, in a coil and sliced into large chunks

2 cloves garlic, finely sliced

2 cups (500 g) canned chopped tomatoes

1 teaspoon tomato paste (concentrate)

2 cups (200 g) canned butter or lima beans, rinsed and drained

4 cups (1 liter) chicken broth or stock + more as needed (see page 56)

1 bouquet garni (see page 168) or sprigs of thyme, rosemary, parsley, and bay leaf, tied together

1 tablespoon coarsely chopped fresh flat-leaf parsley

1¾ cups (100 g) fresh bread crumbs

Preheat the oven to 325°F (170°C/gas 3).

Heat the oil in a large Dutch oven or flameproof casserole over medium heat. Add the onions and bacon and sauté until the onions are softened, about 5 minutes.

Add the pork. Sauté until browned all over, 7–9 minutes.

Season generously with salt and pepper. Stir in the sausage, garlic, tomatoes, tomato paste, beans, and broth. Bring to a boil. Add the bouquet garni. Cover and bake for about 1½ hours, stirring occasionally and adding more broth if the liquid level fails to come halfway up the sides of the dish.

When the meat is tender, remove from the oven, add the parsley, and season with salt and pepper. Sprinkle with the bread crumbs, pressing them down with the back of the spoon. Return to the oven, uncovered, for 30–40 minutes more, or until crispy on top. Serve hot.

Serves: 4–6 • Prep: 20 min • Cooking: 2 ¾ hr

ONIONS

Onions have been grown since the dawn of history, as Mesopotamian and Egyptian wall paintings and records show. Over the millennia, many different types of onions have been bred, from sweet red Spanish onions (great for salads), to strong-flavored, large yellow and white onions, to shallots, pickling onions, and scallions. Such is the popularity of this vegetable that new varieties are being developed all the time. From a nutritional point of view, onions contain a range of sulfide compounds that are believed to help prevent atherosclerosis (hardening of the arteries), lower blood pressure, and lengthen blood-clotting time—all contributing to cardiovascular health. They are also thought to suppress the growth of cancer-causing bacteria in the colon, as well as preventing and slowing tumor growth elsewhere in the body. They also taste good!

Spicy Baked Peanut Lamb

4 tablespoons extra-virgin olive oil

3 pounds (1.5 kg) boneless lamb, cut into bite-size pieces

Salt and freshly ground black pepper

1 large onion, finely chopped

2 cloves garlic, finely chopped

2 tablespoon finely chopped fresh parsley

1–2 fresh red chiles, sliced

3 large tomatoes, chopped

1 cup (150 g) frozen peas

1 cup (250 g) smooth peanut butter

1 tablespoon white wine vinegar

1 tablespoon light brown sugar

2 cups (500 ml) chicken broth or stock (see page 56)

Water (optional)

Freshly cooked long-grain rice, to serve (optional)

Preheat the oven to 350°F (180°C/gas 4).

Heat the oil in a large Dutch oven over medium-high heat. Add the lamb and sauté until browned, 6–8 minutes. Remove the lamb and set aside.

Add the onion, garlic, parsley, chiles, tomatoes, and peas to the pan and sauté for 10 minutes.

Add the peanut butter, vinegar, brown sugar, and broth to the pan and stir over medium heat until the sauce is smooth. Return the lamb to the pan and stir until well coated.

Cover and bake until the lamb is very tender, about $1^1/_2$ hours. Check the pan during baking to make sure the sauce has not dried out too much. Add a few tablespoons of water if it is too dry.

Serve hot, over cooked rice, if desired.

Serves: 6 • Prep: 30 min • Cooking: 2 hr

Baked Lamb and Spinach Frittata

6 tablespoons extra-virgin olive oil

2 pounds (1 kg) fresh spinach, tough stems discarded, leaves shredded

Salt and freshly ground black pepper

1 teaspoon ground cinnamon

12 ounces (300 g) boneless lamb, cut into small cubes

1 large onion, finely chopped

1 cup (100 g) cooked cannellini (white kidney) beans or garbanzo beans (chickpeas)

$1^1/_2$ cups (375 ml) water

4–6 threads saffron, crumbled

$1^1/_4$ cups (150 g) freshly grated Parmesan cheese

$^1/_2$ cup (50 g) coarsely grated day-old bread

6 large eggs, lightly beaten

Preheat the oven to 350°F (180°C/gas 4).

Heat 3 tablespoons of the oil in a large ovenproof baking pan or Dutch oven over high heat.

Add the spinach and sprinkle with the salt, pepper, and cinnamon. Sauté for 10 minutes. Remove from the pan and set aside.

Heat the remaining 3 tablespoons of oil in the same pan over medium heat. Add the lamb and onion and sauté until lightly browned, about 10 minutes.

Add the beans and spinach and pour in the water. Season with salt and pepper and sprinkle with the saffron.

Simmer over medium-low heat until the sauce has reduced by half, about 20 minutes.

Mix in the cheese, bread, eggs, and season with more salt. Bake until set and lightly browned, about 20 minutes. Serve hot.

Serves: 4 • Prep: 15 min • Cooking: 1 hr

Baked Lamb and Spinach Frittata

ROAST PORK SHANKS WITH VEGETABLES

- 3 pounds (1.5 kg) pork shanks
- ½ cup (75 g) all-purpose (plain) flour
  Salt and freshly ground black pepper
- ⅓ cup (90 ml) extra-virgin olive oil
- ¾ cup (180 ml) dry white wine
- 1–2 cups (500 ml) beef broth or stock (see page 28)

- 4 large carrots, sliced
- 6 stalks celery, coarsely chopped
- 4 medium onions, coarsely chopped
- 4 large potatoes, peeled and diced
- 4 medium zucchini (courgettes), diced

Preheat the oven to 400°F (200°C/gas 6). Roll the shanks in the flour and season with salt and pepper.

Heat ¼ cup (60 ml) of the oil in a Dutch oven or flameproof casserole over medium heat. Add the shanks and sauté over high heat until browned, about 10 minutes.

Transfer to the oven and bake for 20 minutes.

Add the wine and cook for 40 minutes more, adding a little broth if the pan becomes too dry.

When the shanks have been in the oven for about 1 hour, add the carrots, celery, onions, potatoes, and zucchini. Drizzle with the remaining oil.

Bake until tender, about 1 hour. Arrange the meat and vegetables on a heated serving dish and serve hot.

Serves: 4–6 • Prep: 30 min • Cooking: 2 ¼ hr

BACON AND CORN BAKE

- 1 pound (500 g) fairly lean bacon, cut into small strips
- 1 large white onion, chopped
- 2 cloves garlic, finely chopped
- 2 tablespoons finely chopped fresh parsley
- 1 green bell pepper (capsicum), seeded and diced

- 2 (14-ounce/400-g) cans creamed corn (sweet corn)
- 2 cups (300 g) fine dry bread crumbs
- 1 cup (120 g) freshly grated Parmesan cheese
  Freshly ground black pepper (optional)

Preheat the oven to 350°F (180°C/gas 4).

Sauté the bacon in a Dutch oven or flameproof casserole over medium-high heat until lightly browned, about 5 minutes. Remove the bacon.

Add the onion, garlic, parsley, and bell pepper and sauté until softened, 6–8 minutes.

Stir in the corn. Remove from the heat and sprinkle with the bread crumbs followed by the cheese. Top with a generous grinding of black pepper, if desired.

Bake until the dish is heated through and the cheese is bubbling on the top, about 25 minutes. Serve hot.

Serves: 4–6 • Prep: 20 min • Cooking: 40 min

VENISON CASSEROLE

- 2 tablespoons extra-virgin olive oil
- 1¾ pounds (750 g) venison, cut into small chunks
- ¾ cup (90 g) diced pancetta
- 1 clove garlic, finely chopped
- 2 red onions, finely chopped
- 2 large carrots, finely chopped
- 2 firm-ripe tomatoes, coarsely chopped

- ½ cup (125 ml) dry red wine
- 1 cup (250 ml) water + more as needed
- 1 sprig fresh rosemary
- 1 bay leaf
- 10 ounces (300 g) canned chestnuts
  Freshly cooked polenta, to serve (see page 176)

Preheat the oven to 300°F (150°C/gas 2).

Heat the oil in a Dutch oven or flameproof casserole over medium-high heat. Working in small batches, add the venison with the pancetta and sauté until browned, 5–8 minutes for each batch.

Return all the browned meat to the pan and add the garlic, onions, carrots, and tomatoes. Pour in the wine and water. Bring to a boil.

Add the rosemary and bay leaf. Cover and bake for 1 hour. Stir in the chestnuts. Bake, adding more water if the sauce starts to dry out, for 1 hour more, or until the venison is very tender. Serve hot over the polenta.

Serves: 4–6 • Prep: 15 min • Cooking: 2 ¼ hr

ROAST PORK AND VEGETABLES WITH GARLIC AND ROSEMARY

1 bone-in pork loin roast, about 5 pounds (2.5 kg)

4 cloves garlic, thinly sliced
  Salt and coarsely ground black pepper

2 tablespoons fresh or dried rosemary leaves

4–6 sweet potatoes, about 2 pounds (1 kg), peeled and cut into chunks

1 small rutabaga (swede), about 1 pound (500 g), peeled and chopped

2–4 parsnips, about 1 pound (500 g), peeled and sliced

2–4 carrots, about 1 pound (500 g), sliced

4 tablespoons extra-virgin olive oil
  Freshly ground black pepper

1 tablespoon cornstarch (cornflour)
  Cold water

1½ cups (375 ml) boiling water

Preheat the oven to 350°F (180°C/gas 4).

Cut about a dozen ½-inch (1-cm)-deep slits in the pork and insert a slice or two of garlic into each. Mix 1 teaspoon salt, ½ teaspoon pepper, and rosemary leaves in a small bowl and rub all over the pork.

Place the pork roast, fat side up, in a large roasting pan.

Combine the sweet potatoes, rutabaga, parsnips, and carrots in a large bowl and drizzle with the oil. Season with salt and pepper and toss well so that the vegetables are all coated in oil. Arrange the vegetables around the pork in the roasting pan.

Roast the pork and vegetables for about 1½ hours, until the meat is tender and the vegetables are cooked and crisp, basting the pork and vegetables two or three times during cooking. Use a roasting fork to turn the vegetables so that they don't stick to the roasting pan.

When cooked, arrange the pork and vegetables on a large heated platter and keep in a warm oven.

Drain and discard most of the fat from the roasting pan. Place the pan over medium heat. Mix the cornstarch in a small bowl with enough cold water to make a smooth paste. Pour this mixture into the roasting pan along with the boiling water. Use a spatula to stir the mixture, scraping the bottom of the pan. Simmer until the sauce has thickened. Pour into a gravy boat. Serve the pork and vegetables with the gravy passed separately.

Serves: 6–8 • Prep: 15 min • Cooking: 1 ½ hr

ROAST LEG OF LAMB WITH VEGETABLES

5 pound (2.5 kg) leg of lamb, bone removed

1 teaspoon cracked black peppercorns

1 teaspoon salt

2 tablespoons finely chopped fresh rosemary

1 small lemon

¾ cup (200 g) butter, softened

4 medium potatoes, cut in bite-size chunks

2 medium carrots, cut in bite-size chunks

2 medium onions, peeled and cut in half

Preheat the oven to 375°F (190°C/gas 5).

Lay the lamb out on a work surface and rub with the peppercorns, salt, and rosemary. Fold the meat over and tie with kitchen string. Let rest for 1 hour.

Place the lamb in a large roasting pan and rub with half the butter. Drizzle with the lemon juice. Rub the potatoes, carrots, and onions with the remaining butter. Place them around the lamb in the roasting pan.

Bake for about 1¾ hours, or until the lamb is cooked but still lightly pink. If you like lamb well done, bake for 2 hours, or more.

Deglaze the pan with 1 tablespoon of boiling water and drizzle over the hot lamb.

Serves: 6 • Prep: 20 min + 1 hr to rest • Cooking: 2 hr

KIELBASA, PEA, AND POTATO BAKE

Kielbasa is a generic name for most Polish sausages. They are generally made from pork, flavored with garlic, and smoked. They are usually sold pre-cooked.

1½ pounds (750 g) kielbasa, sliced
4 large potatoes, peeled and cubed
2 cups (300 g) frozen peas
4 cloves garlic, finely chopped
2 cups (500 ml) milk

1 (10-ounce/300-ml) can cream of mushroom soup
Salt and freshly ground black pepper

Preheat the oven to 350°F (180°C/gas 4).

Combine the kielbasa, potatoes, peas, garlic, milk, and soup in a large casserole dish. Season with salt and pepper and stir gently until well mixed.

Cover the dish and bake until the potatoes are tender, about 1½ hours. Serve hot.

Serves: 4–6 • Prep: 20 min • Cooking: 1 ½ hr

CURRIED SAUSAGE AND APPLE BAKE

2 medium onions, thinly sliced
2 pounds (1 kg) sausage meat
1–2 tablespoons curry powder
1 tablespoon dark brown sugar
2 cups (500 g) applesauce

2 pounds (1 kg) potatoes, cooked and mashed, or 1½ cups (225 g) instant potato flakes (prepared according to the instructions on the package)
1 cup (125 g) freshly grated Parmesan cheese

Preheat the oven to 350°F (180°C/gas 4).

Place half the onions in the bottom of a large, shallow ovenproof dish.

Flour your hands and shape the sausage meat into walnut-sized balls. Place them on top of the onions in a single layer. Sprinkle with the remaining onions.

Mix the curry powder and brown sugar and sprinkle over the sausages.

Spoon the applesauce over the sausages. Spoon the mashed potatoes over the sausage and spread out in an even layer. If desired, use a fork to roughen the surface attractively. Sprinkle with the grated cheese.

Bake for about 1 hour, until golden brown. Serve hot or at room temperature.

Serves: 4–6 • Prep: 15 min • Cooking: 1 hr

PORK, SWEET POTATO, AND APPLE BAKE

2 tablespoons extra-virgin olive oil
6 boneless loin pork chops, about 1½ inches (4 cm) thick
4–6 medium sweet potatoes, peeled and cut into ½-inch (1-cm) cubes
2 Granny Smith apples, diced
½ cup (125 ml) maple syrup
2 cloves garlic, finely chopped

1 tablespoon finely chopped fresh sage leaves
1 teaspoon ground ginger
½ teaspoon ground cinnamon
Salt and freshly ground black pepper
1 cup (250 ml) chicken broth or stock (see page 56)

Preheat the oven to 375°F (190°C/gas 5).

Heat the oil in a Dutch oven over medium-high heat and brown the pork chops on both sides, 8–10 minutes.

Drain off as much of the fat as possible. Cover the pork chops with the sweet potatoes and apples.

Combine the maple syrup, garlic, sage, ginger, cinnamon, salt, pepper, and broth in a small bowl and mix well. Pour this mixture over the chops and vegetables in the pan.

Bake, uncovered, for 15 minutes. Turn the chops and vegetables carefully and bake until the sweet potatoes are soft and the meat is cooked, about 15 minutes more. Serve hot.

Serves: 4–6 • Prep: 15 min • Cooking: 40 min

Kielbasa, Pea, and Potato Bake

Hawaiian Casserole with Italian Sausages

6–8 Italian sausages, cut into bite-size chunks

1½ pounds (750 g) potatoes, peeled and cut into ½-inch (1-cm) cubes

1 (15-ounce/450 g) can pineapple chunks, drained, juice reserved

1 large white onion, coarsely chopped

2 large carrots, sliced

2 large tomatoes, sliced

Water

2 tablespoons dark brown sugar

2 tablespoons cornstarch (cornflour)

Salt and freshly ground black pepper

1 tablespoon butter, cut into small pieces

Preheat the oven to 350°F (180°C/gas 4)

Layer the sausages, potatoes, pineapple chunks, onion, carrots, and tomatoes in a casserole dish.

Add enough water to the pineapple juice to make 1¼ cups (375 ml). Place ½ cup (60 ml) of the pineapple liquid in a small bowl. Add the brown sugar and cornstarch and stir until smooth. Season with salt and pepper to taste. Don't add too much salt because the sausages are fairly salty; ¼ teaspoon should be plenty. Add the remaining pineapple liquid and stir until smooth.

Pour the cornstarch mixture over the ingredients in the casserole. Top with the butter. Cover tightly and bake until the potatoes are tender, about 1 hour. Serve hot.

Serves: 4–6 • Prep: 15 min • Cooking: 1 hr

Beef, Sausage, and Bean Bake

1 tablespoon extra-virgin olive oil

1 pound (500 g) ground (minced) beef

1 pound (500 g) Italian garlic sausages, cut into 1-inch (2.5-cm) chunks

1 large onion, chopped

2 cloves garlic, finely chopped

1 small yellow bell pepper (capsicum), seeded and diced

1 (14-ounce/400-g) can cannellini (white kidney) beans, rinsed and drained

1 (14-ounce/400-g) can whole tomatoes, chopped, with juices

2 tablespoons finely chopped fresh sage

Salt and freshly ground black pepper

1 tablespoon sweet paprika

4 scallions (spring onions), trimmed and sliced, to serve

1 cup (120 g) freshly grated cheddar cheese, to serve

Preheat the oven to 350°F (180°C/gas 4).

Heat the oil in a Dutch oven or flameproof casserole over medium-high heat.

Add the beef, sausage, onion, garlic, and bell pepper and sauté until the beef and sausages are lightly browned, 8–10 minutes.

Add the beans, tomatoes, sage, salt, pepper, and paprika and stir gently to mix. Cover and bake for 60 minutes. Uncover, stir gently, and bake for 30 more minutes.

Remove from the oven and stir in the scallions and cheese. Serve hot.

Serves: 4–6 • Prep: 20 min • Cooking: 1 ¾ hr

Baked Sausages and Beans

2 tablespoons extra-virgin olive oil

6–8 fresh sausages, each one cut into 4 pieces

1 large white onion, coarsely chopped

3 cloves garlic, finely chopped

6 slices bacon, chopped

1 (14-ounce/400-g) can cannellini (white kidney) beans, rinsed and drained

1 (14-ounce/400-g) can red kidney beans, rinsed and drained

1 (14-ounce/400-g) can garbanzo beans (chickpeas), rinsed and drained

1 (14-ounce/400-g) can tomatoes, chopped, with juice

½ cup (125 ml) ketchup

½ cup (125 ml) molasses

2 tablespoons dark brown sugar

1 tablespoon Dijon mustard

1 tablespoon Worcestershire sauce

6–8 fresh sage leaves, torn

Preheat the oven to 350°F (180°C/gas 4).

Heat the oil in a Dutch oven or flameproof casserole over high heat. Add the sausages, onion, garlic, and bacon and sauté until the onion is translucent, the sausages are browned, and the bacon is beginning to get crisp, 5–7 minutes.

Add the cannellini, red kidney, and garbanzo beans, tomatoes, ketchup, molasses, brown sugar, mustard, Worcestershire sauce, and sage and stir well. Bake for 1 hour. Serve hot.

Serves: 6–8 • Prep: 15 min • Cooking: 70 min

Hawaiian Casserole with Italian Sausages

SAUSAGE AND BREAD BAKE

1 tablespoon extra-virgin olive oil
1 small onion, finely chopped
1 stalk celery, finely chopped
1 tablespoon finely chopped fresh parsley
1 pound (500 g) sweet Italian sausages
2 cups (200 g) day-old bread, cut into small cubes

4 leaves fresh sage, torn
4 large eggs
1¼ cups (300 ml) chicken broth or stock (see page 56)
Salt and freshly ground black pepper

Preheat the oven to 350°F (180°C/gas 4).

Heat the oil in a large Dutch oven or flameproof casserole over medium heat. Sauté the onion, celery, and parsley until softened, 5 minutes.

Add the sausages and cook until browned, 7–8 minutes. Chop the sausages into thick slices.

Drain the fat from the pan, pouring 4 tablespoons into a large bowl and discarding the rest. If there is not this much fat in the pan, add extra olive oil.

Mix in the cubes of bread, sage, and sausages. Season with salt and pepper.

Beat the eggs lightly, then stir them into the chicken broth. Pour this liquid over the sausage-and-bread mixture. Stir well.

Cover and bake for 40 minutes. Uncover and cook for 15 minutes more. Serve hot.

Serves: 4 • Prep: 25 min • Cooking: 70 min

PILAF WITH CHICKEN

4–6 threads saffron
1 tablespoon hot water
4 tablespoons extra-virgin olive oil
2 pounds (1 kg) boneless, skinless chicken thighs, cut into bite-size pieces
1 red onion, finely chopped
2 red bell peppers (capsicums), seeded and finely chopped
3 cloves garlic, finely chopped
1–2 sliced fresh red or green chiles
2 teaspoons cumin seeds, freshly ground or whole

1 tablespoon coriander seeds, freshly ground
1½ cups (250 g) basmati rice
2 tablespoons finely grated lemon zest
2 cups (500 ml) chicken broth or stock, heated (see page 56)
Salt and freshly ground black pepper
Black olives, to garnish

Preheat the oven to 350°F (180°C/gas 4).

Soak the saffron in the water for 10 minutes.

Heat 2 tablespoons of the oil a large Dutch oven or flameproof casserole over medium heat. Add the chicken and sauté until the meat turns white, 7–9 minutes. Remove from the pan and set aside.

Heat the remaining 2 tablespoons of oil in the same pan and sauté the onion and bell peppers until softened, 8–10 minutes.

Add the garlic, chiles, cumin, and coriander and cook for 2–3 minutes. Stir in the rice and the lemon zest. Arrange the chicken on top of the rice.

Mix the saffron into the broth and pour over the chicken and rice. Season with salt and pepper. Cover and bake for 50 minutes.

Sprinkle with the olives and serve.

Serves: 4–6 • Prep: 30 min • Cooking: 70 min

BAKED CHICKEN WITH VEGETABLES

- 1 chicken, weighing about 2 pounds (1 kg), cut into 4 pieces
  Salt and freshly ground white pepper
- ½ cup (125 g) butter
- 1¾ cups (250 g) frozen peas
- 3 medium carrots, thinly sliced
- 1 pound (500 g) potatoes, peeled and thinly sliced
- 1 medium onion, finely chopped
- 1 cup (250 ml) dry white wine
- 2 tablespoons water
- 2 large tomatoes, peeled and thinly sliced
- 2 tablespoons finely chopped fresh parsley

Preheat the oven to 350°F (180°C/gas 4). Season the chicken with salt and pepper.

Melt 4 tablespoons of butter a large Dutch oven or flameproof casserole over medium heat. Add the peas, carrots, and potatoes and sauté until lightly browned, 8–10 minutes. Remove and set aside.

Melt the remaining butter in the same pan and sauté the chicken and onion until lightly browned, 8–10 minutes. Pour in the wine, water, and tomatoes. Cover and bake for 30 minutes.

Add the sautéed vegetables. Sprinkle with the parsley and season with salt and white pepper. Cover and bake until the chicken and vegetables are tender, about 1 hour.

Serves: 4 • Prep: 20 min • Cooking: 2 hr

EASY CHEESY CHICKEN AND VEGETABLE CASSEROLE

- ½ cup (75 g) all-purpose (plain) flour
  Salt and freshly ground white pepper
- 4 medium boneless, skinless chicken breasts, sliced in thin strips
- 2 tablespoons extra-virgin olive oil
- 1 pound (500 g) potatoes, peeled and thinly sliced
- 1 pound (500 g) chopped frozen broccoli
- 1 (10-ounce/300 ml) can cream of chicken soup
- 1 (10-ounce/300 ml) cream of celery soup
- ¾ cup (180 ml) milk
- 1 cup (150 g) freshly grated cheddar or Monteray Jack cheese

Preheat the oven to 350°F (180°C/gas 4).

Generously season the flour in a bowl with salt and white pepper. Dredge the chicken in the flour, coating well and shaking off any excess.

Heat the oil in a Dutch oven or flameproof casserole over medium-high heat. Sauté the chicken in two batches until well browned, 7–9 minutes.

Arrange the potatoes and broccoli over the chicken in the pan. Pour in the chicken soup, celery soup, and milk. Stir gently. Sprinkle with the cheese and bake until the chicken and vegetables are tender, about 1 hour.

Serves: 4–6 • Prep: 15 min • Cooking: 1 ¼ hr

CHICKEN AND APRICOT CASSEROLE

- 2 pounds (1 kg) chicken pieces
- 1 (14-ounce/400 g) can apricots, drained, juice reserved
- 1 pound (500 g) tiny new potatoes, scrubbed
- 1½ cups (250 g) frozen peas
  Handful of coarsely chopped fresh cilantro (coriander) leaves
- 1 (4-ounce/125-g) package powdered onion soup
  Salt and freshly ground black pepper
  About 1 cup (250 ml) dry white wine

Preheat the oven to 375°F (190°C/gas 5).

Place the chicken in a casserole dish. Cover with the apricots, potatoes, peas, and cilantro. Sprinkle with the powdered soup and season lightly with salt and pepper.

Add enough wine to the reserved apricot juice to make 1½ cups (375 ml) of liquid. Pour over the ingredients in the casserole dish and let stand for 15 minutes.

Stir gently, then cover tightly. Bake for 1 hour, until the chicken is very tender. Check from time to time, adding more wine if the sauce is dry. Serve hot.

Serves: 4 • Prep: 15 min + 15 min to stand • Cooking: 1 hr

Chicken and Apricot Casserole

BAKED CHICKEN BREASTS WITH FENNEL

¼ cup (60 ml) extra-virgin olive oil
3 cloves garlic, finely chopped
    Salt and freshly ground black
    pepper
6 skinless chicken breasts
2 bulbs fennel, trimmed and thickly
    sliced

2 red onions, cut into wedges
1¼ cups (310 ml) dry white wine
    Freshly cooked egg noodles,
    to serve
2 tablespoons butter

Preheat the oven to 400°F (200°C/gas 6).

Mix 2 tablespoons of the oil and garlic in a roasting pan. Season generously with salt and pepper. Add the chicken and coat it in the garlic mixture.

Add the fennel and onions and drizzle with the remaining 2 tablespoons of oil. Bake for 15 minutes.

Increase the oven temperature to 450°F (225°C/gas 8). Drizzle the wine over the chicken. Bake for 10–15 minutes, or until the chicken and vegetables are tender.

Place the noodles in a large serving dish and toss with the butter. Place the chicken and vegetables on top and serve at once.

Serves: 4–6 • Prep: 15 min • Cooking: 30 min

CHICKEN CASSEROLE WITH LEEKS AND POTATOES

4 tablespoons extra-virgin olive oil
8 chicken thighs
    Salt and freshly ground black
    pepper
4 large leeks, white parts only,
    thinly sliced
2 cloves garlic, finely chopped
4 tablespoons all-purpose (plain)
    flour
½ cup (125 ml) dry white wine

3 cups (750 ml) chicken broth or
    stock (see page 56)
2 bay leaves
8 threads saffron
4 large carrots, thinly sliced
4 large potatoes, peeled and cut
    into bite-size cubes
2 tablespoons finely chopped fresh
    flat-leaf parsley

Preheat the oven to 350°F (180°C/gas 4).

Heat the oil in a Dutch oven or flameproof casserole over medium-high heat. Season the chicken with salt and pepper then add the chicken in a single layer and cook until browned all over, about 10 minutes. Remove the chicken from the pan and set aside.

Add the leeks to the same pan and sauté until softened, about 5 minutes. Add the garlic and sauté for 1–2 minutes more.

Add the flour and stir until golden, about 5 minutes. Add the wine and cook until it has evaporated, about 4 minutes.

Pour in the broth and add the bay leaves, saffron, carrots, and potatoes. Bring to a boil and simmer for 10 minutes.

Add the chicken pieces and their juices, pushing the chicken down into the vegetables and sauce.

Cover the pan and transfer to the oven. Bake until the chicken is tender and the vegetables are done, about 30 minutes. Discard the bay leaves. Serve hot, garnished with the parsley.

Serves: 4 • Prep: 10 min • Cooking: 65 min

Chicken Casserole with Leeks and Potatoes

Savoy Cabbage Turkey Loaf

1½ pounds (750 g) ground turkey breast

8 ounces (250 g) Italian pork sausage, skinned and crumbled

¼ cup (60 g) finely chopped pancetta

1 cup (120 g) freshly grated Parmesan cheese

1 egg + 1 egg yolk

½ cup (75 g) soft fresh bread crumbs
Pinch of nutmeg
Salt and freshly ground black pepper

10 leaves savoy cabbage, soaked in boiling water for 5 minutes

1 small onion, finely chopped

1 pound (500 g) peeled and chopped tomatoes

½ cup (125 ml) extra-virgin olive oil

½ cup (125 ml) dry white wine

½ cup (125 ml) beef broth or stock (see page 28)

Preheat the oven to 400°F (200°C/gas 6).

Combine the turkey, sausage, pancetta, Parmesan, egg and egg yolk, bread crumbs, nutmeg, salt, and pepper in a large bowl and mix well.

Drain the cabbage leaves and dry with a clean kitchen towel. Arrange on a clean work surface in a rectangle; they should be overlapping so that there is no space between the leaves. Place the turkey mixture in the middle of the leaves and shape into a loaf.

Wrap the cabbage leaves around the loaf, taking care not to tear them. Tie with a few twists of kitchen string.

Carefully transfer the turkey loaf to an ovenproof dish. Mix the onion, tomatoes, and oil together and pour over the top. Bake for 1¼ hours, basting frequently with the wine and broth.

Slice the loaf and serve hot.

Serves: 4 • Prep: 30 min • Cooking: 1¼ hr

Spanish Lunch Pot

2 cups (300 g) dried garbanzo beans (chickpeas), soaked overnight and drained

1 chicken, about 3 pounds/1.5 kg, cut into 8 pieces

8 ounces (250 g) Spanish chorizo sausage, thickly sliced

4 ounces (125 g) salt pork, thickly sliced

4 cloves garlic, lightly crushed but whole

4 sprigs rosemary
Salt and freshly ground black pepper

4 threads saffron, dissolved in 12 cups (3 liters) boiling water

Put the beans in a large Dutch oven or casserole with the chicken, chorizo, salt pork, garlic, and rosemary. Season with salt and pepper. Pour in the saffron water to cover the contents of the pot completely.

Cover and place in the oven. Turn on the oven to 350°F (180°C/gas 4).

Bake for 5–6 hours, or until the chicken and beans are very tender. Serve hot.

Serves: 4–6 • Prep: 20 min + 12 hr to soak the beans • Cooking: 5–6 hr

Guinea Fowl Casserole

If guinea fowl is not available, replace with the same weight of chicken.

3 leeks, trimmed and thinly sliced

2 large carrots, thickly sliced

2 large potatoes, thickly sliced

2 red onions, cut into wedges

2 cloves garlic, finely chopped

1 guinea fowl or chicken, weighing about 3 pounds (1.5 kg)

Salt and freshly ground black pepper

1⅓ cups (330 ml) dry white wine

5 ounces (150 g) porcini mushrooms, thickly sliced

5 ounces (150 g) chestnut or button mushrooms, thickly sliced

Preheat the oven to 350°F (180°C/gas 4).

Arrange the leeks, carrots, potatoes, onions, and garlic in a large roasting pan.

Season the cavity of the guinea fowl with salt and pepper. Lay the guinea fowl on top of the vegetables.

Pour the wine over the bird. Cover with aluminum foil and bake for 1¼ hours. Arrange the mushrooms around the bird. Cover with the foil and bake for 30 minutes more, or until the juices run clean and all the vegetables are tender. Serve hot.

Serves: 4–6 • Prep: 15 min • Cooking: 1¾ hr

BAKED SALT COD WITH POTATOES AND CARROTS

1½ pounds (750 g) salt cod
4 tablespoons (60 ml) extra-virgin olive oil
1½ pounds (750 g) potatoes, cut into large cubes
4 large carrots, sliced
4 large tomatoes, sliced
2 tablespoons finely chopped fresh parsley

2 medium onions, thinly sliced
2 cloves garlic, finely chopped
1 teaspoon dried oregano
Salt and freshly ground black pepper
¼ cup (60 g) fine dry bread crumbs

Cut the salt cod into large pieces, removing the center bone (sometimes this has already been removed). Soak in a large bowl of cold water for 24 hours, changing the water at least four times.

Preheat the oven to 350°F (180°C/gas 4). Grease a large, shallow ovenproof dish with 2 tablespoons of the oil.

Arrange the pieces of cod in the dish in a single layer and cover with the potatoes and carrots. Top with the slices of tomatoes. Sprinkle with the parsley, onions, garlic, oregano, a little salt, and a generous sprinkling of pepper. Drizzle with the remaining 2 tablespoons oil.

Cover the pan with a piece of aluminum foil and bake until the fish, potatoes, and carrots are tender, about 45 minutes.

Remove the foil and sprinkle with the bread crumbs.

Bake until the bread crumbs are browned, about 10 minutes. Serve hot

Serves: 4 • Prep: 15 min • Cooking: 55 min

BAKED FISH AND POTATOES

2 pounds (1 kg) firm-textured fish fillets, such as sea bass, carp, mullet, trout, or tuna
Salt and freshly ground white pepper
½ teaspoon dried oregano
5 cloves garlic, finely chopped
3 tablespoons finely chopped fresh parsley

¾ cup (180 ml) extra-virgin olive oil
2 pounds (1 kg) potatoes, peeled and cut into bite-size pieces
2 large tomatoes, sliced
3 tablespoons fresh lemon juice
1 cup (250 ml) dry white wine

Preheat the oven to 325°F (170°C/gas 3). Set out a large roasting pan.

Season the fish with salt and white pepper. Sprinkle with oregano.

Combine the garlic, parsley, and 4 tablespoons of the oil in the pan. Cover with the potatoes and tomatoes and drizzle with 4 tablespoons of oil. Season with salt and pepper.

Cover the pan with aluminum foil and bake until the potatoes are almost tender, 20–25 minutes. Remove from the oven and place the fish on top of the potatoes and tomatoes.

Return to the oven, uncovered, and bake for 15–20 minutes more, until the fish is cooked through. Mix the lemon juice, wine, and remaining 4 tablespoons oil and drizzle over the cooked dish. Serve hot.

Serves: 4 • Prep: 15 min • Cooking: 45 min

BAKED SEA BASS WITH VEGETABLES

Saffron turns dishes the color of sunshine. This recipe uses just 1 teaspoon (about 100 threads) of the most expensive spice in the world. The finest saffron comes from Kashmir, and about 70,000 hand-picked crocus flowers are needed to make just one pound of saffron. You can replace it with turmeric, a yellow powder with a light taste but a strong color. Turmeric is sometimes called the "saffron of the poor."

- 1 teaspoon saffron (or substitute 2 teaspoons ground turmeric)
- 1/2 cup (125 ml) boiling water (or substitute cold water if using turmeric)
- 1 sea bass or grouper, weighing about 3 pounds (1.5 kg)
- Salt and freshly ground black pepper
- 2 tablespoons finely chopped mixed fresh mint, fennel, and parsley
- 3 pounds (1.5 kg) small waxy potatoes, peeled and sliced
- 20 cherry tomatoes, halved
- 5 cloves garlic, whole
- 3 green bell peppers (capsicums), seeded and cut into large strips
- 1 yellow bell pepper (capsicum), seeded and cut into large strips
- 1 red bell pepper (capsicum), seeded and cut into large strips
- 6 sun-dried tomatoes, soaked in hot water for 5 minutes and drained
- 1 cup (250 ml) fish stock (see page 98) or water
- 1 cup (250 ml) extra-virgin olive oil
- 15 green olives, pitted
- 2 tomatoes, thinly sliced
- Juice and shredded zest of 1 lemon
- 2 green chile peppers, seeded and finely chopped
- 5 tablespoons finely chopped fresh cilantro (coriander)
- Lemon wedges, to serve
- Small bunch fresh mint, torn

Preheat the oven to 350°F (180°C/gas 4).

Combine the saffron and boiling water in a small bowl and let steep for at least 5 minutes.

Make 3 or 4 deep gashes along the top of the sea bass. Season the fish with salt and pepper and stuff the mixed herbs into the gashes.

Sprinkle the potatoes with salt and pepper. Cover the base of a large tajine or Dutch oven with the potatoes. Place the cherry tomatoes on top and add the whole garlic cloves. Arrange the bell peppers on top of the tomatoes and season with salt and pepper.

Chop the dried tomatoes coarsely. Add to the vegetables.

Mix together the stock, oil, and half the saffron water and pour it over the vegetables. Bake, uncovered, in the oven for 20 minutes.

Add the olives and place the fish on top of the vegetables. Arrange the tomato slices on top and garnish with strips of lemon zest and the chiles.

Mix the lemon juice with the remaining 1/2 cup (125 ml) oil and the remaining saffron water. Drizzle over the fish. Bake, uncovered, for 20 minutes.

Remove from the oven and sprinkle with cilantro. Bake, uncovered, until the fish is tender, 10 minutes.

Serve with lemon wedges and mint leaves.

Serves: 6 • Prep: 30 min • Cooking: 1 hr

FOCACCIA

Focaccia is a delicious Italian bread that is surprisingly easy to make. It goes beautifully with almost all soups, stews, and baked dishes. Preparing the dough does take a little time, but since you will have the oven on anyway to prepare the recipes in this chapter, why not try it? If you like, incorporate 1 tablespoon finely chopped fresh rosemary or sages leaves to the dough.

- 1 ounce (25 g) fresh yeast or 2 (1/4-ounce/7-g) packages active dry yeast
- 1 teaspoon sugar
- About 3/4 cup (200 ml) warm water
- 3 1/2 cups (500 g) all-purpose (plain) flour
- 1 teaspoon salt
- 6 tablespoons extra-virgin olive oil

Place the yeast in a small bowl. Add the sugar and half the water and stir until dissolved. Set aside until creamy, 10–15 minutes.

Place the flour and salt in a large bowl. Pour in the yeast mixture, remaining water and half the oil. Stir until the flour is absorbed.

Sprinkle a work surface with a little flour. Knead the dough until smooth and elastic, about 15 minutes; it should show air bubbles beneath the surface and spring back if you flatten it with your palm.

Place in a large, lightly oiled bowl and cover with a cloth. Let rise until doubled in volume, about 1 1/2 hours. To test if ready, poke your finger gently into the dough; if the impression remains, then it is ready.

Preheat the oven to 425°F (220°C/gas 8).

Place the dough on an oiled baking sheet and, using your fingertips, spread it into a circular shape about 14 inches (36 cm) in diameter and 1/2 inch (1 cm) thick.

Bake until golden brown, about 20 minutes. Drizzle with the remaining oil and serve hot.

Serves: 4–6 • Prep: 30 min + 1 1/2 hr to rise • Cooking: 20 min

Baked Sea Bass with Vegetables

FISH AND VEGETABLE BAKE

- 4 tablespoons extra-virgin olive oil
- 5 cloves garlic, finely chopped
- 1 teaspoon freshly ground cumin seeds
- ¾ cup (180 ml) fresh lemon juice
  Salt and freshly ground black pepper
- 4 medium potatoes, thinly sliced
- 4 medium carrots, thinly sliced
- 2 large tomatoes, finely chopped
- 3 pounds (1.5 kg) fresh or frozen fish fillets, such as sole or plaice, thawed if frozen
- ½ cup (90 g) pine nuts
- 1 bunch parsley

Preheat the oven to 350°F (180°C/gas 4).

Pour the oil into a large baking dish. Add 4 cloves of the garlic, cumin, 4 tablespoons of the lemon juice, salt, and pepper.

Place a layer of potatoes, carrots, and tomatoes on top and cover with the fish fillets. Arrange the remaining vegetables over the fish.

Bake until the fish and vegetables are tender, 40–45 minutes.

Just before the fish comes out of the oven, combine the pine nuts, parsley, the remaining ½ cup (125 ml) lemon juice, and remaining clove garlic in a food processor and process until smooth.

Spoon the sauce over the fish and vegetables. Serve hot.

Serves: 6–8 • Prep: 20 min • Cooking: 45 min

TUNA AND CASHEW BAKE

- 2 (6-ounce/180-g) cans tuna (canned in oil), drained
- 6 ounces (180 g) white button mushrooms, sliced
- 1 cup (120 g) unsalted cashews
- 3 scallions (green onions), trimmed and sliced
- 3 stalks celery, sliced
- 4 (3-ounce) packages ramen noodles (350 g instant Chinese-style egg noodles), flavor packet discarded, soaked in boiling water for 10 minutes (or according to instructions on the package) and drained
- 1 (14-ounce/400-g) can cream of mushroom soup
- 4 tablespoons water
- 1 tablespoon dark soy sauce

Preheat the oven to 325°F (160°C/gas 3).

Place the tuna in a bowl and crumble with a fork. Add the mushrooms, cashews, scallions, celery, and about two-thirds of the cooked noodles. Stir gently. Spoon this mixture into a Dutch oven or casserole dish.

Pour the soup into the bowl and mix in the water and soy sauce. Pour the soup mixture over the casserole. Top with the remaining noodles.

Bake for 45 minutes. Serve hot.

Serves: 4–6 • Prep: 15 min • Cooking: 45 min

BÉCHAMEL SAUCE

Béchamel is a very versatile French sauce. It can be used to flavor and thicken soups and stews, or as a base for soufflés, or to bind together ingredients in a baked dish. Consistency can very from very thin to almost solid, depending on how the sauce will be used. This recipe is suitable for baked dishes.

- 4 cups (1 liter) milk
- 4 tablespoons butter
- ½ cup (75 g) all-purpose (plain) flour
- Salt and freshly ground black or white pepper
- Pinch of freshly grated nutmeg (optional)

Melt the butter in a medium saucepan over medium-low heat. Stir in the flour and nutmeg, if using. Cook, stirring constantly for 1–2 minutes.

Pour in the milk all at once. Season with salt and pepper, and nutmeg, if using. Bring to a boil and simmer, stirring almost constantly, for 10 minutes.

Makes: 4 cups (1 liter) • Prep: 5 min • Cooking: 15 min

TUNA FISH LAGAN

Lagan is an Indian dish that is a bit like a savory cake, baked in the oven. You can have sweet or savory lagans, with or without meat, fish, or vegetables. The variety is endless. Lagans always taste and look good and they are extremely versatile. They're simple to make and a delight to serve.

- ¼ cup (60 ml) vegetable oil
- ¼ cup (60 ml) butter or margarine, at room temperature
- 2 eggs + 1 egg white, lightly beaten
- ½ cup (125 ml) pineapple juice from can
- 4 tablespoons finely chopped fresh parsley
- 2 teaspoons finely chopped fresh chile (or green chile paste)
- 2 cloves garlic, finely chopped
- 1 teaspoon crushed red pepper flakes
- ¼ teaspoon salt
- 1 medium onion, peeled and grated
- 1 cup (125 g) canned tuna, drained and flaked
- ½ cup (50 g) fresh or frozen corn kernels
- ½ cup (50 g) cooked cubed potatoes
- ⅓ cup (50 g) garbanzo bean (chickpea) flour
- ⅓ cup (50 g) cornstarch (cornflour)
- ⅓ cup (50 g) all-purpose (plain) flour + more as needed
- 1 teaspoon baking powder
- ½ cup (50 g) canned pineapple chunks
  Milk (optional)
- 1 tablespoon poppy seeds
  Tamarind or green chutney, to serve

Preheat the oven to 350°F (180°C/gas 4).

Butter a deep 10-inch (26-cm) baking pan.

Use a handheld blender to blend together the oil, butter, whole eggs, pineapple juice, parsley, green chile, garlic, red pepper flakes, and salt in a large bowl.

Stir in the onion, tuna, corn, and potatoes.

Fold in the garbanzo bean flour, cornstarch, all-purpose flour, and baking powder. Mix in the pineapple.

The mixture should have the consistency of a cake batter. If it is too soft, add little more all-purpose (plain) flour; if too stiff add some milk.

Pour the batter into the pan. Bake for 25 minutes.

Remove from the oven. Spread with the whisked egg white and sprinkle with the poppy seeds. Bake until golden brown, about 10 minutes.

Remove from the pan and cut in thick slices. Serve hot or at room temperature with tamarind or green chutney.

Serves: 4–6 • Prep: 10 min • Cooking: 35 min

VEGETABLE LAGAN

- ¼ cup (60 ml) vegetable oil
- ¼ cup (60 ml) butter
- 2 whole large eggs, lightly beaten
- ½ cup (125 ml) milk + more as needed
  Generous handful of finely chopped fresh cilantro (coriander)
- 2 teaspoons finely chopped green chile
- 2 cloves garlic, finely chopped
- 1 teaspoon crushed red pepper flakes
- ¼ teaspoon salt
- 6 ounces (180 g) zucchini (courgette), peeled and coarsely grated
- 1 medium onion, grated
- ⅓ cup (70 g) fresh or frozen corn (sweet corn) kernels
- ½ green bell pepper (capsicum), seeded and thinly sliced
- ⅓ cup (50 g) garbanzo bean (chickpea) flour
- ⅓ cup (50 g) cornstarch (cornflour)
- ⅓ cup (50 g) all-purpose (plain) flour + more as needed
- 1 teaspoon baking powder
- 1 egg white
  Milk (optional)
- 1 tablespoon poppy seeds
  Mango chutney, to serve

Preheat the oven to 350°F (180°C/gas 4). Butter a large loaf pan.

Use a handheld blender to blend together the oil, butter, whole eggs, milk, cilantro, green chile, garlic, red pepper flakes, and salt in a large bowl.

Mix in the zucchini, onion, corn, and bell peppers. Fold in garbanzo bean flour, cornstarch, all-purpose flour, and baking powder. The mixture should have the consistency of a cake batter. If it is too soft, add a little more flour; or if too stiff, add some milk.

Pour the batter into the prepared pan. Bake for 30 minutes. Do not open the oven during this time.

Remove from the oven. Whisk the egg white and spread on top of the lagan. Sprinkle with the poppy seeds.

Bake until the lagan is golden brown and starts to come away from the sides, about 10 minutes.

Remove from the pan and cut in thick slices. Serve hot or at room temperature with the chutney.

Serves: 4–6 • Prep: 10 min • Cooking: 40 min

BAKED PASTA AND VEGETABLES

This hearty vegetarian dish comes from southern Italy, where pasta and vegetable bakes are common fare. If you are using fresh tomatoes, make sure that they are plump and filled with juice. It is the juices that they release during cooking, together with the oil, that provide the liquid and steam in which the pasta and potatoes can cook.

- ½ cup (125 ml) extra-virgin olive oil
- 3 pounds (1.5 kg) juicy, ripe tomatoes or (28-ounce/800-g) canned Italian tomatoes, with juice
  Handful of fresh basil leaves
- 1 pound (500 g) small penne pasta
- 1 pound (500 g) potatoes, peeled and cut into ¼-inch (0.5-cm) slices
- 8 ounces (250 g) black Italian olives, pitted and sliced
- 1 large onion, sliced
- 1 tablespoon finely chopped fresh oregano
  Salt and freshly ground black pepper
- 1 cup (100 g) freshly grated pecorino or Parmesan cheese
- ½ cup (75 g) fine dry bread crumbs
- 4 tablespoons pine nuts

Preheat the oven to 350°F (180°C/gas 4).

Oil a large deep baking dish with 2 tablespoons of the oil. Spread with a layer of tomatoes and basil followed by a layer of pasta, potatoes, olives, onion, and oregano. Repeat, seasoning each layer with a little salt and pepper, until all the tomatoes, basil, pasta, potatoes, olives, onion, and oregano are in the casserole.

Mix the cheese, bread crumbs, and pine nuts in a small bowl and sprinkle over the top. Drizzle with the remaining 2 tablespoon of oil.

Cover the dish and bake for 1 hour, or until the pasta and potatoes are tender. Serve hot.

Serves: 4–6 • Prep: 10 min • Cooking: 1 hr

BEEF AND SPAGHETTI BAKE

- 2 tablespoons extra-virgin olive oil
- 1 medium onion, finely chopped
- 2 cloves garlic, finely chopped
- 1 tablespoon finely chopped fresh parsley
- 1 pound (500 g) ground beef
- 8 ounces (250 g) spaghetti (uncooked)
- 2 (12-ounce/300-g) jars tomato-based spaghetti sauce
- 2 cups (500 ml) water
- 1½ cups (180 g) freshly grated Parmesan cheese
  Freshly ground black pepper

Preheat the oven to 325°F (160°C/gas 3). Heat the oil in a Dutch oven over medium-high heat.

Add the onion, garlic, and parsley and sauté until the onion is softened, about 5 minutes. Add the beef and sauté until browned, 6–8 minutes.

Break the spaghetti into short lengths and add to the pan. Pour in the spaghetti sauce and water. Stir, then sprinkle with the cheese. Season generously with freshly ground black pepper. Cover and bake for 1½ hours. Serve hot.

Serves 4 • Prep: 15 min • Cooking: 1 hr 40 min

LAMB CASSEROLE WITH PASTA

- 1 boned leg of lamb, weighing about 2 pounds (1 kg), cut into 12 pieces
- 6 tablespoons butter
  Salt and freshly ground black pepper
  Juice of 1 lemon
- 1 onion, finely chopped
- 1 pound (500 g) firm-ripe tomatoes, peeled and chopped
- ¼ teaspoon sugar
- 6 cups (1.5 liters) boiling water
- 1 pound (500 g) rice-shaped soup pasta
- 4 tablespoons freshly grated Parmesan cheese

Preheat the oven to 400°F (200°C/gas 6).

Place the lamb in a Dutch oven. Dot with 4 tablespoons of the butter and season with salt and pepper. Drizzle with the lemon juice. Bake for 20 minutes, turning several times during cooking. Remove the lamb and set aside.

Melt the remaining 2 tablespoons of butter in the Dutch oven over medium heat. Add the onion and sauté until lightly browned, 7–8 minutes. Add the tomatoes and season with salt and pepper. Stir in the sugar. Cook for 10 minutes over medium-high heat, stirring often.

Return the lamb to the pan. Stir in the boiling water. Add the pasta and cover the pan. Bake until the lamb is very tender and the pasta is cooked, about 30 minutes. Sprinkle with the cheese and serve hot.

Serves 4–6 • Prep: 30 min • Cooking: 70 min

Baked Eggs, French-Style

10 firm-ripe tomatoes, peeled and sliced
    Salt and freshly ground black pepper
    Handful of large black Greek olives, pitted and sliced
6   hard-cooked eggs, peeled and sliced
2   tablespoons finely chopped fresh flat-leaf parsley

2   leeks, whites only, finely sliced
2   cups (500 ml) Béchamel sauce (see page 212)
½   cup (75 g) fine dry bread crumbs
½   cup (100 g) freshly grated Parmesan cheese

Preheat the oven to 350°F (180°C/gas 6).

Butter a large ovenproof baking dish.

Cover the bottom of the dish with a layer of tomatoes. Season lightly with salt and pepper. Cover with half the olives, half the eggs, half the parsley and a little more salt and pepper. Top with a layer of leeks and Béchamel. Repeat, finishing with the Béchamel.

Sprinkle with the bread crumbs and Parmesan cheese and bake for about 30 minutes, until the top is golden brown and lightly bubbling.

Serve hot.

Serves: 4–6 • Prep: 25 min • Cooking: 30 min

Tomato and Egg Bake

16 cherry tomatoes
    Salt
3   large whole eggs and 1 large egg yolk
½   cup (125 ml) heavy (double) cream
½   cup (125 ml) milk

4   tablespoons freshly grated Emmentaler cheese
4   tablespoons freshly grated Parmesan cheese
    Freshly ground black pepper
⅔   cup (100 g) fine dry bread crumbs
1   cup (250 ml) pesto (see page 46)

Slice the tops off the tomatoes. Scoop out the seeds and sprinkle with salt. Drain upside-down in a colander.

Preheat the oven to 350°F (180°C/gas 4). Oil a 10 or 12-inch (25 or 30-cm) round baking dish.

Beat the whole eggs and egg yolk, cream, milk, Emmentaler, and Parmesan in a medium bowl until frothy. Season with salt and pepper.

Mix the bread crumbs with the pesto and spoon the mixture inside the tomatoes.

Arrange the tomatoes in the prepared baking dish, not too close together. Put the tops back on and drizzle with the remaining oil. Pour the egg mixture into the dish around the tomatoes. Bake until set, about 30 minutes. Serve warm.

Serves: 4 • Prep: 25 min • Cooking: 30 min

Baked Herb Omelet

2   tablespoons butter, melted
¾   cup (100 g) finely chopped ham
2   tomatoes, peeled and sliced
6   large eggs
½   cup (125 ml) cream or milk
    Salt and freshly ground black pepper

2   tablespoons finely chopped mixed fresh herbs (chives, cilantro/coriander, parsley, oregano, basil, or other)
    Hot buttered triangles of toast, to serve

Preheat the oven to 400°F (200°C/gas 6).

Grease a medium ovenproof dish with the butter.

Place the ham and tomatoes in the bottom and bake until the ham begins to get crisp and the tomatoes are lightly cooked, 4–5 minutes.

Break the eggs into a medium bowl, add the cream, salt, pepper, and herbs and beat lightly.

Take the dish out of the oven and carefully pour the egg mixture over the ham and tomatoes.

Bake until set and lightly browned, 15–20 minutes. Serve immediately, with the toast.

Serves: 2–4 • Prep: 15 min • Cooking: 25 min

Baked Eggs, French-Style

BAKED VEGETABLE FRITTATA

2 tablespoons extra-virgin olive oil
3 large potatoes, peeled and diced
1 teaspoon bouillon granules dissolved in 4 tablespoons hot water
1 large eggplant (aubergine), peeled and diced
1 cup (125 g) Swiss chard (silver beet) or spinach, shredded

9 large eggs
Salt and freshly ground black pepper
1 tablespoon finely chopped fresh mint
1 tablespoon finely chopped fresh thyme

Preheat the oven to 425°F (220°C/gas 7).

Heat the oil in a Dutch oven or 8-inch (20-cm) flameproof casserole over medium-high heat. Add the potatoes and sauté until lightly browned, 5–7 minutes.

Pour in the bouillon. Add the eggplant and Swiss chard and cook for 8 minutes. Increase the heat and cook until the liquid has reduced by half, about 2 minutes.

Beat the eggs in a large bowl. Season with salt and pepper. Pour the egg mixture into the pan. Cover and bake for 10 minutes. Uncover and bake for 5 minutes more.

Set aside for 2 minutes. Cut into squares to serve.

Serves: 4–6 • Prep: 25 min • Cooking: 30 min

STUFFED EGGPLANT

4 large round eggplants (aubergines)
12 ounces (35 g) pecorino romano cheese, cut into small cubes
½ cup (75 g) diced pancetta
4 cloves garlic, finely chopped
⅓ cup (90 ml) extra-virgin olive oil

1 pound (500 g) peeled and chopped fresh tomatoes
⅓ cup (45 g) freshly grated Parmesan cheese
Salt and freshly ground black pepper

Preheat the oven to 350°F (180°C/gas 4).

Cut the eggplants in half lengthwise and use a sharp knife to open crosswise slits in the pulp.

Mix together the pecorino cheese, pancetta, and garlic in a bowl.

Grease an ovenproof dish with half the oil and place the eggplants in it, cut sides up. Cover with the pecorino mixture, pushing it into the slits. Cover with the tomatoes, drizzle with the remaining oil, and sprinkle with the Parmesan. Season with salt and pepper.

Bake until the eggplants are tender, about 40 minutes. Serve hot or at room temperature.

Serves: 4 • Prep: 15 min • Cooking: 40 min

CHEESE AND VEGETABLE CASSEROLE

This casserole is as quick and easy to make as it is delicious to eat. To cut preparation time even more, use frozen vegetables instead of fresh.

2 tablespoons butter
2 onions, finely chopped
2–3 medium potatoes, peeled and thinly sliced
2–3 medium carrots, thinly sliced
2 cups (300 g) broccoli, divided into small florets
2 cups (300 g) green beans, trimmed and cut into short lengths
4 ounces (125 g) water chestnuts, sliced

4 ounces (125 g) white mushrooms, thinly sliced
1 (10-ounce/300-ml) can cream of mushroom soup
1½ cups (250 g) freshly grated cheddar or Monterey Jack cheese
1 large firm-ripe tomato, thinly sliced
Freshly ground black pepper

Preheat the oven to 350°F (180°C/gas 4).

Heat the butter in a Dutch oven over medium heat. Add the onions and sauté until softened, about 5 minutes.

Place layers of potatoes, carrots, broccoli, green beans, water chestnuts, mushrooms, and onions in the prepared dish. Pour the mushroom soup over the top. Sprinkle with the cheese and season with pepper.

Bake for 30 minutes. Remove from the oven and arrange the slices of tomatoes on top. Bake for 10 minutes more, or until the vegetables are tender and the cheese is bubbling and golden brown. Serve hot.

Serves: 4 • Prep: 10 min • Cooking: 40 min

Cheese and Vegetable Casserole

HAM AND CHEESE BAKE

You will need a casserole or Dutch oven that can be used both on the stovetop and in the oven. Because the last step in this recipe involves broiling (grilling), make sure that handles on your casserole or Dutch oven will withstand the heat of the broiler.

2 tablespoons butter	6 slices whole-wheat (wholemeal) bread, cut into small cubes
1 medium onion, finely chopped	
1 clove garlic, finely chopped	4 large eggs
1 tablespoon finely chopped fresh parsley	2 cups (500 g) milk
	1½ cups (250 g) coarsely grated Monterey Jack or cheddar cheese
10 ounces (300 g) frozen mixed vegetables	
	Salt and freshly ground black pepper
1 pound (500 g) boiled ham, cut into ½-inch (1-cm) cubes	
	1 tablespoon Djion mustard

Preheat the oven to 350°F (180°C/gas 4).

Melt the butter in a Dutch oven over medium heat.

Add the onion, garlic, and parsley and sauté until softened, about 5 minutes. Add the mixed vegetables and cook, stirring often, until heated through, 3–4 minutes. Add the ham and bread and toss well.

Beat the eggs with the milk and 1 cup (150 g) of the cheese. Season with salt, pepper, and the mustard. Pour the mixture over the ham-and-bread mixture. Cover the pan and bake until golden brown and a toothpick in the center comes out clean, 30–35 minutes.

Remove the lid and sprinkle with the remaining ½ cup cheese. Broil (grill) until the cheese is bubbling and golden brown, about 5 minutes. Serve hot.

Serves: 4 • Prep: 15 min • Cooking: 45 min

POTATO AND CHEESE BAKE

1½ pounds (750 g) potatoes, peeled and finely shredded	2 large eggs, lightly beaten
	1 teaspoon baking powder
2 large carrots, finely shredded	1 teaspoon dried oregano
2 large onions, finely shredded	Salt and freshly ground black pepper
2 cloves garlic, finely chopped	
2 tablespoons extra-virgin olive oil	1 cup (250 ml) plain yogurt
1½ cups (180 g) grated cheddar cheese	

Preheat the oven to 350°F (180°C/gas 4).

Squeeze as much of the starchy juices out of the shredded potatoes as possible and put them in a large bowl. Add the carrots, onions, garlic, oil, 1 cup (120 g) cheese, eggs, baking powder, oregano, and salt and mix well.

Spoon the mixture into a casserole dish and sprinkle with the remaining cheese. Season with a generous grinding of black pepper.

Bake, uncovered, until puffed and golden brown, about 1½ hours. Serve hot with the yogurt passed on the side.

Serves 4 • Prep: 15 min • Cooking: 1 ½ hr

LEEK AND POTATO GRATIN

4 medium potatoes, peeled and very thinly sliced	1 cup (125 g) grated cheddar or Gruyère cheese
8 leeks, trimmed and cut into ½-inch (1-cm) rounds	1¾ cups (430 ml) heavy (double) cream
6 ounces (180 g) ham, diced	Generous ⅓ cup (100 ml) milk
Salt and freshly ground black pepper	⅛ teaspoon freshly grated nutmeg
2 cloves garlic, finely chopped	1 tablespoon freshly grated Parmesan cheese
2 tablespoons coarsely chopped fresh flat-leaf parsley	Handful of flat-leaf parsley leaves, to garnish
2 tablespoons butter, melted	

Preheat the oven to 375°F (190°C/gas 5). Butter a 12-inch (30-cm) oval ovenproof baking dish.

Arrange a layer of potatoes in the pan, followed by a layer of leeks. Top with a layer of ham. Season with salt and pepper. Sprinkle with the garlic and parsley. Drizzle with butter. Repeat the layers until all the vegetables and ham are used up, finishing with a layer of potatoes. Sprinkle with ½ cup (60 g) of cheddar.

Mix the cream, milk, the remaining ½ cup (60 g) of cheddar, and nutmeg in a medium bowl. Pour over the vegetables and sprinkle with the Parmesan. Bake until the potatoes are soft and golden, about 1 hour. Garnish with the parsley leaves and serve hot.

Serves: 4 • Prep: 20 min • Cooking: 1 hr

TABLETOP POT

SLOW-COOKER SOUPS AND STEWS, AND FONDUES

This chapter features a selection of recipes for fondues, hot pots, and slow cookers. Fondue and hot-pot meals are fun ways to entertain family and close friends. With the preparations complete before the guests arrive and any cooking to be done shared at the table, these meals are relaxing and convivial. However, we have devoted most space in this chapter to slow-cooker recipes, because there really is no more convenient way to prepare delicious and nutritious meals with so little effort.

Slow-Cooker Black Bean Soup

- 1 cup (150 g) dried black beans
- 2 cups (500 ml) chicken broth or stock (see page 56)
- 2 cups (500 ml) boiling water
- 1 large white onion, coarsely chopped
- 2 stalks celery, finely chopped
- 2 cloves garlic, finely chopped
- 4 large fresh sausages, sliced 1-inch (2.5-cm) thick

- Salt and freshly ground white pepper
- 4 tablespoons dry sherry
- ½ cup (100 g) shredded cheddar cheese
- 2 tablespoons finely chopped fresh cilantro (coriander)

Soak the beans in 6 cups (1.5 liters) boiling water in a large pot for 8 hours.

Combine the broth, 2 cups (500 ml) boiling water, onion, celery, garlic, sausages, and salt and white pepper in a slow cooker. Drain the beans and add to the cooker. Stir well.

Cover and cook on low for 8 hours.

Stir in the sherry and cook for 1 more hour.

Ladle the soup into individual bowls and garnish with the shredded cheese and cilantro. Serve hot.

Serves: 4 • Prep: 30 min + 8 hr to soak beans • Cooking: 9 hr

Split Pea and Ham Soup

- 1 pound (500 g) split peas
- 2 cups (350 g) diced cooked ham
- 1 large potato, peeled and diced
- 2 large carrots, diced
- 1 large onion, chopped
- 2 cloves garlic, finely chopped

- 1 bay leaf
- Salt and freshly ground black pepper
- 4 cups (1 liter) boiling water
- 2 cups (500 ml) milk
- 1 tablespoon finely chopped fresh parsley

Combine the split peas, ham, potato, carrots, onion, garlic, and bay leaf in a slow cooker. Season with salt and pepper. Pour the boiling water and milk over the top.

Cover and cook on high until the split peas are tender, 4–6 hours.

Remove the bay leaf and stir in the parsley before serving.

Serves: 6–8 • Prep: 10 min • Cooking: 4–6 hr

Broccoli, Cheese, and Potato Soup

- 1 pound (500 g) potatoes, peeled and diced
- 12 ounces (350 g) broccoli, divided into florets
- 1 medium onion, finely chopped
- 2 tablespoons butter
- 2 cloves garlic, finely chopped (optional)

- Salt and freshly ground black pepper
- 2 tablespoons all-purpose (plain) flour
- 2 cups (500 ml) milk
- 4 cups (1 liter) boiling water
- 1 cup (150 g) diced cheddar cheese

Combine the potatoes, broccoli, onion, butter, and garlic, if using, in a slow cooker. Season with salt and pepper. Mix the flour with a little milk in a small bowl. Pour over the ingredients in the slow cooker. Pour the boiling water over the top.

Cover and cook on low for 10–12 hours. Sprinkle with the cheese and serve hot.

Serves: 4–6 • Prep: 10 min • Cooking: 10–12 hr

Manhattan Clam Chowder

This recipe can also be made using fresh clams in their shells. In that case you will have to soak them for an hour in cold water and then cook them in a large pan over medium-high heat until they open. You will need 3 pounds (3 kg).

- 3 (8-ounce/250-g) cans clams, with juice
- 2 (14-ounce/400-g) cans tomatoes, chopped, with juice
- 2 ounces (60 g) bacon, diced
- 1 pound (500 g) potatoes, peeled and diced
- 1 large onion, finely chopped

- 1 large carrot, thinly sliced
- 2 stalks celery, thinly sliced
- 2 tablespoons finely chopped fresh parsley
- ½ cup dry white wine
- Salt and freshly ground black pepper

Combine the clams, tomatoes, bacon, potatoes, onion, carrot, celery, parsley, and wine in a slow cooker. Season with salt and pepper.

Cover and cook on low until the vegetables are tender, 10–12 hours.

Serves: 6–8 Prep: 10 min • Cooking: 10–12 hr

Slow-Cooker Black Bean Soup

SLOW-COOKER CHICKEN AND VEGETABLE SOUP

This recipe is an excellent way to use up any leftover roast or grilled chicken. Remove all the skin and bones and then chop the chicken finely with a large knife.

- 2 (14-ounce/400-g) cans tomatoes, chopped, with juice
- 2 cups (500 ml) chicken broth or stock (see page 56)
- 1 cup (150 g) frozen corn (sweet corn)
- 1 cup (150 g) frozen peas
- 2 stalks celery, finely chopped
- ½ cup (100 g) short-grain rice
- 4 tablespoons tomato paste

- 1 tablespoon Worcestershire sauce
- 2 tablespoons finely chopped fresh parsley
- Salt and freshly ground white pepper
- 2 cups (350 g) cooked lean chicken, shredded
- 1 tablespoon finely chopped fresh basil

Combine the tomatoes, broth, corn, peas, celery, rice, tomato paste, Worcestershire sauce, parsley, and salt and pepper in a slow cooker. Stir well. Cover and cook on low until the rice and vegetables are tender, 6–8 hours.

One hour before the cooking time is complete, stir in the chicken. Sprinkle with the basil just before serving.

Serves: 6–8 • Prep: 10 min • Cooking: 6–8 hr

PEARL BARLEY AND CHAMPIGNON SOUP

- 1 pound (500 g) small white button mushrooms, cleaned and sliced
- 2 cups (400 g) pearl barley
- 1 medium onion, finely chopped
- 2 cloves garlic, finely chopped
- 2 tablespoons finely chopped fresh thyme

- 1 tablespoon finely chopped fresh parsley
- Salt and freshly ground black pepper
- 6 cups (1.5 liters) beef broth or stock (see page 28)

Combine the mushrooms, barley, onion, garlic, thyme, parsley, salt, and pepper in a slow cooker. Pour the broth in over the top.

Cover and cook on low until the barley is tender and well cooked, 6–8 hours. Serve hot.

Serves: 4–6 • Prep: 15 min • Cooking: 6–8 hr

TOMATO AND LENTIL SOUP

- 1 pound (500 g) lentils, rinsed and drained
- 1 medium onion, finely chopped
- 2 large carrots, sliced
- 2 large celery stalks, sliced
- 2 cloves garlic, finely chopped
- 2 tablespoons finely chopped fresh basil + extra, to garnish
- 2 (14-ounce/400-g) cans tomatoes, chopped, with juice

- ¾ cup (180 ml) tomato paste (concentrate)
- ½ cup (125 ml) dry red wine
- ½ teaspoon crushed red pepper flakes
- ½ teaspoon dried oregano
- Salt and freshly ground black pepper
- 3 cups (750 ml) water

Combine the lentils, onion, carrots, celery, garlic, basil, tomatoes, tomato paste, wine, red pepper flakes, and oregano in a slow cooker. Season with salt and pepper. Pour the water over the top.

Cover and cook on low until the lentils are tender and well cooked, 10–12 hours. Garnish with the extra fresh basil and serve hot.

Serves: 8 • Prep: 15 min • Cooking: 10–12 hr

SLOW-COOKER LENTIL SOUP

- 1 pound (500 g) lentils, rinsed and drained
- 8 cups (2 liters) beef broth or stock (see page 28)
- 2 tablespoons extra-virgin olive oil
- 1 onion, finely chopped
- 2 large carrots, sliced
- 1 large celery stalk, sliced

- 2 cloves garlic, finely chopped
- 1 bay leaf
- ½ teaspoon dried oregano
- Salt and freshly ground black pepper
- ½ cup (125 ml) tomato sauce
- 2 tablespoons red wine vinegar

Combine the lentils and broth in a slow cooker.

Heat the oil in a large frying pan over medium heat and sauté the onion, carrots, celery, and garlic until softened, about 5 minutes. Add to the slow cooker.

Add the bay leaf and oregano. Season with salt and pepper. Cover and cook on low until the lentils are almost tender, 9–11 hours.

Stir in the tomato sauce and vinegar and cook 30 minutes more. Serve hot.

Serves: 8 • Prep: 15 min • Cooking: 9½–11½ hr

Slow-Cooker Chicken and Vegetable Soup

SLOW-COOKER VEGETARIAN CURRY

Walk in the door to the enticing odors of Asia! This light yet nourishing curry makes a perfect evening meal. Serve it with freshly baked naan (pick it up at an Indian deli or supermarket on your way home) or quickly boil some basmati or other long-grain rice.

4 tablespoons peanut or olive oil	1 cup (150 g) frozen peas
4 medium white onions, coarsely chopped	2 tangy green apples (Granny Smiths are ideal)
3 cloves garlic, finely chopped	1 medium red bell pepper (capsicum), seeded and chopped
1 teaspoon grated fresh ginger	1 cup (180 g) dried apricots
1 teaspoon cumin seeds	½ cup (90 g) golden raisins (sultanas)
1 teaspoon ground turmeric	½ cup (125 ml) coconut milk
2 tablespoons finely chopped fresh parsley	½ cup (125 ml) water
2 tablespoons finely chopped fresh dill	1 cup (100 g) walnuts, toasted
2 large carrots, chopped	2 tablespoons finely chopped fresh cilantro (coriander)
2 medium zucchini (courgettes), chopped	Freshly cooked basmati rice or naan, to serve
4 large potatoes with peel, diced	

Combine all the ingredients, except the walnuts and cilantro, in a slow cooker. Stir gently.

Cover and cook on high until the vegetables are very tender, 5–6 hours.

Sprinkle with the walnuts and cilantro just before serving.

Serves: 6–8 • Prep: 20 min • Cooking: 5–6 hr

CREAM OF LEEK AND POTATO SOUP

½ cup (75 g) all-purpose (plain) flour	Salt
4 cups (1 liter) chicken broth or stock (see page 56)	Cayenne pepper
	1 (13-oz/350 g) can evaporated milk
4 large potatoes, peeled and diced	½ cup (125 ml) sour cream
4 leeks, white part only, chopped	1 cup (200 g) shredded sharp cheddar cheese
2 stalks celery, diced	
2 cloves garlic, finely chopped	1–2 tablespoons finely chopped fresh chives, to garnish (optional)
1 tablespoon finely chopped fresh parsley	

Place the flour in a small bowl and gradually stir in about 1 cup (250 ml) of broth until smooth.

Combine the potatoes, leeks, celery, garlic, parsley, salt, and cayenne in a slow cooker. Pour in the broth and flour mixture and the remaining 3 cups (750 ml) of the broth. Stir gently to mix.

Cover and cook on low until the vegetables are very tender, 7–9 hours.

Stir in the evaporated milk, sour cream, and cheese and cook for 1 hour more.

Serve hot, garnished with the chives, if desired.

Serves: 4–6 • Prep: 15 min • Cooking: 8–10 hr

POTATO AND CORN CHOWDER

3 ounces (90 g) bacon, diced	1 tablespoon finely chopped fresh parsley
3 large potatoes, peeled and diced	Salt
1 large onion, chopped	Cayenne pepper
5 cups (1.25 liters) chicken broth or stock (see page 56)	1 cup (250 ml) milk
2 cups (300 g) frozen corn (sweet corn)	½ cup (125 ml) sour cream

Sauté the bacon over medium-high heat in a nonstick skillet until crispy and brown, about 5 minutes. Drain off the bacon grease.

Combine the bacon, potatoes, onion, broth, corn, parsley, salt, and cayenne pepper in a slow cooker.

Cover and cook on low heat for 8 hours. Stir in the milk and sour cream and cook for 30 minutes more.

Serves: 4–6 • Prep: 20 min • Cooking: 8 hr 35 min

ITALIAN SAUSAGE AND BEAN SLOW-COOKER STEW

2 cups (300 g) dried cannellini (white kidney) beans

4 cups (1 liter) beef broth or stock (see page 28)

½ cup (125 ml) water

6–8 sweet or hot Italian sausages, sliced 1-inch (2.5-cm) thick

1 pound (500 g) broccoli, broken into florets, stems diced

1 (14-ounce/400-g) can tomatoes, chopped, with juice

1 large white onion, coarsely chopped

1 teaspoon dried oregano

2 cloves garlic, finely chopped

2 bay leaves

Soak the beans in 6 cups (1.5 liters) boiling water in a large pot for 8 hours.

Drain the beans and transfer to a slow cooker. Add the broth, water, sausages, broccoli, tomatoes, onion, oregano, garlic, and bay leaves. Stir gently and cook on high until the beans are very tender, 6–8 hours.

Skim off any fat and remove the bay leaves before serving.

Serves: 6–8 • Prep: 30 min + 8 hr to soak beans • Cooking: 6–8 hr

BEEF AND TOMATO CASSEROLE

2 pounds (1 kg) stewing beef, cut into bite-size cubes

6 large tomatoes, peeled and chopped

4 large potatoes, peeled and diced

4 large carrots, sliced

3 stalks celery, sliced

1 large onion, chopped

½ cup (75 g) quick-cooking tapioca

2 bay leaves

1 tablespoon finely chopped fresh parsley

1 tablespoon finely chopped fresh basil

Salt

½ teaspoon freshly ground black pepper

1 cup (250 ml) beef broth or stock (see page 28)

Combine the beef, tomatoes, potatoes, carrots, celery, onion, tapioca, bay leaves, parsley, basil, salt, and pepper in a slow cooker. Pour the beef broth over the top and stir gently.

Cover and cook on low until the beef is tender, 6–8 hours. Remove the bay leaves. Serve hot.

Serves: 6–8 • Prep: 20 min • Cooking: 6–8 hr

GROUND BEEF AND POTATO DINNER

1½ pounds (750 g) ground (minced) beef

4 large potatoes, peeled and diced

1 large onion, chopped

1 (14-ounce/400-g) can tomatoes, chopped, with juice

1 cup (150 g) frozen peas

1 cup (150 g) frozen corn (sweet corn)

2 cloves garlic, finely chopped

1 tablespoon finely chopped fresh parsley

1 teaspoon ground ginger

½ teaspoon crushed cumin seeds

Salt and freshly ground black pepper

1 tablespoon finely chopped fresh basil

1 tablespoon finely chopped fresh cilantro

Combine the beef, potatoes, onion, tomatoes, peas, corn, garlic, parsley, ginger, cumin, salt, and pepper in a slow cooker. Stir gently.

Cover and cook on low heat until the meat is well cooked and the vegetables are tender, 6–8 hours.

Stir in the basil and cilantro and serve hot.

Serves: 4–6 • Prep: 20 min • Cooking: 6–8 hr

GROUND BEEF SLOW-COOKER CASSEROLE

1½ pounds (750 g) lean ground (minced) beef

2 cloves garlic, finely sliced

1 tablespoon finely chopped fresh parsley

½ teaspoon salt, or more to taste

½ teaspoon freshly ground white pepper

1½ pounds (750 g) tiny new potatoes, scrubbed

2 large onions, thinly sliced

1 large carrot, diced

8 ounces (250 g) white mushrooms, thinly sliced

1 cup (150 g) frozen peas

3 tablespoons all-purpose (plain) flour

½ cup (125 ml) milk

1 tablespoon Worcestershire sauce

Stir together the ground beef, garlic, parsley, salt, and pepper in the slow cooker.

Add the potatoes, onions, carrot, mushrooms, and peas.

Combine the flour in a small bowl with the milk and stir until smooth. Pour the milk mixture and Worcestershire sauce in over the top.

Cook on low until the meat and potatoes are tender, 8–10 hours. Serve hot.

Serves: 4–6 • Prep: 30 min • Cooking: 8–10 hr

GROUND BEEF AND MUSHROOM STEW

1½ pounds (750 g) ground (minced) beef

6 large potatoes, peeled and diced

1 large onion, chopped

2 cloves garlic, finely chopped

1 cup (150 g) frozen peas

1 tablespoon finely chopped fresh parsley

1 tablespoon finely chopped fresh thyme

1 (4-oz/125 g) package dry mushroom soup mix

Freshly ground black pepper

5 cups (1.25 liters) boiling water

4 tablespoons cornstarch (cornflour)

½ cup (125 ml) cold water

Combine the beef, potatoes, onion, garlic, peas, parsley, and thyme in a slow cooker. Sprinkle with the mushroom soup and a generous grinding of black pepper. Pour the boiling water over the top.

Cover and cook on low heat until the potatoes are tender, 8–9 hours.

Combine the cornstarch in a small bowl with the water and stir until smooth. Stir the cornstarch mixture into the stew and cook for 1 more hour. Serve hot.

Serves: 4–6 • Prep: 20 min • Cooking: 9–10 hr

SLOW-COOKER BEEF STEW

2 tablespoons extra-virgin olive oil

1½ pounds (750 g) chuck steak, cut into bite-size cubes

1 large onion, chopped

2 cloves garlic, finely chopped

3 large carrots, sliced

3 large potatoes, peeled and diced

2 stalks celery, sliced

2 (14-ounce/400 g) cans tomatoes, chopped, with juice

1 cup (250 ml) beef broth or stock (see page 28)

4 tablespoons ketchup

1 tablespoon finely chopped fresh parsley

1 bay leaf

Salt and freshly ground black pepper

4 tablespoons quick-cooking tapioca

Heat the oil in a large frying pan over medium-high heat. Add the meat and sauté until browned, 8–10 minutes.

Transfer the beef to a slow cooker with the onion, garlic, carrots, potatoes, celery, tomatoes, broth, ketchup, parsley, bay leaf, salt, pepper, and tapioca.

Cover and cook on low heat until the steak is tender, 8–10 hours. Remove the bay leaf. Serve hot.

Serves: 6 • Prep: 20 min • Cooking: 8–10 hr

SLOW-COOKER BEEF AND VEGETABLE STEW

2 pounds (1 kg) beef chuck roast, cut into 1½-inch (4-cm) chunks

1 tablespoon extra-virgin olive oil

1 pound (500 g) small red potatoes, quartered

4 medium carrots, sliced

1 (10-ounce/300-ml) can cream of mushroom soup

1 cup (250 ml) beef broth or stock (see page 28)

1 (4-ounce/125-g) package onion soup mix

½ teaspoon dried thyme

2 cups (300 g) fresh or frozen peas

Combine all the ingredients in a slow cooker. Stir gently and cook on low for 8–10 hours. Serve hot.

Serves: 4–6 • Prep: 15 min • Cooking: 8–10 hr

BEEF CASSEROLE WITH WILD RICE

This is the ideal casserole to have slow cooking while you are out all day at work or running errands. To freshen up the flavors, stir in some fresh parsley and lemon zest just before serving.

2 pounds (1 kg) boneless round steak, cut into bite-sized cubes

1 cup (200 g) wild rice

2 stalks celery, sliced

2 large carrots, sliced

1 large onion, chopped

2 large tomatoes, chopped

1½ cups (225 g) frozen peas

½ cup (75 g) slivered almonds

3 cups (750 ml) beef broth or stock (see page 28)

Salt

1 tablespoon finely chopped fresh parsley (optional)

2 teaspoons finely grated lemon zest (optional)

Combine the steak, wild rice, celery, carrots, onion, tomatoes, peas, and almonds in a slow cooker.

Pour in the broth and stir gently. Cover and cook on low until the steak is tender, 6–8 hours.

If desired, stir in the parsley and lemon zest. Serve hot.

Serves: 6–8 • Prep: 20 min • Cooking: 6–8 hr

BEEF AND VEGETABLE STEW WITH BARLEY

1 pound (500 g) boneless round steak, cut into bite-sized pieces

2 carrots, sliced

1 large onion, chopped

1 small red bell pepper (capsicum), seeded and diced

1 cup (150 g) frozen peas

8 ounces (250 g) white mushrooms, sliced

1 cup (200 g) pearl barley

2 tablespoons extra-virgin olive oil

Salt and freshly ground black pepper

1 bay leaf

1 tablespoon finely chopped fresh parsley

5 cups (1.25 liters) beef broth or stock (see page 28)

1 tablespoon finely chopped fresh cilantro (coriander)

Combine the steak, carrots, onion, bell pepper, peas, mushrooms, barley, oil, salt, pepper, bay leaf, and parsley in a slow cooker. Pour in the broth and stir gently.

Cover and cook on low until the steak and pearl barley are tender, 8–10 hours.

Stir in the cilantro and remove the bay leaf before serving.

Serves: 4–6 • Prep: 20 min • Cooking: 8–10 hr

SLOW-COOKER BRAISED PORK AND VEGETABLES

- 1 pound (500 g) small red potatoes, cut in half
- 1 pound (500 g) carrots, thickly sliced
- ¼ cup (60 ml) French mustard
- 3 pounds (1.5 kg) boneless pork loin roast, cut in chunks
- ½ teaspoon dried marjoram
- ½ teaspoon dried thyme
- ½ teaspoon salt
- ¼ teaspoon freshly ground black pepper
- 1 onion, finely chopped
- 2 cloves garlic, finely chopped
- 1½ cups (375 ml) beef broth or stock (see page 28)
- Freshly cooked short-grain or brown rice, to serve

Preheat a 6-quart (6-liter) slow cooker to high.

Layer the potatoes and carrots in the bottom of the slow cooker.

Spread the mustard all over the pork. Sprinkle with the marjoram, thyme, salt, and pepper. Place the pork in the slow cooker. Add the onion and garlic. Pour in the broth.

Cover the slow cooker and cook on the lowest setting for 9 hours, or until the pork and vegetables are tender.

Place the rice on a large serving platter and spoon the braised pork, vegetables, and cooking juices over the top.

Serves: 6 • Prep: 20 min • Cooking: 9 hr

SPICY PORK STEW

Half a teaspoon each of black pepper and red pepper flakes, along with the fresh ginger and garlic, will make a fairly peppery stew. However, if you like really spicy food, add a whole teaspoon of crushed red pepper flakes.

- 2 pounds (1 kg) boneless pork, cut into cubes
- 3 large potatoes, peeled and diced
- 2 large carrots, diced
- 1 large onion, chopped
- 2 cloves garlic, finely chopped
- 1 tablespoon minced fresh ginger
- 1 teaspoon salt
- ½ teaspoon freshly ground black pepper
- ½ teaspoon crushed red pepper flakes
- 1 (14-ounce/400-g) can tomatoes, chopped, with juices
- 2 cups (500 ml) boiling water
- 1 cup (150 g) frozen peas

Combine the pork, potatoes, carrots, onion, garlic, and ginger in a slow cooker. Sprinkle with the salt, pepper, and red pepper flakes. Pour the tomatoes and water over the top.

Cover and cook on high for 1 hour. Turn down to low and cook for 7 hours.

Add the peas and cook for 1 hour. Serve hot.

Serves: 6–8 • Prep: 15 min • Cooking: 9 hr

SPICY PORK STEW WITH CUMIN

This is another slow-cooker stew that can be "freshened up" just before serving with the addition of 1–2 tablespoons of finely chopped fresh herbs (basil, parsley, cilantro/coriander). You might also like to add half a slice of fresh chile pepper for extra verve.

- 2 pounds (1 kg) lean pork, cut in bite-size pieces
- 2 large onions, chopped
- 4 cloves garlic, finely chopped
- 1 cinnamon stick
- 1 teaspoon cumin seeds
- 1–2 fresh chiles, sliced (more, if you like spicy food)
- 1 pound (500 g) tiny new potatoes
- 1 pound (500 g) tiny new carrots
- Salt and freshly ground black pepper
- About 2 cups (500 ml) water
- 2 tablespoons white wine vinegar

Place the pork, onions, garlic, cinnamon stick, cumin, chiles, potatoes, carrots, salt, and pepper in a slow cooker. Pour in as much of the water as needed to just cover the other ingredients.

Cover and cook on low until the pork is tender, 6–8 hours.

Remove the cinnamon stick and stir in the vinegar just before serving.

Serves: 4–6 • Prep: 20 min • Cooking: 6–8 hr

SLOW-COOKER CHICKEN, BEAN, AND CORN STEW

- 1 chicken, weighing 3 pounds (1.5 kg), cut into 8 pieces
- 1 onion, finely chopped
- 2 cups (250 g) cubed ham
- 2 potatoes, peeled and chopped
- 8 cups (2 liters) water
- 2 cups (500 g) canned chopped tomatoes
- 3 cups (300 g) canned cannellini (white kidney) beans, rinsed and drained
- 3 cups (300 g) frozen or fresh corn kernels
- 2 teaspoons salt
- 1 teaspoon sugar
- 1/4 teaspoon freshly ground black pepper
- 1/4 teaspoon dried oregano

Preheat a 6-quart (6-liter) slow cooker to high.

Combine the chicken, onion, ham, and potatoes in the slow cooker. Pour in the water. Cover and cook on the lowest setting for 4–5 hours, or until the chicken is tender.

Remove the chicken from the pot and strip the meat from the bones. Return the meat to the pot. Discard the skin and bones.

Add the tomatoes, beans, corn, salt, sugar, pepper, and oregano. Cover and cook on the highest setting for 1 hour.

Serve hot.

Serves: 6–8 • Prep: 20 min • Cooking: 5–6 hr

SLOW-COOKER CHICKEN AND DUMPLINGS

- 1 pound (500 g) boneless, skinless chicken breasts, cut into small cubes
- 2 large potatoes, peeled and cut into small cubes
- 2 large carrots, thinly sliced
- 1 large onion, finely chopped
- 1 medium red bell pepper (capsicum), seeded and diced
- 1 cup (150 g) frozen peas
- 1 cup (150 g) frozen corn (sweet corn) kernels
- 1 tablespoon butter
- 1 tablespoon finely chopped fresh parsley
  Salt and cayenne pepper
- 3 cups (750 ml) chicken broth or stock (see page 56)
  Biscuit dough (see below—reduce the buttermilk or yogurt to 4 tablespoons)

Combine the chicken, potatoes, carrots, onion, bell pepper, peas, corn, butter, and parsley in a slow cooker. Season with salt and cayenne. Pour 2^1/$_2$ cups (625 ml) of the broth over the top.

Cover and cook on low until the chicken and vegetables are tender, 6–8 hours.

Place the biscuit mix in a small bowl and stir in the remaining 1/2 cup (125 ml) of broth.

Drop tablespoons of the mixture over the chicken and vegetables in the slow cooker.

Cover and cook on high for 15 minutes. Uncover and cook on high for 20 minutes more. Serve hot.

Serves: 4–6 • Prep: 20 min • Cooking: 6½–8½ hr

BUTTERMILK BISCUITS

Warm, fragrant biscuits are the perfect accompaniment to soups, chilis, and stews. They are also simple to make. Here is a quick and easy recipe that will never fail. If serving them with a very spicy dish, increase the sugar to 1–2 tablespoons for a scrumptious contrast of flavor.

- 2 cups (300 g) all-purpose (plain) flour
- 2 teaspoons baking powder
- 1/2 teaspoon baking soda (bicarbonate of soda)
- 2 teaspoons sugar
- 1/2 teaspoon salt
- 1/2 cup (125 g) cold butter, cut up
- 3/4 cup (180 ml) buttermilk or low-fat yogurt

Preheat the oven to 425°F (220°C/gas 7).

Combine the flour, baking powder, baking soda, sugar, and salt in a large bowl. Cut in the butter until the mixture resembles coarse crumbs.

Stir in the buttermilk with fork until the dough forms a soft, sticky ball. Place on a lightly floured work surface and roll to coat in flour.

Divide the dough into 12 pieces and roll into balls. Place on an ungreased baking sheet.

Bake until golden brown, 10–12 minutes.

Serves: 4–6 • Prep: 20 min • Cooking: 10–12 min

Slow-Cooker Chicken, Bean, and Corn Stew

TABLETOP POT ▪ 243

SLOW-COOKER PINEAPPLE CHICKEN

3–4 large potatoes, peeled and sliced ¼-inch (5-mm) thick
6–8 chicken drumsticks
1 medium yellow bell pepper (capsicum), seeded and chopped
1 medium red bell pepper (capsicum), seeded and chopped
1 cup (150 g) frozen peas
2 large white onions, coarsely chopped
½ cup (125 ml) chicken broth (see page 56)

1 (14-ounce/400-g) can unsweetened pineapple chunks, drained, reserving the juice
½ cup (125 ml) chili sauce (spicy ketchup)
2 tablespoons dark soy sauce
1 tablespoon Dijon mustard
Freshly ground black pepper
1 tablespoon cornstarch (cornflour)
2 tablespoons finely chopped cilantro (coriander)

Put the potatoes in a slow cooker. Cover with the chicken drumsticks. Add the bell peppers, peas, and onions. Mix the chicken broth, pineapple juice, chili sauce, soy sauce, and mustard in a small bowl. Pour over the chicken and vegetables. Season generously with black pepper.

Cover and cook on low until the chicken and vegetables are very tender, 8–10 hours.

Transfer the chicken and vegetables to a heated serving platter.

Mix the cornstarch in the small bowl with ½ cup (125 ml) of the cooking juices. Stir until smooth and pour back into the cooker.

Add the pineapple chunks to the slow cooker. Cover and cook on high until they are at serving temperature.

Spoon the pineapple sauce over the chicken and vegetables. Sprinkle with the cilantro and serve hot.

Serves: 6–8 • Prep: 30 min • Cooking: 8–10 hr

GREEN APPLE AND CHICKEN SLOW-COOKER STEW

1 pound (500 g) potatoes, peeled and sliced ¼-inch (5-mm) thick
1 pound (500 g) carrots, sliced ¼-inch (5-mm) thick
1 large tangy green apple (a Granny Smith is ideal), with peel, thinly sliced
6 boneless, skinless chicken breast halves
2 cloves garlic, finely chopped

1 tablespoon dark brown sugar
1 teaspoon salt
½ teaspoon cayenne pepper
¼ teaspoon freshly grated nutmeg
⅛ teaspoon ground cloves
1 cup (250 ml) unsweetened apple juice
2 tablespoons fresh lemon juice

Layer the potatoes, carrots, and apple in a slow cooker. Cover with the chicken breasts.

Sprinkle with the garlic, brown sugar, salt, cayenne, nutmeg, and cloves. Pour the apple juice and lemon juice over the top.

Cover and cook on low until the chicken and vegetables are very tender, 6–8 hours. Serve hot.

Serves: 6 • Prep: 30 min • Cooking: 6–8 hr

CHICKEN AND PINEAPPLE CASSEROLE

1 pound (500 g) tiny new potatoes, scrubbed
1 pound (500 g) baby carrots
1 large onion, chopped
3 boneless, skinless chicken breasts, cut into bite-size pieces
2 (12-ounce/300-g) cans pineapple chunks, drained, juice reserved
4 tablespoons dark brown sugar
2 tablespoons melted butter
1 tablespoon dark soy sauce

1 chicken bouillon cube, crumbled
1 clove garlic, finely chopped
1 teaspoon minced fresh ginger
Salt
Cayenne pepper
3 tablespoons cornstarch (cornflour)
5 tablespoons water
Freshly cooked long-grain rice, to serve

Combine the potatoes, carrots, and onion in a slow cooker. Cover with the chicken.

Scatter the pineapple over the chicken. Mix the reserved pineapple juice, brown sugar, butter, soy sauce, bouillon cube, garlic, ginger, salt, and cayenne pepper in a small bowl. Pour over the chicken.

Cover and cook on low until the chicken and vegetables are almost tender, 6–7 hours.

Combine the cornstarch and water in a small bowl and stir until smooth. Stir this mixture into the chicken casserole and cook for 1 hour more. Serve hot.

Green Apple and Chicken Slow-Cooker Stew

Serves: 4–6 • Prep: 30 min • Cooking: 7–8 hr

STEAK AND CHICKEN FONDUE WITH FRESH VEGETABLES

To serve this dish, you will need a fondue set and dipping forks. The idea is to choose tender, high-quality meat, chop it into small cubes or pieces, and fry it at the table by dipping it into a fondue pot of boiling oil. Serve with a large platter of crisp, garden fresh vegetables, newly baked bread, and little bowls of ketchup, soy sauce, yogurt, relishes, and pickles. Make sure that salt and pepper are within hands reach of each diner so that they can season the food to taste.

Peanut, canola, or olive oil, for frying	2–3 large carrots, cut in long thin strips
1 pound (500 g) best-quality steak, cut in ½-inch (1-cm) cubes	6–8 radishes, cleaned
1 pound (500 g) chicken thighs, boned and cut in ½-inch (1-cm) cubes or pieces	4–6 tender stalks celery
	2–3 artichokes, cleaned and cut into wedges
6–8 scallions (green onions), trimmed and whole	Fresh bread
	Dipping sauces

Pour the frying oil into a fondue pot until about half full. Place on the stove and heat until the oil reaches 375°F (190°C).

Take the fondue pot to the table and place over the burner set to highest temperature.

Set the meats out on a platter. Give each diner a plate and a dipping fork.

Arrange the fresh vegetables on another platter and place the bread on a board. Your guests can spear pieces of meat and dip them into the boiling oil until tender and cooked.

Serves: 4–6 • Prep: 30 min • Cooking: 15 min

CHINESE BEEF HOT POT

Serve with diced firm bean curd and a selection of dipping sauces, such as soy sauce, sesame paste, mustard, chili oil, and peanut sauce.

1½ pounds (750 g) sirloin steak, sliced paper thin	2 cups (500 ml) beef broth or stock (see page 28)
8 ounces (250 g) button mushrooms, cut into bite-size pieces	2 tablespoons dry white wine
	2 tablespoons dark soy sauce
8 ounces (250 g) spinach, tough stems removed, coarsely chopped	1 scallion (spring onion), trimmed and sliced
6 cups (1.5 liters) water	2 thin slices fresh ginger

Lay the beef, mushrooms, and spinach on separate platters on the table.

Bring the water and broth to a boil in a large saucepan with the wine, soy sauce, scallion, and ginger.

Ladle enough of the broth mixture into a Chinese hot pot or fondue pot to fill it three-quarters full. Place the pot on the burner and let it simmer.

Spear the food with dipping forks and cook briefly in the broth until tender. Add more broth as needed during the meal. It is traditional to drink the broth at the end of the meal.

Serves: 4–6 • Prep: 30 min • Cooking: 20 min

MONGOLIAN HOT POT

A fun alternative to the Swiss fondue. Ideal for informal gatherings and New Year's celebrations. Serve with a selection of dipping sauces, such as dark soy sauce, light soy sauce, sesame paste, chili oil, hoisin sauce, and red rice vinegar, poured into small individual bowls.

3 pounds (1.5 kg) boneless lamb, sliced paper thin	1 tablespoon dark soy sauce
2 (10-ounce/600 g) blocks firm tofu (bean curd), cut in ½-inch (1-cm) cubes	1 teaspoon minced fresh ginger
	2 scallions (spring onions), white and tender green parts, finely chopped
1 pound (500 g) bok choy, sliced	
6 cups (1.5 liters) chicken broth or stock (see page 56)	

Lay the lamb, bean curd, and bok choy on separate platters on the table.

Bring the broth to a boil in a large saucepan with the soy sauce, ginger, and scallions.

Fill a Chinese hot pot or fondue pot three-quarters full with broth. Place on the heat source or burner and let it simmer.

Your guests can use chopsticks to pick up slices of meat and pieces of tofu or bok choy and dip them into the simmering broth until heated through and tender. Add more stock as needed during the meal.

At the end of the meal, ladle the stock into small bowls and serve to your guests to drink.

Serves: 4–6 • Prep: 30 min • Cooking: 20 min

Mongolian Hot Pot

CHEDDAR FONDUE WITH SMOKED SALMON

- 1 cup (250 ml) sour cream
- 4 ounces (125 g) mascarpone cheese
- 1 pound (500 g) aged cheddar cheese, shredded (about 4 cups, tightly packed)
- 2 tablespoons finely chopped fresh chives
- 1 teaspoon Worcestershire sauce
- 6 ounces (180 g) smoked salmon, thinly sliced and chopped
  Herb croutons (see below) or crusty fresh bread, lightly toasted and cut into cubes

Stir together the sour cream and mascarpone in a medium saucepan until well blended. Place the pan over low heat and gradually stir in the cheddar. Cook until melted and smooth. Do not allow the mixture to boil.

Stir in 1 tablespoon of the chives, the Worcestershire sauce, and smoked salmon.

Pour the mixture into a fondue pot. Place over the burner and sprinkle with the remaining 1 tablespoon of chives.

Arrange the croutons or bread on a platter. Your guests will use their fondue forks to dip the croutons or bread into the fondue.

Serves: 4–6 • Prep: 15 min • Cooking: 20 min

SWISS FONDUE WITH TOMATOES

- 1 pound (500 g) tasty fresh tomatoes, peeled, seeded and finely chopped
- 2 cloves garlic, finely chopped
- ½ cup (125 ml) tomato juice
- 12 ounces (350 g) Gruyere cheese, grated
- 12 ounces (350 g) Emmentaler cheese, grated
- 1 tablespoon cornstarch (cornflour)
- 1 tablespoon whipping cream
  Freshly ground white pepper
- ½ teaspoon dried oregano
- 1 cup (150 g) diced ham, to serve
  Crusty fresh bread, lightly toasted and cut in cubes

Combine the tomatoes and garlic in a medium saucepan over low heat. Stirring continuously, cook until soft, about 5 minutes.

Add ¼ cup (60 ml) of the tomato juice and cook until very hot, about 3 minutes.

Add the cheeses. Mix the cornstarch with remaining ¼ cup (60 ml) of tomato juice and the cream until smooth. Add the oregano. Stir into tomato-cheese mixture and cook, stirring until the cheese is melted and the mixture has thickened, about 5 minutes. Season with white pepper and oregano.

Serves: 4–6 • Prep: 15 min • Cooking: 20 min

HERB CROUTONS

These crisp little herb croutons are great with all kinds of fondue and are also excellent with vegetable soups. They will keep in an airtight container for up to a week.

- 1 pound (500 g) crusty fresh bread, cut into 1-inch (2.5-cm) cubes
- 3 tablespoons finely chopped fresh mixed herbs (parsley, cilantro/coriander, basil, dill, oregano)
- ¾ cup (180 ml) extra-virgin olive oil
- 2 large cloves garlic, peeled and halved
  Salt and freshly ground black pepper

Preheat the oven to 350°F (180°C/gas 4). Sprinkle the bread with the herbs in a large bowl.

Combine the oil and garlic in a small saucepan over medium heat and cook until the garlic turns pale golden brown, 2–3 minutes. Do not let the garlic darken, because it will add a bitter flavor to the oil. Remove the garlic and discard.

Drizzle the oil over the bread and herbs in the bowl, mixing constantly as you add the oil. Season generously with salt and pepper, mixing well.

Place the croutons on a large baking sheet and toast in the oven for about 10 minutes, until golden brown and crisp. Turn the croutons as they brown.

Cheddar Fondue with Smoked Salmon

ITALIAN CHEESE FONDUE

- 1 pound (500 g) (net weight without rind) Fontina Val d'Aosta cheese, thickly sliced
- 1 cup (250 ml) whole milk
- 2 tablespoons butter
- 4–5 large egg yolks
- Salt and freshly ground white pepper

- Crusty fresh bread, lightly toasted and cut in cubes
- Wedges of raw fennel, to serve
- Carrot sticks, to serve
- Seedless green (white) grapes, to serve

Cover the cheese with the milk in a shallow bowl. Let stand for 2–4 hours.

Melt the butter in a double boiler over simmering water.

Drain the milk off from the cheese, reserving the milk. Add the cheese to the melted butter together with 3–4 tablespoons of the reserved milk.

Stir continuously with a balloon whisk or wooden spoon over the gently simmering water until the cheese has melted and threads start to form. At no point during preparation should the cheese be allowed to boil.

Adding one at a time, stir the first 4 egg yolks into the cheese, incorporating each of them very thoroughly. The mixture should be glossy and smooth. If it still looks a little grainy, add the final, fifth egg yolk and stir well for 1 minute.

Season with salt and white pepper. Serve with the bread, fennel, carrot, and grapes.

Serves: 4 • Prep: 10 min + 2–4 hr to stand • Cooking: 10 min

ONION AND GORGONZOLA FONDUE

Italian Gorgonzola cheese is probably best known in its sweet, creamy version. But about a quarter of the Gorgonzola produced in Italy is actually piccante *(literally "spicy"). Look out for this type when making this dish. If you can't get it, substitute another sharp-flavored blue cheese.*

- 3½ cups (350 g) fontina cheese, grated
- ¾ cup (100 g) freshly grated Parmesan cheese
- 1 scant tablespoon cornstarch (cornflour)
- 2 tablespoons extra-virgin olive oil
- 1 pound (500 g) sweet white onions, thinly sliced
- 1½ cups (375 ml) dry white wine
- 1 tablespoon white wine vinegar
- ¾ cup (100 g) crumbled piccante (sharp) Gorgonzola cheese

- Crusty baguette (French loaf), diced, to serve
- 6–8 stalks celery, cut into short lengths, to serve
- 1–2 Granny Smith apples, cored and cut into wedges (drizzled with 1–2 tablespoons freshly squeezed lemon juice to prevent them from darkening), to serve
- 2 large carrots, cut in long thin strips, to serve

Combine the Fontina, Parmesan, and cornstarch in a large bowl.

Heat the oil in a large heavy saucepan over low heat. Add the onions, cover, and cook until very tender, about 30 minutes. Stir from time to time during cooking.

Remove the lid and increase the heat to medium. Cook, stirring often until the liquid had reduced, about 5 minutes.

Pour in half the wine and cook until the wine has evaporated and the onions are golden brown, about 5 minutes. Add the remaining wine and the vinegar and cook until heated through.

Gradually add the Fontina mixture, stirring to melt as you add it. Add half the Gorgonzola. Decrease the heat to low and cook until the fondue just begins to bubble, 2–3 minutes. Do not let it boil.

Pour the sauce into a warmed fondue pot and place over a burner set to low. Sprinkle with the remaining Gorgonzola.

Serve with the bread, celery, apples, and carrots for dipping.

Serves: 4–6 • Prep: 30 min • Cooking: 15 min

Italian Cheese Fondue

INDEX